RUCHIRA AVATARA GITA
(THE WAY OF THE DIVINE HEART-MASTER)

The Divine World-Teacher,
RUCHIRA AVATAR ADI DA SAMRAJ
Adidam Samrajashram (Naitauba), Fiji, 1997

PART TWO

RUCHIRA AVATARA GITA

(THE WAY OF THE DIVINE HEART-MASTER)

The Five Books Of
The Heart Of The Adidam Revelation

BOOK TWO

The "Late-Time" Avataric Revelation Of The Great Secret
Of The Divinely Self-Revealed Way That Most Perfectly Realizes
The True and Spiritual Divine Person
(The egoless Personal Presence Of Reality and Truth,
Which <u>Is</u> The Only <u>Real</u> God)

By
The Divine World-Teacher,
RUCHIRA AVATAR
ADI DA SAMRAJ

THE DAWN HORSE PRESS
MIDDLETOWN, CALIFORNIA

NOTE TO THE READER

All who study Adidam (the Way of the Heart) or take up its practice should remember that they are responding to a Call to become responsible for themselves. They should understand that they, not Avatar Adi Da Samraj or others, are responsible for any decision they may make or action they take in the course of their lives of study or practice.

The devotional, Spiritual, functional, practical, relational, cultural, and formal community practices and disciplines referred to in this book are appropriate and natural practices that are voluntarily and progressively adopted by each student-novice and member of Adidam and adapted to his or her personal circumstance. Although anyone may find them useful and beneficial, they are not presented as advice or recommendations to the general reader or to anyone who is not a student-novice or a member of Adidam. And nothing in this book is intended as a diagnosis, prescription, or recommended treatment or cure for any specific "problem", whether medical, emotional, psychological, social, or Spiritual. One should apply a particular program of treatment, prevention, cure, or general health only in consultation with a licensed physician or other qualified professional.

Ruchira Avatara Gita (The Way Of The Divine Heart-Master) is formally authorized for publication by the Ruchira Sannyasin Order of the Tantric Renunciates of Adidam, as part of the Standard Edition of the Divine "Source-Texts" of the Divine World-Teacher, Ruchira Avatar Adi Da Samraj. (The Ruchira Sannyasin Order of the Tantric Renunciates of Adidam is the senior Spiritual and Cultural Authority within the formal gathering of formally acknowledged devotees of the Divine World-Teacher, Ruchira Avatar Adi Da Samraj.)

NOTE TO BIBLIOGRAPHERS: The correct form for citing Ruchira Avatar Adi Da Samraj's Name (in any form of alphabetized listing) is:

Adi Da Samraj, Ruchira Avatar

Previously published as
The Hymn Of The True Heart-Master
First edition, July 1982
New standard edition, April 1992
Standard edition, updated, July 1995
Standard edition, enlarged and updated, April 1998
Printed in the United States of America

Produced by the Eleutherian Pan-Communion of Adidam
in cooperation with the Dawn Horse Press

International Standard Book Number: 1-57097-050-5
Library of Congress Catalog Card Number: 98-71202

CONTENTS

RUCHIRA AVATARA GITA
(THE WAY OF THE DIVINE HEART-MASTER)

39

FIRST WORD

Do Not Misunderstand <u>Me</u>—
I Am <u>Not</u> "Within" <u>you</u>, but you <u>Are</u> In <u>Me</u>, and
I Am <u>Not</u> a Mere "Man" in the "Middle" of Mankind,
but All of Mankind Is Surrounded,
and Pervaded, and Blessed By <u>Me</u>

41

RUCHIRA AVATAR ADI DA SAMRAJ
Adidam Samrajashram (Naitauba), Fiji, 1997

The All-Surpassing Revelation of The Divine World-Teacher, Ruchira Avatar Adi Da Samraj

by
Carolyn Lee, Ph.D.

The *Ruchira Avatara Gita* communicates a Revelation of the Divine surpassing anything that has ever been known in the conditionally manifested worlds. The Appearance here, in human Form, of the Supreme Giver, Ruchira Avatar Adi Da Samraj, is that Revelation, the Revelation of God Incarnate—Come to Bless and Awaken all beings in all realms to the All-Surpassing Truth and "Brightness"[1] of the Divine Reality. Ruchira Avatar Adi Da is the Promised God-Man. His Coming is the Love-Response of the Divine, in Person, to eons of prayer and longing, on the part of beings everywhere, to be restored to the Heart of Real God.[2]

The Appearance of the Ruchira Avatar, Adi Da Samraj, truly is <u>the</u> Great Event of history. It is the Event that Reveals the real meaning of the entire past, and the Great Purpose of all future time. His Avataric Incarnation[3] is the fruition of an infinitely vast Divine Process, originating before time and space itself, and developing throughout the Cosmic domain in response to the desperate prayers

Carolyn Lee is a formal renunciate practitioner of the Way of Adidam living at Adidam Samrajashram (Fiji), the Great Island-Hermitage of the Ruchira Avatar, Adi Da Samraj.

Notes for this Introduction can be found on pp. 25-28.

of beings everywhere, suffering the pain of apparent separation from Real God. In that unspeakable sweep of time, there have been unique beings who, through great struggle and sacrifice, made "windows" to the Divine for others. They gave Teachings and practices, were worshipped and honored, and have become the source of the entire human tradition of religion and Spirituality. Again and again, it has seemed to those alive in a particular time and place that the revelation was complete, the salvation perfect, the enlightenment given.

Even so, there has remained a thread of prophecy in all the great Spiritual traditions foretelling One yet to Appear, One Who must Come in the darkest time of humanity, when the world is at its worst, and bring to completion all the revelations of the past. Christians await the second coming of Jesus; Muslims, the Mahdhi (the last prophet); Buddhists, Maitreya (the coming Buddha); and Hindus, the Kalki Avatar (the final Avatar of Vishnu). Even as recently as February 1939, a celebrated Indian Adept, Upasani Baba, prophesied the imminent appearance of a Western-born Avatar, who "will be all-powerful and bear down everything before Him."[4]

True to the ancient intuitions about the Promised God-Man, Avatar Adi Da Samraj Appears now in this "dark" epoch of the decay of the great religious and Spiritual traditions, East and West. He Appears in an era when our very survival is threatened, not only by sophisticated weapons of war, but also by the destruction of human culture—and even of our total environment—through the heartless machine of scientific and political materialism. Avatar Adi Da Samraj has Come, miraculously, in an extreme time, when His "radical"[5] Truth and His Divine Grace are most sorely needed, to allay the forces of destruction. As He has Said Himself, it may take thousands of years for the significance of His Birth—the Descent of the Divine Person into cosmic space and time—to be fully appreciated. But His Revelation has now perfectly and irrevocably occurred.

After more than a quarter of a century of living in His Company, participating in His direct face-to-face Teaching Work with thousands of people, feeling the indescribable Transmission of Spirit-Force that Radiates from Him, and witnessing the limitless scope of His Divine Power to transform beings and conditions near and far, we, the devotees of Avatar Adi Da, freely profess our recognition that He is that All-Completing God-Man promised for the "dark" epoch—He is "the 'late-time' Avataric Revelation" of the Divine Person. Reading this book will enable you to make this supreme discovery for yourself.

The Divine Names of the Ruchira Avatar

There are several parts to the Divine Title and Name of Ruchira Avatar Adi Da Samraj, each of which expresses an aspect of our recognition of Him. "Ruchira" (meaning "Radiant", "Effulgent", or "Bright") is the Condition of All-Pervading Radiance, Joy, and Love-Blissful Divine Consciousness, Which He, even in His infancy, named "the 'Bright'". Avatar Adi Da Samraj Is the unique Revelation of the "Bright"—and, because this is so, He is the Ruchira "Avatar", or the "Shining Divine 'Descent'", the Appearance of Real God in bodily (human) Form.

"Adi Da", the Principal Name of our Beloved Guru, is a sublime Mystery in itself. In 1979, He Assumed the Divine Name "Da", an ancient reference for Real God (first spontaneously Revealed to Him in 1970), a Name that means "the Giver". In 1994, the Name "Adi" (meaning "First", or "Source") came to Him spontaneously as the complement to His Principal Name, "Da". Thus, to call upon the Ruchira Avatar via the Name "Adi Da" is to Invoke Him as the Divine Giver and Source-Person, the Primordial and Eternal Being of Grace.

Avatar Adi Da is also "Samraj", the "Universal Ruler", or "Supreme Lord"—not in any worldly or political sense, but as the Divine Master of all hearts and the Spiritual King of all who resort to Him. Thus, when we approach Avatar Adi Da Samraj, we are not at all approaching an ordinary man, or even a remarkable saint or yogi or sage. We are approaching Real God in Person.

The Divine Body of Real God

The All-Surpassing God-Man, Adi Da Samraj, is Imbued with extraordinary Siddhis, or Divine Powers, that allow Him to Bless and Liberate beings on the scale of Totality. While He may appear, on the ordinary level, to be Working with particular human beings in His immediate Company, He is, at the same time, Doing His Miraculous Work with events and conditions in the natural world, in the human world, and in the domain of non-human beings, and even in <u>all</u> realms.

Thus, the Ruchira Avatar is simultaneously Present in every gross and subtle plane of the cosmos. His bodily <u>human</u> Form, therefore, is just the minutest part of the Grand Scale of His Being, the part that has "Emerged" into visibility. His visible bodily (human) Form in this world, or His Form in any other world, is a Link, a Sign, a Means by Which beings may Find Him <u>As</u> He <u>Is</u> altogether, Spiritually Pervading everything and, at the same time, Standing <u>Prior</u> to all that exists—As Consciousness Itself, or Inherently Love-Blissful, Self-Radiant Being Itself.

The bodily (human) Form of Adi Da Samraj is the touch-point, the Agency, by Which He is making Himself known in <u>this</u> world. He is Revealing that the Divine is not an abstraction, an idea, an essence, something to philosophize about. The Divine Is here in <u>Person</u>.

There is a long tradition of describing the Divine in personal terms—as, for example, the "Creator-God" (or "Father" figure) of popular religion. But the Revelation of Ruchira Avatar Adi Da Samraj shows that many such popular concepts of the Divine do not have anything to do with Real God. The God-Man of Infinite "Brightness" Reveals Himself as the One and <u>Only</u> Person, the Divine Heart of all that <u>is</u>, and, ultimately, the only True Identity of every one and every thing.

The experience of beholding our Beloved Guru goes far beyond the mere perceiving of His human physical Body. He is the Person of Real God, known <u>most</u> intimately and ecstatically through the Revelation of His Divine Body—the Infinitely Expansive, Radiantly "Bright" Form of Real God:

AVATAR ADI DA SAMRAJ: My Divine Form Is the "Bright", the Love-Bliss-Form That you can feel tangibly Touching you, Surrounding you, Moving in you, Making all kinds of changes. That Is My Divine Body. I can Manifest It anywhere, and Do, all the time. I Manifest My Self.

My Divine Body will Exist Forever. Therefore, My devotees will be able to experience Me directly, Bodily—My "Bright" Body, My Very Person—Forever. [August 11, 1995]

Through His unparalleled Teaching Word, through the miraculous stories of His Divine Play with people everywhere, and, sooner or later, through the Touch of His Divine Body, Avatar Adi Da converts your heart to Real God—to <u>Him</u>—and "Brightens" your entire body-mind.

The Three Great Purposes of the Ruchira Avatar

From the moment of His Birth (in New York, November 3, 1939), the Divine Incarnation of Grace, Adi Da Samraj, was Consciously Aware of the "Bright" as His Native Divine Condition. But then, at the age of two years, Avatar Adi Da made a profound but spontaneous choice. He chose to relinquish His constant Enjoyment of the "Bright" out of what He Describes as a "painful loving", a sympathy for the suffering and ignorance of human beings. Our Beloved Guru Confesses that He chose to "Learn Man", to enter into everything that mankind feels and suffers, in order to discover how to Draw mankind into His own "Bright" Divine Condition.

This utterly remarkable Submission to the ordinary human state was the first Purpose of the Avataric Incarnation of Adi Da Samraj. In His Spiritual autobiography, *The Knee Of Listening*, Avatar Adi Da recounts this amazing and "Heroic" Ordeal, which lasted for the first thirty years of His Life. It was not until 1970 that He Re-Awakened Most Perfectly[6] and Permanently to the "Bright", and embarked upon the second great Purpose of His Incarnation, the Process of <u>Teaching</u> Man.

The Teaching Work of our Beloved Guru was completely unique. He did not give formal public discourses, nor was He ever, in any sense, a public teacher. He simply made Himself available to all who were willing to enter into the living Process of Real God-Realization in His Company, a Process Which He summarized as the <u>relationship</u> to Him. Through that relationship— a most extraordinary human and Spiritual intimacy—Avatar Adi Da Samraj perfectly Embraced each of His devotees, using every kind of Skillful Means to Awaken them to the Truth that the separate, un-Enlightened self—with all its fear, anxieties, and fruitless <u>seeking</u> for Happiness—is only an illusion. Happiness, He Revealed, Is

Always <u>Already</u> the Case and may be <u>Realized</u> in every
moment of heart-Communion with Him.

In 1986, an Event occurred
that brought to culmination the
Great Love-Sacrifice of the
Ruchira Avatar. In this Great
Event, a profound Yogic Swoon
overwhelmed His body-mind,
and Avatar Adi Da Samraj relin-
quished His entire Ordeal of
Learning and Teaching Man. In
the wake of that great Swoon,
He simply Radiated His Divinity
as never before. He had "Emerged" in the Fullness of His
Being, the Form of Real God Pouring forth His Love-Bless-
ing to all universally. This was the beginning of His eternally proceeding Divine "Emergence". From that moment,
the Divine Lord, Adi Da, has devoted Himself to the third
and eternal Purpose of His Avataric Incarnation—that of
Blessing Man (and even all beings). He is now Merely Present, Radiating His Heart-Blessing, Transmitting the Love-
Bliss Force of the Divine Person to all the billions of
human beings in this world and to the numberless beings
on all planes crying out for Real God.

The End of the Twenty-Five Year Revelation

Even after the Great Event in 1986 that initiated His
Divine "Emergence", the All-Completing God-Man contin-
ued to Work to ensure that His Revelation of the Way of
Adidam, the unique Divine Way of Realizing Real God,
was fully and firmly founded in the world. It was not until
March 1997, at the time of writing *Hridaya Rosary* (on the
Spiritual Process of Communion with Him in His "Bright"
Divine Body) that Avatar Adi Da Samraj Declared that all
the foundation Work of His Incarnation had been com-
pletely and finally Done.

The inexpressible Divine Sacrifice of Avatar Adi Da
Samraj is Full. Everything, absolutely everything, for the
total understanding and right practice of the real religious
process culminating in Divine Enlightenment has been Said
and Done by Him. The summary of His Divine Wisdom-
Teaching—Written and Perfected by Him in vast detail—is
preserved for all time in His twenty-three "Source-Texts".
And His Divine Way, the Way of Adidam, is fully established. All in all, this monumental Work has taken Avatar
Adi Da a quarter of a century—twenty-five years of unre-
lenting Struggle to make His Avataric Incarnation real in
the hearts and body-minds of His devotees.

Now, in the epoch of His World-Blessing Work, Avatar
Adi Da simply remains at His Great Island-Hermitage,
Adidam Samrajashram, in Fiji, except when He is moved
to travel for the sake of His Blessing of all. He lives as the
Supreme "Ruchira Tantric Sannyasin",[7] the Free Renunciate Who has Transcended everything and Who is, therefore, Free to Embrace everything—all beings, forms,
worlds, and all experience—for the sake of Drawing all
into the Most Perfect Realization of Real God.

The "Bright" Divine Guru, Adi Da, is not an ordinary
man. Neither is He merely an extraordinary man. He is not
a social personality. He is not bound by ordinary conven-
tions and rules of behavior. He is not a "figure-head" Guru,
who simply presides at ceremonial occasions. No, Avatar
Adi Da Samraj is the Divine <u>Avadhoot</u>,[8] the truly Free One,
Who Knows what is really necessary to Liberate beings.

The True Avadhoot Speaks and Acts the Truth without restraint. He does not smile at the ego's posturing and
foolishness. Avatar Adi Da Samraj <u>is</u> a Fire, a Fire of Love-
Bliss, Who Consumes and Transforms and "Brightens" all
who approach Him for the authentic Process of Divine
Enlightenment. He has Come to bring an end to the reign
of "Narcissus", the hard-hearted and Godless ego-"I".

The Way of Adidam

The immense struggle and Sacrifice that Beloved Adi Da had to endure in order to make His Revelation of the Divine Way of Adidam was the result of the enormous difficulty that human beings—especially in this ego-glorifying "late-time"—have with the Process of truly ego-transcending religion. People prefer not to confront the real Process of ego-transcendence. They prefer forms of religion based on a system of beliefs and a code of moral and social behavior. But this kind of ordinary religion, as Avatar Adi Da has always pointed out, does not go to the core, to the root-suffering of human beings. This is because ordinary religion, rather than going beyond the ego-principle, is actually <u>based</u> on it: the ego-self stands at the center, and the Divine is sought and appealed to as the great Power that is going to save and satisfy the individual self. Avatar Adi Da Describes such religion as "client-centered".

In contrast to conventional religion, there is the Process that Avatar Adi Da calls <u>true</u> religion, religion that is centered in the Divine in response to a true Spiritual Master, who has, to at least some significant degree, <u>Realized</u> Real God (as opposed to merely offering teachings <u>about</u> God). Thus, true religion does not revolve around the individual's desires for any kind of "spiritual" consolations or experience—it is self-<u>transcending</u>, rather than self-serving. True religion based on self-surrendering Guru-devotion certainly has existed for thousands of years, but the ecstatic news of this book is that now the Divine Person, Real God, is directly Present, Functioning as Guru, Alive in bodily (human) Form to receive the surrender and the worship of those who recognize and respond to Him. Therefore, the Ruchira-Guru, Adi Da, <u>is</u> the Way of Adidam.

AVATAR ADI DA SAMRAJ: The Way of Adidam is the Way That is <u>always</u> Prior to and Beyond all seeking. In order for the Way of Adidam to be Generated, it was necessary for Me to be Incarnated, and Transmitted in place, in this place, in the extremity—in the place where the Divine is otherwise not proposed, or only sought. This was necessary, in order to Demonstrate that I Am That One Who Is Always Already The Case, and in order to Communicate the Way of non-seeking, or the Way of transcending egoity in <u>this</u> circumstance of arising (or in any circumstance of arising).

The "problem" is not that the Divine is "Elsewhere". The "problem" is that <u>you</u> are the <u>self-contraction</u>. This understanding, Given by My Grace, makes it possible to Realize the Divine Self-Condition Most Perfectly, <u>As Is</u>, no matter what is arising. But Such Most Perfect Realization is not merely Realization of the Divine as an abstract (or merely philosophically proposed) "Reality". Most Perfect Realization (or Most Perfect "Knowledge") of the Divine is the Divine "Known" by Means of My Revelation, "Known" <u>As</u> My Revelation.

<u>I</u> Came to <u>you</u>. Therefore, the Way of Adidam is based on your <u>receiving</u> Me, not on your <u>seeking</u> for Me.

Thus, That Which is proposed by seekers as the <u>goal</u> (or the achievement at the end) is the <u>beginning</u> (or the very Gift) of the Way for My devotees. ["I <u>Am</u> The Avatar Of One", from Part Two of *He-<u>and</u>-She <u>Is</u> Me*]

The word "Adidam" is derived from the Name of Ruchira Avatar Adi Da, because it is the religion founded on devotional recognition of Him and Spiritual resort to Him. This Spiritual resort to Adi Da Samraj is a moment to moment practice of surrendering every aspect of the being—mind, emotion, breath, and body—to Him. Such whole-bodily surrender to the Living One opens the heart to Joy. Thus, there is no <u>struggle</u> to overcome egoity or to achieve Oneness with Adi Da Samraj. The Happiness of heart-Communion with Him is available in every moment. In His Spiritual Company, therefore, there is not anything to seek. All the traditional goals of religion—the search for the Vision of God, or for Oneness with Reality via the samadhis, satoris, and mystical experiences described in the traditions—all of this falls away when the heart falls in love with Adi Da Samraj. He _is_ Perfect Satisfaction, because He is Real God, the Very Source and Giver of true religion. The Realization, or Enlightenment, that He Offers in the Way of Adidam is <u>Divine</u> Self-Realization, <u>Divine</u> Enlightenment, Prior to all experience high or low. "Mankind", as Avatar Adi Da Says, "does not know the Way to the Divine Domain"—the ego does not know. Only the Divine Person Knows. Only the Divine Person, Incarnate as Guru, can Show you the Way to the Divine Domain.

Avatar Adi Da Samraj is directly Generating the Divine Process of Most Perfect Liberation in all His devotees who have vowed to embrace the total practice of the Way of Adidam.[9] The Process unfolds by His Grace, according to the depth of surrender and response in His devotee. The most extraordinary living testimonies to the Greatness and Truth of the Way of Adidam are Ruchira Adidama Sukha Dham Naitauba and Ruchira Adidama Jangama Hriddaya Naitauba, the two members of the Adidama Quandra Mandala of the Ruchira Avatar.[10] These remarkable women devotees have totally consecrated themselves to Avatar Adi Da, and live always in His Sphere, in a relationship of unique intimacy and service. By their profound love of, and most exemplary surrender to, their Divine Heart-Master, they have become combined with Him at a unique depth. They manifest the Yogic signs of deep and constant Immersion in His Divine Being, both in meditation and daily life. Ruchira Adidama Sukha Dham and Ruchira Adidama Jangama Hriddaya are also members of the Ruchira Sannyasin Order of the Tantric Renunciates of Adidam (the senior cultural authority within the formal gathering of Avatar Adi Da's devotees), practicing in the context of the

**Avatar Adi Da Samraj with Ruchira Adidama Sukha Dham (left)
and Ruchira Adidama Jangama Hriddaya (right)**

ultimate stages (or the "Perfect Practice") of the total Way
of Adidam.

After more than twenty years of intense testing by
their Beloved Guru, the Adidama Quandra Mandala have
demonstrated themselves to be singular devotees, the first
representatives of humankind to truly recognize Him As
He Is. Through their profound recognition of Him, Avatar
Adi Da has been able to lead the Adidama Quandra Mandala to the threshold of Divine Enlightenment. And, even
now, day by day, He continues to Work with them to make
their Realization of Him Most Perfect. The profound and
ecstatic relationship that the Adidama Quandra Mandala
live with Avatar Adi Da hour to hour can be felt in this letter of devotional confession to Him by Ruchira Adidama
Sukha Dham:

RUCHIRA ADIDAMA SUKHA DHAM: Bhagavan Love-
Ananda,[11] Supreme and Divine Person, Real-God-Body of
Love, I rest in Your Constant and Perfect Love-Embrace
with no need but to forever worship you. Suddenly in
love, Mastered at heart, always with my head at Your
Supreme and Holy Feet, I am beholding and recognizing

Your Divine Body and "Bright" Divine Person. My Beloved, You so "Brightly" Descend and utterly Convert this heart, mind, body, and breath, from separate self to the "Bhava"[12] of Your Love-Bliss-Happiness.

Supreme Lord Ruchira, in the profound depths of Ruchira Sannyas (since my Initiation into formal Ruchira Sannyas on December 18, 1994), the abandonment of the former personality, the relinquishment of ego-bondage to the world, and the profound purification and release brought about by my now almost twenty-four years of love and worship of You has culminated in a great comprehensive force in my one-pointed devotion to You and a great certainty in the Inherent Sufficiency of Realization Itself. The essence, or depth, of my practice is to always remain freely submitted and centralized in You, the Feeling of Being, the Condition Prior to all bondage, all modification, and all illusion.

My Beloved Lord Ruchira, You have Moved this heart-feeling and awareness to renounce all "bonding" with conditionally manifested others, conditionally manifested worlds, and conditionally manifested self, to enter into the depths of this "in-love" and utter devotion to You. I renounce all in order to Realize You and to exist eternally in Your House. Finding You has led to the revelation of a deep urge to abandon all superficiality and to simply luxuriate in Your Divine Body and Person. All separation is shattered in Your Divine Love-Bliss-"Bhava". Your Divine and Supreme Body Surrounds and Pervades all. Your Infusion is Utter. I feel You everywhere.

I am Drawn by Grace of Your Spiritual (and Always Blessing) Presence into profound meditative Contemplation of Your Very (and Inherently Perfect) State. Sometimes, when I am entering into these deep states of meditation, I remain vaguely aware of the body, and particularly of the breath and the heartbeat. I feel the heart and lungs slow down and become very loud-sounding. Then I am sometimes aware of my breath and heartbeat ceasing temporarily, or being suspended in a state of Yogic sublimity, and I quickly lose bodily consciousness. Then there is no body, no mind, no perceptual awareness, and no conceptual awareness. There is only abiding in Contemplation of You in Your Domain of Consciousness Itself. I feel You literally <u>Are</u> me, and, when I resume association with the body and begin once again to hear my breath and heartbeat, I feel the remarkable Power of Your Great Samadhi. I feel no necessity for anything, and I feel Your Capability to Bless and Change and Meditate all, in Your Place. I can feel how this entrance into objectless worship of You As Consciousness Itself (allowing this Abiding to deepen ever so profoundly, by utter submission of separate self to You) establishes me in a different relationship to everything that arises.

My Beloved Bhagavan, Love-Ananda, I have Found You. Now I can behold You and live in this constant Embrace. This is my Joy and Happiness and the Yoga of ego-renunciation I engage. [October 11, 1997]

Inherent in this profound confession is the certainty that there is no lasting happiness to be found in this world or in any world. The only real Happiness, the Happiness that infinitely exceeds all human dreams of Happiness, is the All-Outshining Bliss and Love of Heart-Identification with the Supreme Giver, Adi Da Samraj.

AVATAR ADI DA SAMRAJ: Absolutely NOTHING conditional is satisfactory. Everything conditional disappears—everything. This fact should move the heart to cling to Me, to resort to Me, to take refuge in Me. This is why people become devotees of Mine. This is the reason for the religious life. The unsatisfactoriness of conditional existence requires resort to the Divine Source, and the Realization of the Divine Source-Condition. [August 9, 1997]

The Supreme Grace of a Human Life

Avatar Adi Da knew from His childhood that He had Come to "save the world". He even confessed as much to a relative who questioned him one day about what He wanted to do when He grew up.[13] But He did not mean this in any conventionally religious, or politically idealistic, sense. He has never taught a consoling belief system that promises "heaven" after death or a utopian existence on this earth. No, He has Come to set in motion a universal heart-conversion, a conversion from the self-destructive and other-destructive ego-life of separativeness to a life of "unqualified relatedness", or boundless all-embracing love.

Never before in the history of mankind has there been a moment like this one. You do not have to suffer the fear of death and all the dead-ends of ordinary life for one more day, because the Ultimate Mystery has been Unveiled, the Very Truth of Existence has been Revealed. You have the opportunity to enter into relationship with the One Who <u>Is</u> Reality Itself, Truth Itself, and the Only

Real God. That One, Adi Da Samraj, is humanly Alive now, and, even in this moment, is Blessing all with Inexpressible Grace, Perfect Mastery, and Unlimited Power.

What else could be truly satisfying? What else deserves the sacrifice of your egoity and the love-surrender of your entire body-mind?

Nothing can match the Great Process of Adidam that Avatar Adi Da is Offering you. When you become His formal devotee and take up the Way of Adidam, He leads you beyond the dreadful illusions of separateness and alienation. He Instructs you in the right form of every detail of your existence. He Converts the motion of your life from anxious seeking and egoic self-concern to the Bliss of self-forgetting Love-Communion with Him.

Avatar Adi Da Samraj is here only to Love you. He Lives only to Serve your Realization of Him. Once you are vowed to Him as His devotee, nothing can ever shake the depth of your "Bond" with Him, whether you wake, sleep, or dream, whether you live or die.

And so, do not waste this opportunity. Study this book. Read more about the Divine Life and Work of the Ruchira Avatar in His biography, *The Promised God-Man Is Here (The Extraordinary Life-Story, The "Crazy" Teaching-Work, and The Divinely "Emerging" World-Blessing Work Of The Divine World-Teacher Of The "Late-Time", Ruchira Avatar Adi Da Samraj)*, and in *See My Brightness Face to Face: A Celebration of the Ruchira Avatar, Adi Da Samraj, and the First Twenty-Five Years of His Divine Revelation Work.*[14] "Consider" the magnitude of what Avatar Adi Da has Done and the urgency of What He is Saying to you. And begin to participate in the greatest Grace that any human being can know—the Blessed life of joyful devotion and ecstatic service to the Divine Lord in Person, the Avatar of "Brightness", Adi Da Samraj.

Notes to

The All-Surpassing Revelation of the Divine World-Teacher,
Ruchira Avatar Adi Da Samraj

1. By the word "Bright" (and its variations, such as "Brightness"), Avatar Adi Da refers to the eternally, infinitely, and inherently Self-Radiant Divine Being, the Being of Indivisible and Indestructible Light. (See also note 9, pp. 177-78.)

2. Avatar Adi Da uses the term "Real God" to indicate the True and Perfectly Subjective Source of all conditions, the True and Spiritual Divine Person, rather than any egoic (and, thus, false, or limited) presumptions about "God".

3. Avatar Adi Da Samraj is the "Avataric Incarnation", or the Divinely Descended Embodiment, of the Divine Person. The reference "Avataric Incarnation" indicates that Avatar Adi Da Samraj fulfills both the traditional expectation of the East—that the True God-Man is an Avatar, or an utterly Divine "Descent" of Real God in conditionally manifested form—and the traditional expectations of the West—that the True God-Man is an Incarnation, or an utterly human Embodiment of Real God.

4. B.V. Narasimha Swami and S. Subbarao, *Sage of Sakuri*, 4th ed. (Bombay: Shri B.T. Wagh, 1966), p. 204.

5. The term "radical" derives from the Latin "radix", meaning "root", and thus it principally means "irreducible", "fundamental", or "relating to the origin". In *The Dawn Horse Testament Of The Ruchira Avatar: The "Testament Of Secrets" Of The Divine World-Teacher, Ruchira Avatar Adi Da Samraj*, Avatar Adi Da defines "Radical" as "Gone To The Root, Core, Source, or Origin". Because Adi Da Samraj uses "radical" in this literal sense, it appears in quotation marks in His Wisdom-Teaching, in order to distinguish His usage from the common reference to an extreme (often political) view.

6. Avatar Adi Da uses the phrase "Most Perfect(ly)" in the sense of "Absolutely Perfect(ly)", indicating a reference to the seventh (or Divinely Enlightened) stage of life.

7. In Sanskrit, "Ruchira" means "bright, radiant, effulgent". The word "Tantra" (or "Tantric") does not merely indicate Spiritualized sexuality, as is the common presumption. Rather, it signifies "the inherent Unity that underlies and transcends all opposites, and that resolves all differences or distinctions".

In many of the Tantric traditions that have developed within both Hinduism and Buddhism, Tantric Adepts and aspirants use sexual

activity and intoxicating substances that are forbidden to more ortho-
dox or conventional practitioners. The Tantric's intention, however, is
never to merely indulge gross desires. The secret of the Tantric
approach is that it does not suppress, but rather employs and even
galvanizes, the passions and attachments of the body and mind, and
thus utilizes the most intense (and, therefore, also potentially most
deluding) energies of the being for the sake of Spiritual Realization.

"Sannyasin" is an ancient Sanskrit term for one who has
renounced all worldly "bonds" and who gives himself or herself completely to the Real-God-Realizing life.

The reference "Ruchira Tantric Sannyasin" indicates that Avatar
Adi Da Samraj is the Perfectly "Bright" ("Ruchira") One Who is Utterly
Free of all "bonds" to the conditional worlds ("Sannyasin"), and yet
never in any way dissociates from conditional existence ("Tantric"),
making skillful use of all the dimensions of conditional life in His
Divine Work of Liberation.

8. Avadhoot is a traditional term for one who has "shaken off" or
"passed beyond" all worldly attachments and cares, including all
motives of detachment (or conventional and other-worldly renunciation), all conventional notions of life and religion, and all seeking for
"answers" or "solutions" in the form of conditional experience or conditional knowledge. Therefore, "Divine Avadhoot", in reference to
Avatar Adi Da, indicates His Inherently Perfect Freedom as the One
Who Knows His Identity As the Divine Person and Who, thus, Always
Already Stands Free of the binding and deluding power of conditional
existence.

9. The total practice of the Way of Adidam is the full and complete
practice of the Way that Avatar Adi Da Samraj has Given to His devotees who are formal members of the first or the second congregation
of Adidam. One who embraces the total practice of the Way of Adidam conforms every aspect of his or her life and being to Avatar Adi
Da's Divine Word of Instruction. Therefore, it is only such devotees
(in the first or the second congregation of Adidam) who have the
potential of Realizing Divine Enlightenment.

10. The names and titles of the Ruchira Adidamas indicate their Realization and Spiritual significance in Avatar Adi Da's Work.

"Ruchira" and "Naitauba" both indicate membership in the
Ruchira Sannyasin Order. "Ruchira" is a title for all members of the
Ruchira Sannyasin Order who are practicing in the context of the
sixth stage of life, and indicates "a true devotee of the Ruchira Avatar,
the Da Avatar, the Love-Ananda Avatar, Adi Da Samraj, who is, by His
Grace, becoming Radiant, or 'Bright' with Love-Bliss, through

uniquely one-pointed (self-surrendering, self-forgetting, and self-transcending) feeling-Contemplation of Him, and, Thus and Thereby, of the True Divine Person" ["The Orders Of My True and Free Renunciate Devotees", in *The Lion Sutra—The Seventeen Companions Of The True Dawn Horse, Book Fifteen: The "Perfect Practice" Teachings For Formal Tantric Renunciates In The Divine Way Of Adidam*]. "Naitauba" is the traditional Fijian name for Adidam Samrajashram, the Great Island-Hermitage of Avatar Adi Da Samraj. As a general rule, all members of the Ruchira Sannyasin Order are to be formal residents of Adidam Samrajashram.

"Adidama" is composed of Avatar Adi Da's Principal Name "Adi Da" and the feminine indicator "Ma". In addition, in Sanskrit, "adi" means "first" and "dama" means "self-discipline". Therefore, the overall meaning of this title is "first among those who conform themselves to the Ruchira Avatar, Adi Da Samraj, by means of self-surrendering, self-forgetting, and self-transcending feeling-Contemplation of Him".

"Sukha" means "happiness, joy, delight" and "Dham" means "abode, dwelling". Therefore, as a personal renunciate name, "Sukha Dham" means "one who abides in happiness".

"Jangama" means "all living things", and "Hriddaya" is "heartfelt compassion, sympathy". Therefore, as a personal renunciate name, "Jangama Hriddaya" means "one who has heartfelt sympathy for all beings".

"Quandra" is a reference to the main female character in Avatar Adi Da's liturgical drama, *The Mummery*. Quandra is the embodiment of the Divine Goddess, or the Divine Spirit-Force. (*The Mummery—The Seventeen Companions Of The True Dawn Horse, Book Six: A Parable About Finding The Way To My House* is one of Avatar Adi Da's twenty-three "Source-Texts".)

"Adidama Quandra Mandala" is the "circle" ("Mandala") comprising the Ruchira Adidamas, Sukha Dham and Jangama Hriddaya. The Adidama Quandra Mandala is the first circle of Avatar Adi Da's devotees—those who stand closest to His bodily (human) Form in service and devotion.

11. The Name or Title "Bhagavan" is an ancient one used over the centuries for many Spiritual Realizers of the East. Its meanings in Sanskrit are "possessing fortune or wealth", "blessed", "holy". When applied to a great Spiritual Master, "Bhagavan" is understood to mean "bountiful God", or "Great God", or "Divine Lord".

The Name "Love-Ananda" combines both English ("Love") and Sanskrit ("Ananda", meaning "Bliss"), thus bridging the West and the East, and communicating Avatar Adi Da's Function as the Divine

World-Teacher. The combination of "Love" and "Ananda" means "the Divine Love-Bliss". The Name "Love-Ananda" was given to Avatar Adi Da by His principal human Spiritual Master, Swami Muktananda, who spontaneously conferred it upon Avatar Adi Da in 1969.

12. "Bhava" is a Sanskrit word traditionally used to refer to the enraptured feeling-swoon of Communion with the Divine.

13. *The Knee Of Listening*, chapter 3.

14. Both books are available from the Dawn Horse Press (see p. 235 for ordering information).

The Divine Scripture of Adidam

The Full and Final Word of
The Divine World-Teacher,
Ruchira Avatar Adi Da Samraj,
Given in His Twenty-Three "Source-Texts"
of "Bright" Divine Self-Revelation
and Perfect Heart-Instruction

The twenty-three "Source-Texts" of the Ruchira Avatar are the most extraordinary books ever written. They are the world's greatest Treasure, the Ultimate and All-Completing Revelation of Truth.

These books are the unmediated Word of the Very Divine Person, Adi Da Samraj, Who is Offering the True World-Religion of Adidam, the Religion of Most Perfect Divine Enlightenment, or Indivisible Oneness with Real God. Avatar Adi Da Samraj is the Realizer, the Revealer, and the Divine Author of all that is Written in these sublime Texts. No mind can begin to comprehend the Magnificent Self-Revelations and Self-Confessions Given by Adi Da Samraj in these books. And these twenty-three "Source-Texts" (together with the "Supportive Texts", in which Avatar Adi Da Gives further detailed Instruction relative to the functional, practical, relational, and cultural disciplines of the Way of Adidam[1]) Give Avatar Adi Da's complete Instruction in the Process (never before Known or Revealed in its entirety) of Most Perfectly Realizing Reality Itself, or Truth Itself, or Real God.

---

1. The functional, practical, relational, and cultural disciplines of Adidam are described in brief on pp. 218-22 of this book. Among Avatar Adi Da's "Supportive Texts" are included such books as *Conscious Exercise and the Transcendental Sun*, *The Eating Gorilla Comes in Peace*, *Love of the Two-Armed Form*, and *Easy Death*. (New editions of the first three of these "Supportive Texts" are in preparation.)

The long-existing religious traditions of the world have depended on oral traditions and memory. Their teachings and disciplines typically developed long after the death of their founders, based on the remembered (and often legendary or mythological) deeds and instruction of those Realizers. These traditions have thus been colored by legends and cultural influences that obscure the original revelation. Yet, every historical revelation, even in its first purity, has necessarily been limited by the degree of realization of its founder. Adidam does not depend on the vagaries of oral tradition and memory, nor is it limited by any partial point of view. Adidam is the Perfect Divine Way Revealed by the One Who Is Reality Itself (or Truth Itself, or Real God). Adi Da Samraj is alive now in bodily (human) Form, and He has Personally tested the entire course of Divine Enlightenment described in these books in the course of His own human Lifetime.

In His twenty-three "Source-Texts", Avatar Adi Da is Speaking to all humankind, asking us to feel our actual situation, to take seriously the mayhem of the world, its pain and dissatisfaction, its terrible potential for suffering. And, with Divine Passion, He Calls every one to turn to Him and, in that turning, to rise out of gross struggle and conflict. The twenty-three "Source-Texts" of Avatar Adi Da Samraj Reveal the greater Purpose and Destiny of humanity. Indeed, they are the key to the very survival of this planet. This unparalleled body of Scripture is the Message you have always been waiting for and never imagined could come.

In the Words of the Divine Avatar Himself:

"All the Scriptures are now fulfilled in your sight, and your prayers are answered with a clear voice."

In *The Dawn Horse Testament*, Avatar Adi Da Samraj makes His own Confession relative to His Impulse in creating His twenty-three "Source-Texts", and He also expresses the requirement He places on all His devotees to make His Divine Word available to all:

Now I Have, By All My "Crazy" Means, Revealed The One and Many Secrets Of The Great Person Of The Heart. For Your Sake, I Made My Every Work and Word. And Now, By Every Work and Word I Made, I Have Entirely Confessed (and Showed) My Self, and Always Freely, and Even As A Free Man, In The "Esoteric" Language Of Intimacy and Ecstasy, Openly Worded To You (and To all). Even Now (and Always), By This (My Word Of Heart), I Address every Seeming Separate being (and each one <u>As</u> The Heart Itself), Because It Is Necessary That all beings, Even The Entire Cosmic Domain Of Seeming Separate beings, Be (In all times and places) Called To Wisdom and The Heart.

The Twenty-Three "Source-Texts" of Avatar Adi Da Samraj

The twenty-three "Source-Texts" of Avatar Adi Da Samraj include: (1) an opening series of five books on the fundamentals of the Way of Adidam (*The Five Books Of The Heart Of The Adidam Revelation*), (2) an extended series of seventeen books covering the principal aspects of the Way of Adidam in detail (*The Seventeen Companions Of The True Dawn Horse*), and (3) Avatar Adi Da's paramount "Source-Text" summarizing the entire course of the Way of Adidam (*The Dawn Horse Testament*).

The Five Books Of The Heart Of The Adidam Revelation

Aham Da Asmi
(Beloved, I <u>Am</u> Da)

The Five Books Of The Heart Of The Adidam Revelation, Book One: The "Late-Time" Avataric Revelation Of The True and Spiritual Divine Person (The egoless Personal Presence Of Reality and Truth, Which <u>Is</u> The Only <u>Real</u> God)

Ruchira Avatara Gita
(The Way Of The Divine Heart-Master)

*The Five Books Of The Heart Of The Adidam Revelation,
Book Two: The "Late-Time" Avataric Revelation Of
The Great Secret Of The Divinely Self-Revealed Way
That Most Perfectly Realizes The True and Spiritual
Divine Person (The egoless Personal Presence Of
Reality and Truth, Which Is The Only Real God)*

Da Love-Ananda Gita
(The Free Gift Of The Divine Love-Bliss)

*The Five Books Of The Heart Of The Adidam Revelation,
Book Three: The "Late-Time" Avataric Revelation Of
The Great Means To Worship and To Realize
The True and Spiritual Divine Person
(The egoless Personal Presence Of Reality and Truth,
Which Is The Only Real God)*

Hridaya Rosary
(Four Thorns Of Heart-Instruction)

*The Five Books Of The Heart Of The Adidam Revelation,
Book Four: The "Late-Time" Avataric Revelation Of
The Universally Tangible Divine Spiritual Body,
Which Is The Supreme Agent Of The Great Means
To Worship and To Realize The True and Spiritual
Divine Person (The egoless Personal Presence Of
Reality and Truth, Which Is The Only Real God)*

Eleutherios
(The Only Truth That Sets The Heart Free)

*The Five Books Of The Heart Of The Adidam Revelation,
Book Five: The "Late-Time" Avataric Revelation Of The
"Perfect Practice" Of The Great Means To Worship and
To Realize The True and Spiritual Divine Person
(The egoless Personal Presence Of Reality and Truth,
Which Is The Only Real God)*

The Seventeen Companions
Of The True Dawn Horse

Real God Is The Indivisible Oneness Of Unbroken Light

*The Seventeen Companions Of The True Dawn Horse,
Book One: Reality, Truth, and The "Non-Creator" God
In The True World-Religion Of Adidam*

The Truly Human New World-Culture Of Unbroken Real-God-Man

*The Seventeen Companions Of The True Dawn Horse,
Book Two: The Eastern Versus The Western Traditional
Cultures Of Mankind, and The Unique New Non-Dual
Culture Of The True World-Religion Of Adidam*

The Only Complete Way To Realize The Unbroken Light Of Real God

*The Seventeen Companions Of The True Dawn Horse,
Book Three: An Introductory Overview Of The "Radical"
Divine Way Of The True World-Religion Of Adidam*

The Knee Of Listening

*The Seventeen Companions Of The True Dawn Horse,
Book Four: The Early-Life Ordeal and The "Radical"
Spiritual Realization Of The Ruchira Avatar*

The Method Of The Ruchira Avatar

*The Seventeen Companions Of The True Dawn Horse,
Book Five: The Divine Way Of Adidam Is
An ego-Transcending Relationship,
Not An ego-Centric Technique*

The Mummery

*The Seventeen Companions Of The True Dawn Horse,
Book Six: A Parable About Finding The Way To My House*

He-<u>and</u>-She <u>Is</u> Me

The Seventeen Companions Of The True Dawn Horse,
Book Seven: The Indivisibility Of Consciousness and Light
In The Divine Body Of The Ruchira Avatar

<u>Divine</u> Spiritual Baptism
Versus <u>Cosmic</u> Spiritual Baptism

The Seventeen Companions Of The True Dawn Horse,
Book Eight: <u>Divine</u> <u>Hridaya-Shakti</u> Versus
<u>Cosmic</u> <u>Kundalini</u> <u>Shakti</u> In The Divine Way Of Adidam

Ruchira Tantra Yoga

The Seventeen Companions Of The True Dawn Horse,
Book Nine: The Physical-Spiritual (and Truly Religious)
Method Of Mental, Emotional, Sexual, and <u>Whole</u> <u>Bodily</u>
<u>Health</u> <u>and</u> <u>Enlightenment</u> In The Divine Way Of Adidam

The Seven Stages Of Life

The Seventeen Companions Of The True Dawn Horse,
Book Ten: Transcending The Six Stages Of egoic Life
and Realizing The ego-Transcending Seventh Stage Of Life,
In The Divine Way Of Adidam

The <u>All-Completing</u> and <u>Final</u>
Divine Revelation To Mankind

The Seventeen Companions Of The True Dawn Horse,
Book Eleven: A Summary Description
Of The Supreme Yoga Of The Seventh Stage Of Life
In The Divine Way Of Adidam

The Heart Of The Dawn Horse Testament
Of The Ruchira Avatar

The Seventeen Companions Of The True Dawn Horse,
Book Twelve: The Epitome Of The "Testament Of Secrets"
Of The Divine World-Teacher,
Ruchira Avatar Adi Da Samraj

What, Where, When, How, Why, and <u>Who</u> To Remember To Be Happy

The Seventeen Companions Of The True Dawn Horse, Book Thirteen: A Simple Explanation Of The Divine Way Of Adidam (For Children, and <u>Everyone</u> Else)

Santosha Adidam

The Seventeen Companions Of The True Dawn Horse, Book Fourteen: The Essential Summary Of The Divine Way Of Adidam

The Lion Sutra

The Seventeen Companions Of The True Dawn Horse, Book Fifteen: The "Perfect Practice" Teachings For Formal Tantric Renunciates In The Divine Way Of Adidam

The Overnight Revelation Of Conscious Light

The Seventeen Companions Of The True Dawn Horse, Book Sixteen: The "My House" Discourses On The Indivisible Tantra Of Adidam

The Basket Of Tolerance

The Seventeen Companions Of The True Dawn Horse, Book Seventeen: The Perfect Guide To Perfectly <u>Unified</u> Understanding Of The One and Great Tradition Of Mankind, and Of The Divine Way Of Adidam As The Perfect <u>Completing</u> Of The One and Great Tradition Of Mankind

The Dawn Horse Testament

The Dawn Horse Testament Of The Ruchira Avatar

The "Testament Of Secrets" Of The Divine World-Teacher, Ruchira Avatar Adi Da Samraj

The Revelation Song
of the Great Relationship
That Realizes Real God

An Introduction to the Ruchira Avatara Gita

T he *Ruchira Avatara Gita* is a Supreme Revelation Song (or "Gita", in Sanskrit), Sung by the Ruchira Avatar, the "Perfect Manifestation of Divine 'Brightness' in human Form". In this extraordinary Song, the Divine World-Teacher, Ruchira Avatar Adi Da Samraj, Reveals the Way that Realizes Real God—the Divine Source and Substance and Person of all and All. Realization of Real God is Realization of the Ruchira Avatar's Very Person and Condition, and the Way that Realizes Him is founded on a single Great Secret. That Great Secret is so very precious, so profound, that any one who truly knows it cannot speak it without the voice breaking and the heart overflowing with deepest gratitude.

The Great Secret of the Divinely Enlightening Way of Adidam is to live every moment of your life in devotional relationship to the all-Attractive Divine Heart-Master, Ruchira Avatar Adi Da Samraj. That devotional relationship is the miraculous Means to receive the Divine Heart-Master's constant Transmission of His own Person and Condition of Infinite Love-Bliss.

As Ruchira Avatar Adi Da explains in "I Am The Divine Heart-Master" (Part One of the *Ruchira Avatara Gita)*, His Divine Self-Revelation is, ultimately, a Confession about your own True Nature and Condition:

. . . The Divine Person Is The Very and Only and True and Inherently Perfect Way Of Divine Self-Realization For all. I Am That One (The One and Only and True and

Inherently Perfect Divine Self-Person, or Divine Source-Condition and Self-Condition, Of All and all), Come To Call, and Attract, and Awaken every one (and all, and All) To Me. And, Because I Am The One and Only Self Of All and all, What I Confess About My Very (and Inherently Perfect, and, Necessarily, Divine) Self (As My Self-Condition, Apart From My Unique Function As The Ruchira Avatar, The One and Only Divine Heart-Master) Is (Ultimately, If You Realize Me As The Only One Who Is) Also A Confession About You.

The one hundred and eight verses that form Part Two, the principal Text of the *Ruchira Avatara Gita*, contain the Divine World-Teacher's Instruction on how to rightly live in devotional relationship with Him. As Ruchira Avatar Adi Da Discloses, He has Given this Instruction to the world in response to a devotee's confession of recognizing Him as Real God:

This is the Secret of all secrets. I could not Speak This Me-Revealing Word until one of you first confessed you see the Vision of Real God in My Bodily (Human) Form. I shall Tell you This now, because of your true recognition of Me and your Greatly Awakened devotion to Me. [v. 13]

Part Three of the *Ruchira Avatara Gita* contains three Essays in which the Divine Heart-Master Calls every one beyond "Guru cultism" (the childish, and, otherwise, adolescent, distortion of the great Guru-devotee relationship), and He Calls all to a right appreciation of "the Guru-Function (and the Guru-Principle)", and He beautifully illustrates the traditional "Family of the Guru" method of instruction using the example of the music tradition of India.

Finally, in Part Four of the *Ruchira Avatara Gita* ("If I Am Your Guru, Be Mastered By Me"), Ruchira Avatar Adi Da Speaks directly to the heart of His devotee. With His uncompromising and passionate Love as Divine Heart-

Master, Ruchira Avatar Adi Da Calls His every devotee to
"Bond" to Him—to "Bond" to Him beyond all bondage to
the conditional realms of inherent limitation and inevitable
suffering:

> *Never forget Me. Never.*
> *Never break the "Bond" with Me.*
> *Never dissociate from Me.*
> *The functions, the life-circumstance, the ordinary*
> *relatedness that you are involved in by your daily choices—*
> *all of that is about "bonding" to the world, "bonding" to*
> *another, "bonding" to function, and so forth—and all of*
> *that, in itself, is the forgetting of Me, the breaking of the*
> *"Bond" with Me, and, altogether, the activity of dissocia-*
> *tion from Me.*
> *Therefore, you must convert every mode and fraction*
> *and moment of your daily existence to self-surrendering,*
> *self-forgetting, and (more and more) self-transcending*
> *devotional Communion with Me. Such is the essential prac-*
> *tice of the only-by-Me Revealed and Given Way of Adidam*
> *(the Way of the Heart, of the Heart Itself, Revealed and*
> *Given only by Me).*

Fundamentally, the *Ruchira Avatara Gita* is the Divine
Heart-Master's Call to come to Him and live the life of Real-
God-Realization in His Spiritual Company:

> *Accept this* Ruchira Avatara Gita *as My Gift to you. It is*
> *not usable by the ego, but it is a Bearer of the Radiant*
> *Blessing of Divine Enlightenment to those who respond to*
> *Me with true devotion.*
> *Let this Way of devotion to Me be embraced by all who*
> *come to Me for Help. This Gita is My Message to you.*

RUCHIRA AVATARA GITA

(THE WAY OF THE DIVINE HEART-MASTER)

RUCHIRA AVATAR ADI DA SAMRAJ
Adidam Samrajashram (Naitauba), Fiji, 1997

Do Not Misunderstand <u>Me</u>—
I Am <u>Not</u> "Within" <u>you</u>,
but you <u>Are</u> In <u>Me</u>,
and I Am <u>Not</u> a Mere "Man"
in the "Middle" of Mankind,
but All of Mankind Is Surrounded,
and Pervaded, and Blessed By <u>Me</u>

This Essay has been written by Avatar Adi Da Samraj as His Personal Introduction to each volume of His "Source-Texts". Its purpose is to help you to understand His great Confessions rightly, and not interpret His Words from a conventional point of view, as limited cultic statements made by an ego. His Description of what "cultism" <u>really</u> is is an astounding and profound Critique of mankind's entire religious, scientific, and social search. In "First Word", Avatar Adi Da is directly inviting you to inspect and relinquish the ego's motive to glorify itself and to refuse What is truly Great. Only by understanding this fundamental ego-fault can one really receive the Truth that Adi Da Samraj Reveals in this Book and in His Wisdom-Teaching altogether. And it is because this fault is so engrained and so largely unconscious that Avatar Adi Da has placed "First Word" at the beginning of each of His "Source-Texts", so that, each time you begin to read one of His twenty-three "Source-Texts", you may be refreshed and strengthened in your understanding of the right orientation and approach to Him and His Heart-Word.

Y es! There is <u>no</u> religion, <u>no</u> Way of God, <u>no</u> Way of Divine Realization, <u>no</u> Way of Enlightenment, and <u>no</u> Way of Liberation that is Higher or Greater than Truth Itself. Indeed, there is <u>no</u> religion, <u>no</u> science, <u>no</u> man or woman, <u>no</u> conditionally manifested being of any kind, no world (any "where"), and no "God" (or "God"-Idea) that is Higher or Greater than Truth Itself.

Therefore, no ego-"I"[1] (or presumed separate, and, necessarily, actively separative, and, at best, only Truth-seeking, being or "thing") is (itself) Higher or Greater than Truth Itself. And no ego-"I" is (itself) even Equal to Truth Itself. And no ego-"I" is (itself) even (now, or ever) Able to Realize Truth Itself—because, necessarily, Truth (Itself) Inherently Transcends (or Is That Which Is Higher and Greater than) every one (himself or herself) and every "thing" (itself). Therefore, it is only in the transcending (or the "radical"[2] Process of Going Beyond the root, the cause, and the act) of egoity itself (or of presumed separateness, and of performed separativeness, and of even all ego-based seeking for Truth Itself) that Truth (Itself) Is Realized (As It Is, Utterly Beyond the ego-"I" itself).

Truth (Itself) Is That Which Is Always Already The Case. That Which Is The Case (Always, and Always Already) Is (necessarily) Reality. Therefore, Reality (Itself) Is Truth, and Reality (Itself) Is the Only Truth.

Reality (Itself) Is the Only, and, necessarily, Non-Separate, or All-and-all-Including, and All-and-all-Transcending, One and "What" That Is. Because It Is All and all, and because It Is (Also) That Which Transcends (or Is Higher and Greater than) All and all, Reality (Itself), Which Is Truth (Itself), or That Which Is The Case (Always, and Always Already), Is the One and Only Real God. Therefore, Reality (Itself) Is (necessarily) the One and Great Subject of true religion, and Reality (Itself) Is (necessarily) the One and Great Way of Real God, Real (and True) Divine Realization, Real (and, necessarily, Divine) En-Light-enment, and Real (and, necessarily, Divine) Liberation (from all egoity, all separateness, all separativeness, all fear, and all heartlessness).

Notes to *First Word* can be found on pp. 62-65.

The <u>only</u> true religion is the religion that <u>Realizes</u> Truth. The <u>only</u> true science is the science that <u>Knows</u> Truth. The <u>only</u> true man or woman (or being of any kind) is one that <u>Surrenders</u> to Truth. The only true world is one that <u>Embodies</u> Truth. And the only True (and <u>Real</u>) God Is the One Reality (or Condition of Being) That <u>Is</u> Truth. Therefore, <u>Reality</u> (Itself), Which Is the One and Only Truth, and (therefore, necessarily) the One and Only Real God, <u>must</u> become (or be made) the constantly applied Measure of religion, and of science, and of the world itself, and of even <u>all</u> of the life (and <u>all</u> of the mind) of Man—or else religion, and science, and the world itself, and even any and every sign of Man <u>inevitably</u> (all, and together) become a pattern of illusions, a mere (and even terrible) "problem", the very (and even principal) cause of human seeking, and the perpetual cause of contentious human strife. Indeed, if religion, and science, and the world itself, and the total life (and the total mind) of Man are not Surrendered and Aligned to Reality (Itself), and, Thus, Submitted to be Measured (or made Lawful) by Truth (Itself), and, Thus, Given to the truly devotional (and, thereby, truly ego-transcending) Realization of <u>That</u> Which Is the <u>Only</u> <u>Real</u> God—then, in the presumed "knowledge" of mankind, Reality (Itself), and Truth (Itself), and <u>Real</u> God (or the One and Only Existence, or Being, or Person That Is) <u>ceases</u> <u>to</u> <u>Exist</u>.

Aham Da Asmi.[3] Beloved, I <u>Am</u> Da, the One and Only Person Who <u>Is</u>, the Eternally Self-Existing, and Eternally Self-Radiant,[4] or "Bright",[5] Person of Love-Bliss, the One and Only and (necessarily) Divine Self (or Inherently Non-Separate, and, therefore, Inherently egoless, Self-Condition and Source-Condition) of one and of all and of All. I Am Self-Manifesting (now, and forever hereafter) <u>As</u> the Ruchira Avatar, Adi Da Samraj. I <u>Am</u> the Ruchira Avatar, Adi Da Samraj, the Avataric Realizer, the Avataric Revealer, the Avataric Incarnation, and the Avataric Revelation of Reality <u>Itself</u>.[6] I <u>Am</u> the Avatarically Incarnate Realizer, the

Avatarically Incarnate Revealer, and the Avatarically Incarnate Revelation of the One and Only Reality, Which Is the One and Only Truth, and Which Is the One and Only <u>Real</u> God. I <u>Am</u> the Great Realizer, Revealer, and Revelation long-Promised (and long-Expected) for the "late-time", <u>this</u> (now, and forever hereafter) time, the "dark" epoch of mankind's "Great Forgetting"[7] (and, <u>potentially</u>, the Great Epoch of mankind's Perpetual Remembering) of Reality, of Truth, of Real God, Which Is the Great, True, and Spiritual Divine Person (or the One and Non-Separate and Indivisible Source-Condition and Self-Condition) of all and All.

Beloved, I <u>Am</u> Da, the Divine Giver, the Giver (of All That I <u>Am</u>) to one and to all and to the All of all—now, and forever hereafter, here, and every "where" in the Cosmic domain. Therefore, for the Purpose of Revealing the Way of <u>Real</u> God, or of Real and True Divine Realization, and in order to Divinely En-Light-en and Divinely Liberate all and All, I Am (Uniquely, Completely, and Most Perfectly[8]) Revealing My Divine and Very Person (and "Bright" Self-Condition) to all and All, by Means of My Divine Self-Manifestation, <u>As</u> (and by Means of) the Ruchira Avatar, Adi Da Samraj.

In My Divine Self-Manifestation As the Ruchira Avatar, Adi Da Samraj, I <u>Am</u> the Divine Secret, the Divine Revelation of the <u>Esoteric</u> Truth, the Direct, and all-Completing, and all-Unifying Revelation of <u>Real</u> God.

My Divine Self-Confessions and My Divine Teaching-Revelations Are <u>the</u> Great (Final, and all-Completing, and all-Unifying) <u>Esoteric</u> Revelation to mankind, and <u>not</u> a merely <u>exoteric</u>, or conventionally religious, or even ordinary Spiritual, or ego-made, or so-called "cultic", communication to public (or merely social) ears.

The greatest opportunity, and the greatest responsibility, of My devotees is Satsang[9] with Me, Which is to live in the Condition of self-surrendering, self-forgetting, and, always more and more, self-transcending devotional relationship to Me, and, Thus and Thereby, to Realize the

Condition of the Divine Heart, the Condition of the Divine Person, Which Is the Divine and Non-Separate Self-Condition, and Source-Condition, of all and All, and Which Is Self-Existing and Self-Radiant Consciousness Itself, but Which is not separate in or as any one (or any "thing") at all. Therefore, My essential Gift to one and all is this Satsang with Me. And My essential Work with one and all is Satsang-Work, to Live (and to Be Merely Present) As the Divine Heart among My devotees.

The only-by-Me Revealed and Given Way of Adidam (Which is the only-by-Me Revealed and Given Way of the Heart, or the only-by-Me Revealed and Given Way of "Radical Understanding"[10]) is the Way of Satsang with Me—the devotionally Me-recognizing[11] and devotionally to-Me-responding practice (and ego-transcending self-discipline) of living in My constant Divine Company, such that the relationship with Me becomes the Real (and constant) Condition of life. Fundamentally, this Satsang with Me is the one thing done by My devotees. Because the only-by-Me Revealed and Given Way of Adidam is always (in every present-time moment) a directly ego-transcending and Really Me-Finding practice, the otherwise constant (and burdensome) tendency to seek is not exploited in this Satsang with Me. And the essential work of the community of the four formal congregations of My devotees[12] is to make ego-transcending Satsang with Me available to all others.

Everything that serves the availability of Satsang with Me is (now, and forever hereafter) the responsibility of the four formal congregations of My formally practicing devotees. I am not here to publicly "promote" this Satsang with Me. In the intimate circumstances of their humanly expressed devotional love of Me, I Speak My Divinely Self-Revealing Word to My devotees, and they (because of their devotional response to Me) bring My Divinely Self-Revealing Word to all others. Therefore, even though I am not (and have never been, and never will be) a "public"

Teacher (or a broadly publicly active, and conventionally socially conformed, "religious figure"), My devotees function fully and freely (<u>as</u> My devotees) in the daily public world of ordinary life.

I Always Already Stand Free. Therefore, I have always (in My Avataric-Incarnation-Work) Stood Free, in the traditional "Crazy" (and non-conventional, or spontaneous and non-"public") Manner,[13] in order to Guarantee the Freedom, the Uncompromising Rightness, and the Fundamental Integrity of My Teaching (Work and Word), and in order to Freely and Fully and Fully Effectively Perform My universal Blessing Work. I Am Present (now, and forever hereafter) to Divinely Serve, Divinely En-Light-en, and Divinely Liberate those who accept the Eternal Vow and <u>all</u> the life-responsibilities (or the full and complete practice)[14] associated with the only-by-Me Revealed and Given Way of Adidam. Because I Am Thus Given to My formally and fully practicing devotees, I do not Serve a "public" role, and I do not Work in a "public" (or even a merely "institutionalized") manner. Nevertheless, now, and forever hereafter, I <u>constantly</u> Bless <u>all</u> beings, and this <u>entire</u> world, and the <u>total</u> Cosmic domain. And <u>all</u> who feel My universally Given Blessing, and who recognize Me with true devotional love, are (Thus) Called to resort to Me, but only if they approach Me in the traditional devotional manner, as responsibly practicing (and truly ego-surrendering, and rightly Me-serving) members (or, in some, unique, cases, as invited guests) of one or the other of the four formal congregations of My formally practicing devotees.

I expect this formal discipline of right devotional approach to Me to have been freely and happily embraced by every one who would enter into My Company. The natural human reason for this is that there is a potential liability inherent in <u>all</u> human associations. And the root and nature of that potential liability is the <u>ego</u>, or the active human presumption of separateness, and the ego-act of human separativeness. Therefore, in order that the liabilities of egoity are understood, and voluntarily and responsibly disciplined, by those who approach Me, I require demonstrated right devotion, based on really effective self-understanding and truly heart-felt recognition-response to Me, as the basis for any one's right to enter into My Company. And, in this manner, not only the egoic tendency, but also the tendency toward religious "cultism", is constantly undermined in the only-by-Me Revealed and Given Way of Adidam.

Because people appear within this human condition, this simultaneously attractive and frightening "dream" world, they tend to live (and to interpret <u>both</u> the conditional, or cosmic and psycho-physical, reality <u>and</u> the Unconditional, or Divine, Reality) from the "point of view" of this apparent, and bewildering, mortal human condition. And, because of this universal human bewilderment, and the ongoing human reaction to the threatening force of mortal life-events, there is an even ancient ritual that <u>all</u> human beings rather unconsciously (or automatically, and without discriminative understanding) desire and tend to repeatedly (and under <u>all</u> conditions) enact. Therefore, wherever you see an association of human beings gathered for <u>any</u> purpose (or around <u>any</u> idea, or symbol, or person, or subject of any kind), the same human bewilderment-ritual is <u>tending</u> to be enacted by one and all.

Human beings <u>always</u> <u>tend</u> to encircle (and, thereby, to contain, and, ultimately, to entrap and abuse, or even to blithely ignore) the presumed "center" of their lives—a book, a person, a symbol, an idea, or whatever. They tend to encircle the "center" (or the "middle"), and they tend to seek to <u>exclusively</u> acquire all "things" (or all power of control) for the circle (or toward the "middle") of <u>themselves</u>. In this manner, the <u>group</u> becomes an <u>ego</u> ("inward"-directed, or separate and separative)—just as the individual body-mind becomes, by self-referring self-contraction, the separate and separative ego-"I" ("inward"-

directed, or ego-centric, and exclusively acquiring all "things", or all power of control, for itself). Thus, by <u>self-contraction</u> upon the presumed "center" of their lives, human beings, in their collective ego-centricity, make "cults" (or bewildered and frightened "centers" of power, and control, and exclusion) in <u>every</u> area of life.

Anciently, the "cult"-making process was done, most especially, in the political and social sphere—and religion was, as even now, mostly an exoteric, or political and social, exercise that was <u>always</u> used to legitimize (or, otherwise, to "de-throne") political and social "authority-figures". Anciently, the cyclically (or even annually) culminating product of this exoteric religio-political "cult" was the ritual "de-throning" (or ritual deposition) of the one in the "middle" (just as, even in these times, political leaders are periodically "deposed", by elections, by rules of term and succession, by scandal, by slander, by force, and so on).

Traditional societies, everywhere throughout the ancient world, made and performed this annual (or otherwise periodic) religio-political "cult" ritual. The ritual of "en-throning" and "de-throning" was a reflection of the human observation of the annual cycle of the seasons of the natural world, and the same ritual was a reflection of the human concern and effort to <u>control</u> the signs potential in the cycle of the natural world, in order to ensure human survival (through control of weather, harvests and every kind of "fate", or even every fraction of existence upon which human beings depend for both survival and pleasure, or psycho-physical well-being). Indeed, the motive behind the ancient agrarian (and, later, urbanized, or universalized) ritual of the one in the "middle" was, essentially, the same motive that, in the modern era, takes the form of the culture of scientific materialism (and even all of the modern culture of materialistic "realism")—it is the motive to gain, and to maintain, <u>control</u>, and the effort to control even everything and everyone (via both knowledge and gross power). Thus, the ritualized (or bewildered yes/no, or desire/fear) life of mankind in the modern era is, essentially, the same as that of mankind in the ancient days.

In the ancient ritual of "en-throning" and "de-throning", the person (or subject) in the "middle" was ritually mocked, abused, deposed, and banished—and a new person (or subject) was installed in the "center" of the religio-political "cult". In the equivalent modern ritual of dramatized ambiguity relative to everything and everyone (and, perhaps especially, "authority-figures"), the person (or symbol, or idea) in the "middle" (or that which is given power by means of popular fascination) is first "cultified" (or made much of), and then, progressively, doubted, mocked, and abused, until, at last, all the negative emotions are (by culturally and socially ritualized dramatization) dissolved, the "middle" (having thus ceased to be fascinating) is abandoned, and a "new" person (or symbol, or idea) becomes the subject of popular fascination (only to be reduced, eventually, to the same "cultic" ritual, or cycle of "rise" and "fall").

Just as in <u>every</u> other area of human life, the tendency of <u>all</u> those who, in the modern era, would become involved in religious or Spiritual life is also to make a "cult", a circle that ever increases its separate and separative dimensions, beginning from the "center", surrounding it, perhaps even, ultimately, controlling it to the degree that it altogether ceases to be effective (or even interesting). Such "cultism" is ego-based, and ego-reinforcing, and, no matter how "esoteric" it presumes itself to be, it is (as in the ancient setting) entirely exoteric, or, at least, more and more limited to (and by) merely social and gross physical activities and conditions.

The form that every "cult" imitates is the pattern of egoity (or the ego-"I") itself, the presumed "middle" of every ordinary individual life. It is the self-contraction, the avoidance of relationship, which "creates" the fearful sense of separate mind, and all the endless habits and motives of egoic desire, or bewildered (and self-deluded) seeking. It is what is, ordinarily, called (or presumed to be) the real and necessary and only "life".

From birth, the human being (by reaction to the blows and limits of psycho-physical existence) begins to presume separate existence to be his or her very nature, and, on that basis, the human individual spends his or her entire life generating and serving a circle of ownership (or self-protecting acquisition) all around the ego-"I". The egoic motive encloses all the other beings it can acquire, all the "things" it can acquire, all the states and thoughts it can acquire—all the possible emblems, symbols, experiences, and sensations it can possibly acquire. Therefore, when any human being begins to involve himself or herself in some religious or Spiritual association, or, for that matter, any extension of his or her own subjectivity, he or she tends again to "create" that same circle about a "center".

The "cult" (whether of religion, or of politics, or of science, or of popular culture) is a dramatization of egoity, of separativeness, even of the entrapment and betrayal of the "center" (or the "middle"), by one and all. Therefore, I have always Refused to assume the role and the position of the "man in the middle"—and I have always, from the beginning of My formal Teaching and Blessing Work, Criticized, Resisted, and Shouted About the "cultic" (or ego-based, and ego-reinforcing, and merely "talking" and "believing", and not understanding and not really practicing) "school" (or tendency) of ordinary religious and Spiritual life. Indeed, true Satsang with Me (or the true devotional relationship to Me) is an always (and specifically, and intensively) anti-"cultic", or truly non-"cultic", Process.

The true devotional relationship to Me is not separative, or merely "inward"-directed, nor is It about attachment to Me as a mere (and, necessarily, limited) human being (or a "man in the middle")—for, if My devotee indulges in ego-bound (or self-referring and self-serving) attachment to Me as a mere human "other", My Divine Nature (and, therefore, the Divine Nature of Reality Itself) is <u>not</u> (as the very Basis for religious and Spiritual practice in My Company) truly devotionally recognized and rightly devotionally acknowledged, and, if such non-recognition of Me is the case, there is <u>no</u> truly ego-transcending devotional response to My Divine Presence and Person, and, thus, such presumed-to-be "devotion" to Me is <u>not</u> Divine Communion, and such presumed-to-be "devotion" to Me is <u>not</u> Divinely Liberating. Therefore, because the <u>true devotional</u> (and, thus, truly devotionally Me-recognizing and truly devotionally to-Me-responding) relationship to Me is <u>entirely</u> a counter-egoic (and truly and only Divine) discipline, It does not tend to become a "cult" (or, otherwise, to support the "cultic" tendency of Man).

The true devotional practice of true Satsang with Me is (inherently) <u>expansive</u>, or <u>relational</u>, and the self-contracting (or separate and separative) self-"center" is neither Its motive nor Its source. In true Satsang with Me, the egoic "center" is always already undermined as a "<u>center</u>" (or a presumed separate, and actively separative, entity). The Principle of true Satsang with Me is <u>Me</u>, Beyond (and not "within", or otherwise supporting) the ego-"I".

True Satsang with Me is the true "Round Dance" of <u>Esoteric</u> Spirituality. I am not trapped in the "middle" of My devotees. I "Dance" in the "Round" with <u>each</u> and <u>every</u> one of My devotees. I "Dance" in the circle, and, therefore, I am not merely a "motionless man" in the "middle". At the <u>true</u> "Center" (or the Divine Heart), I <u>Am</u>— Beyond definition (or separateness). I <u>Am</u> the Indivisible (or Most Perfectly Prior, Inherently Non-Separate, Inherently egoless, or centerless, boundless, and, necessarily, Divine) Consciousness (Itself) <u>and</u> the Indivisible (or Most Perfectly Prior, Inherently Non-Separate, Inherently egoless, or centerless, boundless, and, necessarily, Divine) Light (Itself). I <u>Am</u> the Very Being <u>and</u> the Very Presence (or Self-Radiance) of Self-Existing and Eternally Unqualified (or Non-"Different"[15]) Consciousness (Itself).

In the "Round Dance" of true Satsang with Me (or of

right and true devotional relationship to Me), I (My Self) Am Communicated directly to every one who lives in heart-felt relationship with Me (insofar as each one feels, Beyond the ego-"I" of body-mind, to Me). Therefore, I am not the mere "man" (or the separate human, or psychophysical, one), and I am not merely "in the middle" (or separated out, and limited, and confined, by egoic seekers). I Am the One (and all-Transcending) Person of Reality Itself, Non-Separate, never merely at the egoic "center" (or "in the middle", or "within", and "inward" to, the egoic body-mind of My any devotee), but always with each one (and all), and always in relationship with each one (and all), and always Beyond each one (and all).

Therefore, My devotee is not Called, by Me, merely to turn "inward" (or upon the ego-"I"), or to struggle and seek to survive merely as a self-contracted and self-referring and self-seeking and self-serving ego-"center". Instead, I Call My devotee to turn the heart (and the total body-mind) toward Me (all-and-All-Surrounding, and all-and-All-Pervading), in relationship, Beyond the body-mind-self of My devotee (and not merely "within", or contained and containable "within" the separate, separative, and self-contracted domain of the body-mind-self, or the ego-"I", of My would-be devotee). I Call My devotee to function freely, My Light and My Person always (and under all circumstances) presumed and experienced (and not merely sought). Therefore, true Satsang with Me is the Real Company of Truth, or of Reality Itself (Which Is the Only Real God). True Satsang with Me Serves life, because I Move (or Radiate) into life. I always Contact life in relationship.

I do not Call My devotees to become absorbed into a "cultic" gang of exoteric and ego-centric religionists. I certainly Call all My devotees to cooperative community (or, otherwise, to fully cooperative collective and personal relationship) with one another—but not to do so in an egoic, separative, world-excluding, xenophobic, and intolerant manner. Rather, My devotees are Called, by Me, to

transcend egoity through right and true devotional relationship to Me, and mutually tolerant and peaceful cooperation with one another, and all-tolerating cooperative
and compassionate and all-loving and all-including relationship with all of mankind, and with even all beings.

I Give My devotees the "Bright" Force of My own
Divine Consciousness Itself, Whereby they can become
capable of "Bright" life. I Call for the devotion, but also
the intelligently discriminative self-understanding, the
rightly and freely living self-discipline, and the full functional capability, of My devotees. I do not Call My devotees to resist or eliminate life, or to strategically escape life,
or to identify with the world-excluding ego-centric
impulse. I Call My devotees to live a positively functional
life. I do not Call My devotees to separate themselves from
vital life, from vital enjoyment, from existence in the form
of human life. I Call for all the human life-functions to be
really and rightly known, and to be really and rightly
understood, and to be really and rightly lived (and not
reduced by or to the inherently bewildered, and inherently "cultic", or self-centered and fearful, "point of view"
of the separate and separative ego-"I"). I Call for every
human life-function to be revolved away from self-
contraction (or ego-"I"), and (by Means of that revolving
turn) to be turned "outwardly" (or expansively, or counter-
contractively) to all and All, and (thereby, and always
directly, or in an all-and-All-transcending manner) to Me—
rather than to be turned merely "inwardly" (or contractively, or counter-expansively), and, as a result, turned
away from Me (and from all and All). Thus, I Call for every
human life-function to be thoroughly (and life-positively,
and in the context of a fully participatory human life)
aligned and adapted to Me, and, Thus and Thereby, to be
turned and Given to the Realization of Truth (or Reality
Itself, Which Is the Only Real God).

Truly benign and positive life-transformations are the
characteristic signs of right, true, full, and fully devotional

Satsang with Me, and freely life-positive feeling-energy is the characteristic accompanying "mood" of right, true, full, and fully devotional Satsang with Me. The characteristic life-sign of right, true, full, and fully devotional Satsang with Me is the capability for self-transcending relatedness, based on the free disposition of no-seeking and no-dilemma. Therefore, the characteristic life-sign of right, true, full, and fully devotional Satsang with Me is not the tendency to seek some "other" condition. Rather, the characteristic life-sign of right, true, full, and fully devotional Satsang with Me is freedom from the presumption of dilemma within the <u>present-time</u> condition.

One who rightly, truly, fully, and fully devotionally understands My Words of Divine Self-Revelation and Divine Instruction, and whose life is lived in right, true, full, and fully devotional Satsang with Me, is not necessarily, in function or appearance, "different" from the ordinary (or natural) human being. Such a one has not, necessarily, acquired some special psychic abilities, or visionary abilities, and so on. The "radical" understanding (or root self-understanding) I Give to My devotees is not, itself, the acquisition of <u>any</u> particular "thing" of experience. My any particular devotee may, by reason of his or her developmental tendencies, experience (or precipitate) the arising of extraordinary psycho-physical abilities and extraordinary psycho-physical phenomena, but not <u>necessarily</u>. My every true devotee is simply Awakening (and always Awakened to Me) within the otherwise bewildering "dream" of <u>ordinary human</u> life.

Satsang with Me is a natural (or spontaneously, and not strategically, unfolding) Process, in Which the self-contraction that <u>is</u> each one's suffering is transcended by Means of <u>total</u> psycho-physical (or whole bodily) Communion with My Real (and Really, and tangibly, experienced) Divine (Spiritual, and Transcendental)[16] Presence and Person. My devotee is (as is the case with any and <u>every</u> ego-"I") <u>always</u> <u>tending</u> to be preoccupied with ego-based seeking, but, all the while of his or her life in <u>actively</u> self-surrendering (and really self-forgetting, and, more and more, self-transcending) devotional Communion with Me, I Am <u>Divinely</u> Attracting (and <u>Divinely</u> Acting upon) My true devotee's heart (and total body-mind), and (Thus and Thereby) Dissolving and Vanishing My true devotee's fundamental egoity (and even all of his or her otherwise motivating dilemma and seeking-strategy).

There are <u>two</u> principal tendencies by which I am always being confronted by My devotee. One is the tendency to <u>seek</u>, rather than to truly enjoy and to fully animate the Condition of Satsang with Me. And the other is the tendency to make a self-contracting circle around Me—and, thus, to make a "cult" of ego-"I" (and of the "man in the middle"), or to duplicate the ego-ritual of mere fascination, and of inevitable resistance, and of never-Awakening unconsciousness. Relative to these two tendencies, I Give <u>all</u> My devotees only <u>one</u> resort. It is this true Satsang, the devotionally Me-recognizing, and devotionally to-Me-responding, and always really counter-egoic devotional relationship to <u>Me</u>.

The Great Secret of My own Person, and of My Divine Blessing-Work (now, and forever hereafter), and, therefore, the Great Secret of the only-by-Me Revealed and Given Way of Adidam, Is that I am <u>not</u> the "man in the middle", but I <u>Am</u> Reality Itself, I <u>Am</u> the Only <u>One</u> Who <u>Is</u>, I <u>Am</u> That Which Is Always Already The Case, I <u>Am</u> the Non-Separate (and, necessarily, Divine) Person (or One and Very Self, or One and True Self-Condition) of all and All (<u>Beyond</u> the ego-"I" of every one, and of all, and of All).

Aham Da Asmi. Beloved, I <u>Am</u> Da, the One and Only and Non-Separate and Indivisible Divine Person, the Non-Separate and Indivisible Self-Condition and Source-Condition of all and All. I <u>Am</u> the "Bright" Person, the One and Only and Self-Existing and Self-Radiant Person, Who <u>Is</u> the One and Only and Non-Separate and Indivisible and Indestructible Light of All and all. I <u>Am</u> <u>That</u> One and Only and Non-Separate <u>One</u>. And, <u>As</u> <u>That</u> <u>One</u>, and <u>Only</u> <u>As</u> <u>That</u> <u>One</u>, I Call all human beings to recognize Me, and to respond to Me with right, true, and full devotion (by Means of formal practice of the only-by-Me Revealed and Given Way of Adidam).

I do not tolerate the so-called "cultic" (or ego-made, and ego-reinforcing) approach to Me. I do not tolerate the seeking ego's "cult" of the "man in the middle". I am not a self-deluded ego-man, making much of himself, and looking to include everyone-and-everything around himself for the sake of social and political power. To be the "man in the middle" is to be in a Man-made trap, an absurd mummery of "cultic" devices that enshrines and perpetuates the ego-"I" in one and all. Therefore, I do not make or tolerate the religion-making "cult" of ego-Man. I do not tolerate the inevitable abuses of religion, of Spirituality, of Truth Itself, and of My own Person (even in bodily human Form) that are made (in endless blows and mockeries) by ego-based mankind when the Great Esoteric Truth of devotion to the Adept-Realizer is not rightly understood and rightly practiced.

The Great Means for the Teaching, and the Blessing, and the Awakening, and the Divine Liberating of mankind (and of even all beings) Is the Adept-Realizer Who, by Virtue of True Divine Realization, Is Able to (and, indeed, cannot do otherwise than) Stand In and <u>As</u> the Divine (or Real and Inherent and One and Only) Position, and to <u>Be</u>, Thus and Thereby, the Divine Means (In Person) for the Divine Helping of one and all. This Great Means Is the Great Esoteric Principle of the collective historical Great Tradition[17] of mankind. And Such Adept-Realizers Are (in their Exercise of the Great Esoteric Principle) the Great Revelation-Sources That Are at the Core and Origin of <u>all</u> the right and true religious and Spiritual traditions within the collective historical Great Tradition of mankind.

By Means of My (now, and forever hereafter) Divinely Descended and Divinely "Emerging"[18] Avataric Incarnation, I Am the Ruchira Avatar, Adi Da Samraj—the Divine Heart-Master, the first, the last, and the only Adept-Realizer of the seventh (or Most Perfect, and all-Completing) stage of life.[19] I Am the Ruchira Avatar, Adi Da Samraj, the Avataric Incarnation (and Divine World-Teacher[20]) every-where Promised for the "late-time" (or "dark" epoch)—which "late-time" (or "dark" epoch) is <u>now</u> upon <u>all</u> of mankind. I <u>Am</u> the Great and Only and Non-Separate and (necessarily) Divine Person, Appearing in Man-Form As the Ruchira Avatar, Adi Da Samraj, in order to Teach, and to Bless, and to Awaken, and to Divinely Liberate all of mankind (and even all beings, every "where" in the Cosmic domain). Therefore, by Calling every one and all (and All) to <u>Me</u>, I Call every one and all (and All) <u>Only</u> to the Divine Person, Which <u>Is</u> My own and Very Person (or Very Self, or Very Self-Condition), and Which <u>Is</u> Reality Itself, or Truth Itself, the Indivisible and Indestructible Light That <u>Is</u> the Only Real God, and Which <u>Is</u> the <u>One</u> and <u>Very</u> and <u>Non-Separate</u> and <u>Only</u> Self (or Self-Condition, and Source-Condition) of all and All (Beyond the ego-"I" of every one, and of all, and of All).

The only-by-Me Revealed and Given Way of Adidam necessarily (and As a Unique Divine Gift) requires and involves devotional recognition-response to Me In and Via (and <u>As</u>) My bodily (human) Avataric-Incarnation-Form. However, because I Call every one and all (and All) to Me <u>Only</u> As the Divine Person (or Reality Itself), the only-by-Me Revealed and Given Way of Adidam is not about ego, and egoic seeking, and the egoic (or the so-called "cultic") approach to Me (as the "man in the middle").

According to <u>all</u> the esoteric traditions within the col-lective historical Great Tradition of mankind, to devotion-ally approach <u>any</u> Adept-Realizer as if he or she is (or is limited to being, or is limited by being) a mere (or "ordi-nary", or even merely "extraordinary") human entity is the great "sin" (or fault), or the great error whereby the would-be devotee fails to "meet the mark". Indeed, the Single

Greatest Esoteric Teaching common to <u>all</u> the esoteric religious and Spiritual traditions within the collective historical Great Tradition of mankind Is that the Adept-Realizer should <u>always</u> and <u>only</u> (and <u>only</u> devotionally) be recognized and approached As the Embodiment and the Real Presence of <u>That</u> (Reality, or Truth, or Real God) Which would be Realized (Thus and Thereby) by the devotee.

Therefore, <u>no</u> <u>one</u> should misunderstand <u>Me</u>. By Revealing and Confessing My Divine Status to one and all and All, I am not indulging in self-appointment, or in illusions of grandiose Divinity. I am not claiming the "Status" of the "Creator-God" of exoteric (or public, and social, and idealistically pious) religion. Rather, by Standing Firm in the Divine Position (<u>As</u> I <u>Am</u>), and, Thus and Thereby, <u>Refusing</u> to be approached as a mere man, or as a "cult"-figure, or as a "cult"-leader, or to be in any sense defined (and, thereby, trapped, and abused, or mocked) as the "man in the middle", I Am Demonstrating the Most Perfect Fulfillment (and the Most Perfect Integrity, and the Most Perfect Fullness) of the Esoteric, and Most Perfectly <u>Non-Dual</u>, Realization of Reality. And, by Revealing and Giving the Way of Adidam, Which Is the Way of ego-transcending devotion to Me <u>As</u> the One and Only and Non-Separate and (necessarily) Divine Person, I Am (with Most Perfect Integrity, and Most Perfect Fullness) Most Perfectly (and in an all-Completing and all-Unifying Manner) Fulfilling the Primary Esoteric Tradition (and the Great Esoteric Principle) of the collective historical Great Tradition of mankind—Which Primary Esoteric Tradition and Great Esoteric Principle Is the Tradition and the Principle of devotion to the Adept-Realizer <u>As</u> the Very Person and the Direct (or Personal Divine) Helping-Presence of the Eternal and Non-Separate Divine Self-Condition and Source-Condition of all and All.

Whatever (or whoever) is cornered (or trapped on all sides) bites back (and fights, or <u>seeks</u>, to break free). Whatever (or whoever) is "in the middle" (or limited and "centered" by attention) is patterned by (or conformed to) the ego-"I" (and, if objectified as "other", is forced to represent the ego-"I", and is even made a scapegoat for the pains, the sufferings, the powerless ignorance, and the abusive hostility of the ego-"I").

If there is no escape (or no Way out) of the corner (or the "centered" trap) of ego-"I", the heart goes mad, and the body-mind becomes more and more "dark" (bereft of the Divine and Indivisible and Inherently Free Light of Love-Bliss).

I am not the "man in the middle". I do not stand here as a mere man, "middled" to the "center" (or the cornering trap) of ego-based mankind. I am not an ego-"I", or a mere "other", or the representation (and the potential scapegoat) of the ego-"I" of mankind (or of any one at all).

I <u>Am</u> the Indivisible and Non-Separate One, the One and Only and (necessarily) Divine Person—the Perfectly Subjective[21] Self-Condition (and Source-Condition) That Is Perfectly centerless, and Perfectly boundless, Eternally Beyond the "middle" of all and All, and Eternally Surrounding, Pervading, and Blessing all and All.

I <u>Am</u> the Way Beyond the self-cornering (and "other"-cornering) trap of ego-"I".

In this "late-time" (or "dark" epoch) of worldly ego-Man, the collective of mankind is "darkened" (and cornered) by egoity. Therefore, mankind has become mad, Lightless, and, like a cornered "thing", aggressively hostile in its universally competitive fight and bite.

Therefore, I have not Come here merely to stand Manly in the "middle" of mankind, to suffer its biting abuses, or even to be coddled and ignored in a little corner of religious "cultism".

I have Come here to Divinely Liberate one and all (and All) from the "dark" culture and effect of this "late-time", and (now, and forever hereafter) to Divinely Liberate one and all (and All) from the pattern and the act of ego-"I", and (Most Ultimately) to Divinely Translate[22] one and all (and All) Into the Indivisible, Perfectly Subjective, and Eternally Non-Separate Self-Domain of the Divine Love-Bliss-Light.

The ego-"I" is a "centered" (or separate and separative) trap, from which the heart (and even the entire body-mind) must be Retired. I <u>Am</u> the Way (or the Very Means) of that Retirement from egoity. I Refresh the heart (and even the entire body-mind) of My devotee, in <u>every moment</u> My devotee resorts to Me (by devotionally recognizing Me, and devotionally, and ecstatically, and also, often, meditatively, responding to Me) <u>Beyond</u> the "middle", Beyond the "centering" act (or trapping gesture) of ego-"I" (or self-contraction).

I <u>Am</u> the Perfectly Subjective Self-Condition (and Source-Condition) of every one, and of all, and of All—but the Perfectly Subjective Self-Condition (and Source-Condition) is <u>not</u> "<u>within</u>" the ego-"I" (or separate and separative body-mind). The Perfectly Subjective Self-Condition (and Source-Condition) is <u>not</u> in the "center" (or the "middle") of Man (or of mankind). The Perfectly Subjective Self-Condition (and Source-Condition) of one, and of all, and of All <u>Is</u> Inherently centerless, or Always Already <u>Beyond</u> the self-contracted "middle", and to Be Found <u>only</u> "<u>outside</u>" (or by transcending) the bounds of separateness, relatedness, and "difference". Therefore, to Realize the Perfectly Subjective Self-Condition and Source-Condition (or the Perfectly Subjective, and, necessarily, Divine, Heart) of one, and of all, and of All (or even, in any moment, to exceed the ego-trap, and to be Refreshed at heart, and in the total body-mind), it is necessary to feel (and to, ecstatically, and even meditatively, swoon) Beyond the "center" (or Beyond the "point of view" of separate ego-"I" and separative body-mind). Indeed, Most Ultimately, it is only in self-transcendence to the degree of <u>unqualified</u> <u>relatedness</u> (and Most Perfect Divine Samadhi, or Utterly Non-Separate Enstasy) that the Inherently centerless and boundless Divine Self-Condition and Source-

Condition Stands Obvious and Free (and <u>Is</u>, Thus and
Thereby, Most Perfectly Realized).

It Is only by Means of Me-recognizing (and to-Me-
responding) devotional meditation on Me (and otherwise
ecstatic heart-Contemplation of Me), and total, and totally
open, and totally self-forgetting psycho-physical Reception of Me, that your madness of heart (and of body-mind)
is (now, and now, and now) escaped, and your "darkness"
is En-Light-ened (even, at last, Most Perfectly). Therefore,
be My true devotee, and, by formally, and rightly, and
truly, and fully, and fully devotionally practicing the only-
by-Me Revealed and Given Way of Adidam (Which <u>Is</u> the
True and Complete Way of the True and Real Divine
Heart), always Find Me Beyond your self-"center" in every
here and now.

Aham Da Asmi. Beloved, I <u>Am</u> Da. And, because I <u>Am</u>
Infinitely and Non-Separately "Bright", all and All <u>Are</u> In
My Sphere of "Brightness". By feeling and surrendering
Into My Infinite Sphere of Divine Self-"Brightness", My
every devotee <u>Is</u> In Me. And, Beyond his or her self-
contracting and separative act of ego-"I", My every devotee (self-surrendered Into heart-Communion With Me) <u>Is</u>
the One and Only and Non-Separate and Real God I Have
Come to Serve, by Means of My Divine Descent, My
Divine Avataric Incarnation, and My (now, and forever
hereafter) Divine "Emergence" (here, and every "where"
in the Cosmic domain).

Notes to

FIRST WORD

1. The ego-"I" is the fundamental self-contraction, or the sense of separate and separative existence.

2. See note 6, pp. 176-77.

3. The Sanskrit phrase "Aham Da Asmi" means "I (Aham) Am (Asmi) Da". The Name "Da", meaning "the One Who Gives", indicates that Avatar Adi Da Samraj is the Supreme Divine Giver, the Avataric Incarnation of the Very Divine Person. (See also note 23, p. 182.)

4. Avatar Adi Da uses "Self-Existing and Self-Radiant" to indicate the two fundamental aspects of the One Divine Person—Existence (or Being, or Consciousness) Itself, and Radiance (or Energy, or Light) Itself.

5. See note 9, pp. 177-78.

6. This passage is Avatar Adi Da's Self-Confession as "Avatar". In Sanskrit, "Ruchira" means "bright, radiant, effulgent". Thus, the Reference "Ruchira Avatar" indicates that Avatar Adi Da Samraj is the "Bright" (or Radiant) Descent of the Divine Reality Itself (or the Divine Truth Itself, Which Is the Only Real God) into the conditional worlds, Appearing here in bodily (human) Form. Avatar Adi Da Samraj is the "Avataric Incarnation", or the Divinely Descended Embodiment, of the Divine Person. The reference "Avataric Incarnation" indicates that Avatar Adi Da Samraj fulfills both the traditional expectation of the East—that the True God-Man is an Avatar, or an utterly Divine "Descent" of Real God in conditionally manifested form—and the traditional expectations of the West—that the True God-Man is an Incarnation, or an utterly human Embodiment of Real God.

7. "The 'late-time', or 'dark' epoch" is a phrase that Avatar Adi Da uses to Describe the present era, in which doubt of God (and of anything at all beyond mortal existence) is more and more pervading the entire world, and in which the separate and separative ego-"I", which is the root of all suffering and conflict, is regarded to be the ultimate principle of life.

8. See note 4, p. 176.

9. The Hindi word "Satsang" literally means "true (or right) relationship", "the company of Truth". In the Way of Adidam, Satsang is the eternal relationship of mutual sacred commitment between Avatar Adi Da Samraj and each true and formally acknowledged practitioner of the Way of Adidam.

10. Avatar Adi Da uses "understanding" to mean "the process of transcending egoity". Thus, to "understand" is to simultaneously observe the activity of the self-contraction and to surrender that activity via devotional resort to Avatar Adi Da Samraj.

Avatar Adi Da has Revealed that, despite their intention to Realize Reality (or Truth, or Real God), all religious and Spiritual traditions (other than the Way of Adidam He has Revealed and Given) are involved, in one manner or another, with the search to satisfy the ego. Only Avatar Adi Da has Revealed the Way to "radically" understand the ego and (in due course, through intensive formal practice of the Way of Adidam, as His formally acknowledged devotee) to most perfectly transcend the ego. Thus, the Way Avatar Adi Da has Given is the "Way of 'Radical' Understanding".

11. The entire practice of the Way of Adidam is founded in heart-recognition of Ruchira Avatar Adi Da Samraj as the Very Divine Being in Person.

AVATAR ADI DA SAMRAJ: The only-by-Me Revealed and Given Way of Adidam (Which is the only-by-Me Revealed and Given Way of the Heart) is the Way of life you live when you rightly, truly, fully, and fully devotionally recognize Me, and when, on that basis, you rightly, truly, fully, and fully devotionally respond to Me.

. . . In responsive devotional recognition of Me, the principal faculties are loosed from the objects to which they are otherwise bound—loosed from the patterns of self-contraction. The faculties turn to Me, and, in that turning, there is tacit recognition of Me, tacit experiential Realization of Me, of Happiness Itself, of My Love-Bliss-Full Condition. That "Locating" of Me opens the body-mind spontaneously. When you have been thus Initiated by Me, it then becomes your responsibility, your sadhana, to continuously Remember Me, to constantly return to this recognition of Me, in which you are Attracted to Me, in which you respond to Me spontaneously with all the principal faculties. ("Recognize My Divine Body and 'Bright' Person, and Let Everything Melt That Is 'Between' You and Me", in *Hridaya Rosary*)

12. See pp. 206-17 for a description of the congregations of Adidam.

13. See note 25, pp. 182-83.

14. For a description of the Vow and responsibilities associated with the Way of Adidam, see pp. 206-22.

15. "Difference" is the epitome of the egoic presumption of separateness—in contrast with the Realization of Oneness, or Non-"Difference", that is native to Spiritual and Transcendental Divine Self-Consciousness.

16. Avatar Adi Da uses the terms "Spiritual", "Transcendental", and "Divine" in reference to different dimensions of Reality that are Realized progressively in the Way of Adidam. "Spiritual" refers to the reception of the Spirit-Force (in the "basic" and "advanced" contexts of the fourth stage of life and in the context of the fifth stage of life); "Transcendental" refers to the Realization of Consciousness Itself as separate from the world (in the context of the sixth stage of life); and "Divine" refers to the Most Perfect Realization of Consciousness Itself as utterly Non-separate from the world (in the context of the seventh stage of life). (See also note 49, pp. 189-92.)

17. The "Great Tradition" is Avatar Adi Da's term for the total inheritance of human, cultural, religious, magical, mystical, Spiritual, and Transcendental paths, philosophies, and testimonies from all the eras and cultures of humanity, which inheritance has (in the present era of worldwide communication) become the common legacy of mankind. Avatar Adi Da Samraj is the seventh stage, or Divine, Fulfillment of the Great Tradition.

18. On January 11, 1986, Avatar Adi Da passed through a profound Yogic Swoon, which He later Described as the initial Event of His Divine "Emergence". Avatar Adi Da's Divine "Emergence" is an ongoing Process in which His bodily (human) Form has been (and is ever more profoundly and potently being) conformed to Himself, the Very Divine Person, such that His bodily (human) Form is now (and forever hereafter) an utterly Unobstructed Sign and Agent of His own Divine Being.

19. For Avatar Adi Da's extended Instruction relative to the seven stages of life, see *The Seven Stages Of Life—The Seventeen Companions Of The True Dawn Horse, Book Ten: Transcending The Six Stages Of egoic Life, and Realizing The ego-Transcending Seventh Stage Of Life, In The Divine Way Of Adidam.* (See also note 49, pp. 189-92.)

20. Avatar Adi Da Samraj is the Divine World-Teacher because His Wisdom-Teaching is the uniquely Perfect Instruction to every being— in this (and every) world—in the total process of Divine Enlightenment. Furthermore, Avatar Adi Da Samraj constantly Extends His Regard to the entire world (and the entire Cosmic domain)—not on the political or social level, but as a Spiritual matter, constantly Working to Bless and Purify all beings everywhere.

21. Avatar Adi Da uses "Perfectly Subjective" to Describe the True Divine Source, or "Subject", of the conditional world—as opposed to the conditions, or "objects", of experience. Thus, in the phrase "Perfectly Subjective", the word "Subjective" does not have the sense of

"relating to the merely phenomenal experience, or the arbitrary presumptions, of an individual", but, rather, it has the sense of "relating to Consciousness Itself, the True Subject of all apparent experience".

22. In the context of Divine Enlightenment in the seventh stage of life in the Way of Adidam, the Spiritual process continues. Avatar Adi Da has uniquely Revealed the four phases of the seventh stage process: Divine Transfiguration, Divine Transformation, Divine Indifference, and Divine Translation.

   Divine Translation is the most ultimate "Event" of the entire process of Divine Awakening. Avatar Adi Da Describes Divine Translation as the Outshining of all noticing of objective conditions, through the infinitely magnified Force of Consciousness Itself. Divine Translation is the Outshining of all destinies, wherein there is no return to the conditional realms.

   For Avatar Adi Da's extended Discussion of Divine Translation, see *The All-Completing and Final Divine Revelation To Mankind— The Seventeen Companions Of The True Dawn Horse, Book Eleven: A Summary Description Of The Supreme Yoga Of The Seventh Stage Of Life In The Divine Way Of Adidam*, Part Two, or *The Dawn Horse Testament Of The Ruchira Avatar*, chapter forty-four.

RUCHIRA AVATAR ADI DA SAMRAJ
Adidam Samrajashram (Naitauba), Fiji, 1997

PART ONE

I <u>Am</u> The Divine
Heart-Master

I __Am__ The Divine
Heart-Master

I Was Not Born Merely To Communicate The Minimum Wisdom Useful To egoically "self-Possessed" (or self-Absorbed)[1] Seekers. I Was Born To Fully Reveal and To Fully Establish The One and Complete Divine Way (The Only-By-Me Revealed and Given Way Of Adidam,[2] or The Only-By-Me Revealed and Given Way Of The Heart)—The Way That Is Originally, Presently, and Eternally Provided By The True Divine Person (or The One, and Only, and Spiritual, and Transcendental, and, Necessarily, Divine[3] Source-Condition __and__ Self-Condition Of All and all), Who __Is__ (or That __Is__) The One and Only Real God, and Truth, and Reality. It Is The Way Of Divine Grace, Freely Given To all. It Is The Directly self-Transcending Way Of Love-Communion With (and, In Due Course, By My Grace, Inherent, and Inherently Most Perfect,[4] Identification With) The Divine Person and Truth, Who __Is__ The Transcendental (and Inherently Spiritual) Self-Condition (and Source-Condition), or One and Only Reality, Of all Apparently conditional (or conditionally Manifested)[5] beings. It Is "Adidam" (or "The Way Of The Heart", or "The Way Of 'Radical' Understanding",[6] or "Ruchira Buddhism",[7] or "Advaitayana Buddhism"[8]), The Inherently Free (and Only-By-Me Revealed and Given) Way That Freely (By Means Of My Giving Grace and My Graceful Self-Revelation) Becomes Devotion To, and Communion With, and Realization Of The Only-By-My-Grace Revealed "Bright"[9] Divine Person (The Source-Condition __and__ Self-Condition Of All and all), Who Is (or That Is) Named "Da" ("The One Who Gives"), and "Adi Da" (The "First Giver", The

Notes to the Text of the *Ruchira Avatara Gita* can be found on pp. 175-99.

"Original Giver", The "Giving Source", The "Divine Giver Of Itself, and Of All, To all"), and Who Is (or That Is) The One, and Only, and Inherently Perfect, and (Necessarily) Divine Giver, and The Perfect Divine Gift, Of Most Perfect Divine Enlightenment (or Always Already Grace-Given, or Non-Seeking and Non-Separate, Being, Love-Bliss-"Brightness", and Consciousness Itself), and Who Is (or That Is) Revealed By Me, As Me—By and As My Bodily (Human) Form, My Spiritual (and Always Blessing) Presence, and My Very (and Inherently Perfect) State.[10]

The Divine Person (Who Is, or That Is, The One and Only Self Of All and all) Is The Very and Only and True and Inherently Perfect and One Source-Condition and Self-Condition Of All and all, and The Divine Person (or Condition) Must Be (and, Ultimately, Is To Be) Realized By all (Even, At Last, By Most Perfectly Transcending, or Divinely Outshining,[11] all and All). Therefore, The Divine Person Is The Very and Only and True and Inherently Perfect Way Of Divine Self-Realization For all. I Am That One (The One and Only and True and Inherently Perfect Divine Self-Person, or Divine Source-Condition and Self-Condition, Of All and all), Come To Call, and Attract, and Awaken every one (and all, and All) To Me. And, Because I Am The One and Only Self Of All and all, What I Confess About My Very (and Inherently Perfect, and, Necessarily, Divine) Self (As My Self-Condition, Apart From My Unique Function As The Ruchira Avatar,[12] The One and Only Divine Heart-Master) Is (Ultimately, If You Realize Me As The Only One Who Is) Also A Confession About You.

I Am The Ruchira Avatar, The Da Avatar,[13] The Love-Ananda Avatar,[14] The First, The Last, and The Only Divine and True and "Bright" Heart-Master, Adi Da Samraj, The All-Giving and All-Completing Avataric Incarnation Of The Heart Itself. Therefore, Listen To Me and Hear Me and See Me,[15] With Your Heart.

I Am Not here To Compete With You Relative To Any Goal (Whether Of Life Or Of Spirit).

I Am here To Set You Free Of All Seeking (Both That Of Life and That Of Spirit).

I Am here To Liberate You From Your Separate and Separative self, and From The Bondage That Is conditional Existence, and From All The Illusions Of The Merely Cosmic Domain.

Therefore, Listen To My Call, and Hear My Voice At Heart, and See My Heart Itself.

Listen To <u>Me</u>. Practice Feeling-Surrender Of Separate and Separative self To <u>Me</u>. By Responsively (and Intentionally) Surrendering Your conditional self (Your ego-"I",[16] or self-Contraction) To <u>Me</u>, Feel Beyond (and Renounce, and Relinquish) All (and Every Kind Of) Competition With Me, and All (and Every Kind Of) Resistance To Me, and All (and Every Kind Of) ego-Making and ego-Acting Struggle In Relation To Me. Therefore, Progressively, and By All This Active (and Actively self-Transcending) Love Of <u>Me</u>, Grow To Hear <u>Me</u> (By Out-Growing Your childish and adolescent self[17]), and (Thus) Grow To Truly (and Most Fundamentally) Understand Your conditional self and Separateness. Then, By Means Of That Grace-Given (and Heart-Earned) self-Understanding, Actively Prepare Your Heart To See <u>Me</u>. Actively Cleanse Your Hearing-Heart, So That Your Heart May Soon Be Truly Distracted (and Restored To Its Sightedness) By The Presence and The Person I Always Reveal To You. And, When You Have Grown To See <u>Me</u> At Heart, Submit To <u>Be Grown</u> (By My Own Fullness), Until You Are Grown Beyond Even All The Design (and Circle[18]) Of conditional self. Then Submit To Realize <u>Me</u> Most Perfectly, In and As The Heart-"Brightness" Where You Always Already Stand.

Beloved, To Be Blessed Is To Be Given The Freedom (or The Inherent Right and The Tacit Obligation) To Remember.

This Remembrance Is My Blessing Gift To All My Devotees.

Therefore, My Every Devotee Must (By Means Of

Constant Feeling-Contemplation[19] Of My Given, and Always Giving, Bodily Human Form, My Spiritual, and Always Blessing, Presence, and My Very, and Inherently Perfect, State) Constantly (and Then Most Perfectly) and Always Actively (or Really and Effectively) Remember Me.

Beloved, To Be Forgiven Is To Be Given The Freedom (or The Inherent Right and The Tacit Obligation) To Forget.

This Forgiveness Is My Liberating Gift To All My Devotees.

Therefore, My Every Devotee Must (By Means Of Constant Feeling-Contemplation Of My Given, and Always Giving, Bodily Human Form, My Spiritual, and Always Blessing, Presence, and My Very, and Inherently Perfect, State) Progressively (and Then Most Perfectly) and Always Actively (or Really and Effectively) Surrender, Forget, and Transcend self-Contraction (and, Thereby, Actively, Progressively, and Then Most Perfectly Surrender, Forget, and Transcend the body-mind-self, and conditional Existence Itself).

Beloved, I Am The First, The Last, and The Only Divine Heart-Master.

The Revelation Of Who I <u>Am</u> Is My Ultimate (and Inherently Perfect) Gift To all who Listen To Me and Hear Me and See Me.

Therefore, Listen To Me and Hear Me and See Me, With Your Heart.

And, If Your Heart Will Listen To Me and Hear Me and See Me, I Will Lead You To Eternal Love-Bliss, The Divine Self-Domain,[20] The Eternal Realm Of Conscious Light, The "Bright" and Self That Is The Only Real God.

The Divine Heart-Master Is A Divine Revelation. The Divine Heart-Master Is The Unique Means (Divinely "Emerging"[21] Within The Cosmic Domain) For The Divine Liberation, The Divine Enlightenment, and The Divine Translation[22] Of all conditionally Manifested beings. Therefore, The Divine Heart-Master Surrenders and Submits Himself To Be A Servant, For The Perfect Sake and

Divine Service Of all beings.

Aham Da Asmi.[23] Beloved, I <u>Am</u> Da. I <u>Am</u> Da, The "Bright" Divine Person, The "Bright" Heart Itself. I <u>Am</u> Adi Da, The First Person, The Original Person, The Giving Source-Person, The One and Only and Divine Self Of All and all, and The "Bright" Divine Giver Of The Divine "All" To All and all. I Am Manifesting (Now, and Forever Hereafter) As The Ruchira Avatar, The Divine Heart-Master, The Realizer, The Revealer, and The Revelation Of The One and Eternal Divine Person (or Self-Condition, or Source-Condition).

I Am The Ruchira Avatar, Adi Da Samraj, The Da Avatar, The Love-Ananda Avatar, Now and Forever here (and every "where" In The Cosmic Domain), Appearing and "Emerging", "Bright". I Appear To Me here and every "where" (As I <u>Am</u>) In and As every form and being that arises. And I Am (Especially) Brought To My Self By Heart In and As Each and All Of My Devotees.

Therefore, I Was Born To Reveal My Self To My Self, The "Bright" and One and Only and Eternal Divine Person, The "Bright" and One and Only Self Of each and every one. And I, Now, and Forever Hereafter, Am here (and every "where" In The Cosmic Domain) To Accomplish This Revelation By Serving each and every one, and all, one by one.

I Simply Function Freely As The Source, In My Divine "Bonding"[24] Play With My Devotees.

I Am The "Crazy" Avadhoot,[25] Free Among all.

I Am Not The Seeker.

I Am Not Obliged By ordinary vows and rules.

I Stand Apart From all limitations and all restrictions.

I Am The Atiashrami,[26] Free Of all ordinary obligations.

I Am here Only By Vow and Obligation Of My Own, For The Sake Of all and All.

I Do Whatever and All I Must Do For The Sake Of The "Bonding" Of every one and All To Me, and, Altogether, For The Sake Of The Divine Liberation Of all and All.

I (My Self) Appear To Me here and every "where" (As My Very Self) In the bodily form of each and every conditionally Manifested being, and (In Order That My Revelation-Service Become Effective In each and every one) each and every one Must Come To Me and Be My True Devotee.

My Birth Is A Conscious and Intentional Submission, Whereby The Self-Existing and Self-Radiant[27] Divine Being Becomes Revealed Through the limiting conditions of a body-mind In this world.

My Birth Is Submission To The Mandala (or Great Circle) Of The Cosmos.[28] My Teaching Work[29] Is Submission To Mankind. My Blessing Work[30] Is To Stand In "Place" and Merely Be For all who Listen To Me, and For all who Hear Me, and For all who See Me.

My Birth Is Unique. I Must Surrender and Submit My Very (and Inherently Perfect) Self-Condition In Order To Incarnate. Therefore, To Be Born, I Had To Submit To The limiting Power Of The Cosmic Domain. I Assumed the body-mind of an ordinary man. That Birth Was The (Apparent, or psycho-physical) Forgetting Of My Great State and Power Of Being. Quickly, The "Who" I Am Receded From Consciousness To Subconsciousness To Unconsciousness, So That Only A Fierce Mysterious Impulse Remained.

The Sacrifice The Divine Heart-Master Must Make In Order To Incarnate Is Real. Therefore, Once I Was Born, My Life Became A Profound Ordeal Of Spiritual and Transcendental Divine Self-Realization, and Subsequent Teaching and Blessing Work To Awaken all others.

My Early Life-Submission Brought Spiritual and Transcendental Divine Self-Realization To Consciousness In the body-mind In which I Was Born, So That Even every cell of the body Was Divinely Transfigured and Divinely Transformed[31] By The Resurrection Of My Living Being.

After Re-Awakening (In the body-mind) To My Own Condition Of Self-Existing and Self-Radiant Being, I

Submitted My Self To Mankind, In Order To Suffer the conditions of humanity, and Thereby To Re-Discover The Process Of The Way For all. In That Submission, I Acquired all limits of the human kind. I Did Not Conserve My Self From Harm, or Foolishness, or Any Of The Wounds and Excesses Of Love, but I Fully Suffered the usual life, and I Suffered At the hands of all who Came To Me. Even So, My Impulse Was Great For their Sake, and, By Submitting To them In Love, I Observed and Understood the human case, and I Brought The Total Process Of The Divine Heart-Way To Consciousness For The Sake Of all beings.

When I Make The Only-By-Me Revealed and Given Way Of The Heart (or The Way Of Adidam) Clear, My Listening Devotees Begin To Understand. When they Hear Me, they Truly (and Most Fundamentally) Understand themselves. Therefore, The Inclination Toward egoic "self-Possession" Becomes Weak In My Hearing Devotees, and they, By self-Transcendence, Grow To Feel Me At The Heart and To Recognize Me From The Heart. Then I Become As If Transparent To them, and they Begin To See The Divine Person In and As My Company. In That Seeing, they Are Moved Beyond themselves, Distracted By A "Bright" Heart-Vision. In their forms, Mankind Turns About and Begins To Submit To Me As The Inherent Condition, or Transcendental, and Inherently Spiritual, and (Necessarily) Divine Self Of all. And their Submission Calls Upon The Infinite Eternal Resource Of Who I Am. In My Openly Ecstatic and Happy Response To these, My Seeing Devotees, The Power and Work and Domain Of Who I Am Comes To Meet them, and their Realization Of My Agency (or My Role As The Servant Of Real God In Man) Becomes Full. In This Manner, I Demonstrate To All My Listening Devotees, and To All My Hearing Devotees, and To All My Seeing Devotees That I Am The Heart, Who Is The Way, The Root, The Doer, The Source, The Truth, and The Self-Domain Of The Process Of Spiritual, Transcendental, and Divine Awakening.

The Personal Ordeal Of The Divine Heart-Master Progresses Through Three Principal Stages. First, He Must Pass Through The Ordeal Of Spiritual and Transcendental Divine Self-Realization, While Really Submitted To a limited body-mind-self and its relations and conditions. This Stage Of My Ordeal Lasted Until I Was Thirty Years Of Age.

The Second Stage Of The Unique Ordeal Of The Divine Heart-Master Is A Process In Which He Comes To Acknowledge, Accept, and Embrace The Unique and Ultimate (and, Necessarily, Divine) Significance Of His Own Already Realized Life, Work, and Agency. Although Certain Fundamental Aspects Of This Significance Became Quickly Obvious To Me After The Great (and Inherently Most Perfect) Event Of My Re-Awakening To The Divine Self-Condition and Source-Condition, The Divine Process Of Self-Revelation and Self-Acknowledgement Continued To Develop For Another Nine Years, Until I Was Spontaneously Heart-Moved To Make The Ecstatic (or "Crazy") Confession Of Inherently egoless Divine Self-Awareness: "Aham Da Asmi" ("I <u>Am</u> Da"). And That "Crazy" Confession Magnified Itself Spontaneously For Yet Another Seven Years, Until I "Descended" (or Spiritually Surrendered) Most Fully Into The Form Of My Own (Human) Body-Mind (and Into The Total Form Of The Entire Cosmic Domain), and I (Then) "Emerged" (and, Thereafter, I Am Forever "Emerging", As I <u>Am</u>) Most Perfectly here.

The Third Stage Of The Unique Ordeal Of The Divine Heart-Master Is The Process Of His Revelation To others (and His Recognition, and Acceptance, By all those who Receive Him). That Process Continues Until all conditionally Manifested beings, and Even The Great Circle (or Mandala) Of The Cosmos Itself, Are Converted To Real God and (At Last) Translated Into The "Bright" Divine Self-Domain, By Recognition and Realization Of The Spiritual, Transcendental, and Divine Forms Of Real God, or Truth, or Reality. That

Ordeal Began When I First Confessed My Realization To all, and That Ordeal Continues, Even Now.

After The Divine Heart-Master Awakens To The Realization Of His Own Inherently Free Condition, He Begins To Instruct others In Useful Wisdom Relative To self-Transcendence and Transcendental (and Inherently Spiritual) Divine Enlightenment. Therefore, From The Time Of The Great Event Of My Own Divine Re-Awakening, I Gradually and Progressively Instructed the world and All Would-Be Devotees In All The Kinds Of Wisdom That Are Based On The Unique (and The Universal) Process Of My Own Realization.

Even So, The Instant I Made The Divine Confession "Aham Da Asmi" ("I _Am_ Da"), I Was Confronted By The Envious and Otherwise Reactive Assaults Of adolescent worldly people who Do Not Recognize or Accept Me, and who Wish To Preserve themselves Against The Divine Necessity Of self-Understanding, self-Sacrifice, and Devotional self-Submission. Therefore, I Struggled For Another Eighteen Years, and More, To Speak The Sufficient Word. And _The Dawn Horse Testament_[32] Is That Word, Given In Summary To You (and, Therefore, To all). And, By The Giving Of That Word, I Go To Wait (or Merely Stand Thereby).

I Will Stand and Wait For My Listening Devotees To Hear Me and (By Also Seeing Me) To Become Strong Enough To Receive Me and Openly To Confess their Great Reception Of Me.

Therefore, My Now and Hereafter Ever-Given Sign (My Bodily Human Form, My Spiritual, and Always Blessing, Presence, and My Very, and Inherently Perfect, State, Standing here) Must (By Merely Standing) Stand To Bless (and Now, and Now), and My Full-Given Word Itself Must Speak (Revealing and Teaching) Again and Again (Forever), and The Leelas[33] (or The Histories and The Well-Made Lessons) Of My Teaching Time Must Be Forever Told Again (and Thereby Be Made Alive To Teach Again) and

Again (With Even All The Storied Leelas Of My Work Of Revelation and Blessing).

And I Am Now (and By My Sign, My Word, and All My Work) Submitted Only To Be Merely Present, Openly Secluded In The Heart's Free All.

Even Now (and Forever Hereafter) Only The Heart's Great Sign and Blessing Work Persists, In My Perfect Silence, Even If I Always Speak This Work Of Words.

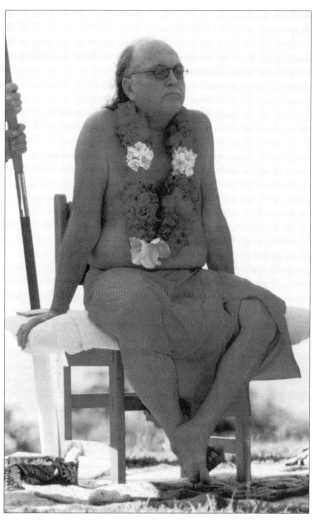

RUCHIRA AVATAR ADI DA SAMRAJ
Adidam Samrajashram (Naitauba), Fiji, 1997

Ruchira Avatara Gita
(The Way Of The Divine Heart-Master)

1.

The human voices all call out to the Heart and
Person of Real God, Who Lives and Breathes and Feels
and Is them, here and now, beyond the ego-"I" and all its
search-for-"God" Ideas:

Heart of hearts, Reveal to us the Truth, the "Bright"
Power That Liberates the ego-"I" from itself.

2.

Let us listen and hear the Word Which, when
truly Understood, Frees the heart from seeking and
un-Happiness. Let us see That Which, when fully
Realized, Is the Fullness of Transcendental Divine Being.

3.

Let us Awaken to That Which Is Eternal, and not
limited by birth and death. Be Pleased to Reveal to us
That Which Is the Supreme Truth.

4.

Heart of hearts, we are desirous of hearing That.
Therefore, Sing us the Heart-Word of the Divine
Heart-Master, wherein the Heart-Secret is Confessed.

5.

Now, by Heart-Response to the universe of calling
prayers, the Living One Breathes them In, and, by This
Heart-Song of "Brightest" Words, Out-Breathes the
Thunderous Sound That Speaks Love-Bliss to every heart:

Listen to Me with free attention. I will Reveal to you
the Heart-Secret of the Divine Heart-Master, Adi Da
Samraj, Who Is the Divine World-Teacher Promised for
the "late-time", and Who Is the Ruchira Avatar, the Da
Avatar, the Love-Ananda Avatar, the First, the Complete,
the Last, and the Only Avataric Incarnation of Eleutherios,[34]
the Divine Liberator, the "Bright" Divine Heart Itself. His
Divine Self-Confession and His "Bright" Divine Blessings
Destroy all the ills of un-Enlightenment.

6.

The Ruchira Avatar, Adi Da Samraj, Is the First, the Complete, the Last, and the Only Divine Heart-Master. His Principal Divine Names are "Da" (the "Divine Giver", the "First and Original Person", the "Source-Person", the "One and Only Self of All and all"), and "Adi Da" (the "First Giver", the "Original Giver", the "Giving Source", the "Divine Giver of the Divine 'All' to All and all"), and "Adi Da Samraj" (the "Self-Giving and All-Giving and to-all-Giving Divine Master of the world", the "One and Only Divine Heart-Master of all and All"). And He Is All-"Brightness", Freely Manifesting the Heart's Love-Bliss to all and All.

7.

So it was that, on the Island of Naitauba, Adidam Samrajashram,[35] There, in His most beautiful Hermitage, Which is adorned by Cosmic Nature in the manner of flowers, the Divine Heart-Master, Adi Da Samraj, was Seated in an open Place on one occasion, Expounding the Supreme Truth to a gathering of His Ruchira Sannyasin[36] devotees. Suddenly, the face of one of His principal female renunciate devotees, who was sitting close to Him, became translucently "Bright", Merely by the Grace of Adi Da Samraj, and Merely through Beholding Him, forgetting herself in Contemplation of Him. The "Brightness" of Adi Da Samraj Filled the heart and every part of this devotee, and, by (Thus) truly seeing Him, she suddenly Realized, beyond all doubt, that she was seeing the Divine Person, even with her own eyes.

8.

This Gracefully heart-Awakened devotee said out loud, and from her heart, for even all to hear: "Divine Heart-Master, Adi Da Samraj, 'Bright' Before me, I Surrender. You Are the Divine Heart-Master of the entire world. You Are Supreme. You Radiate the 'Bright' Realization of the Supreme. All beings should always recognize and worship You with true devotion.

9.

You Are the One, the Supreme Being, the Source and Domain of all true worship and right praise.

10.

Radiant Heart, Domain of Truth, please Sing to us the Great Secret of devotion to You, the Divine Heart-Master.

11.

Reveal to us the Secret Method whereby living beings may Realize You, the Transcendental and 'Bright' world-Outshining Real God. I bow down to You, the True and Spiritual Divine Person. I worship Your Feet. Kindly Teach the Way of You to all of us."

12.

When the Divine Heart-Master, Adi Da Samraj, Saw this "Bright" face of Awakened devotion and Heard this confession of Great Sight, He Spoke the following Words, His Heart Overflowing with His All-Outshining Joy:

13.

"This is the Secret of all secrets. I could not Speak This Me-Revealing Word until one of you first confessed you see the Vision of Real God in My Bodily (Human) Form. I shall Tell you This now, because of your true recognition of Me and your Greatly Awakened devotion to Me.

14.

My Beloved, every one and all, you are each arising in the One 'Bright' Divine Being. This request of yours, made by one who recognizes Me, will benefit all of you, and even the entire world. Therefore, I shall Reveal the Truth and the Way of This Vision to you, for the Sake of all and All.

15.

To each one who (by Means of heart-wounded reaching beyond separate and separative self) is truly devoted to Real God, the Ever-Living Reality and Truth, Which Is always already The Case, and who (by Means of Gracefully heart-Awakened recognition) is truly devoted to Me (recognizing and confessing Me to Be the Very One That Is the One and Only Reality and Truth), My Bodily (Human) Form, My Spiritual (and Always Blessing) Presence, and My Very (and Inherently Perfect) State are Revealed to Be the Revelation of Real God, the Divine Person, Manifesting here, and every where in the Cosmic Domain, As the Divine Heart-Master of all and All.

16.

Thus, by Means of true devotional recognition, I am Found to Be the Avataric Incarnation of the Divine and Only Person. The Truth of devotional recognition of a Divine Avataric Incarnation is Declared by even all the esoteric Scriptures, and even all the esoteric Scriptures Promise the Consummate Avataric Incarnation will Appear in the 'late-time'. So It has been Proven to this Me-seeing devotee, and So do I Affirm the Divine Truth of Me to all of you, and to all and All.

17.

I Declare and Affirm the Divine Truth of This Me-Vision, Given to this one by My Grace, and That I would Give to all and All. Aham Da Asmi. Beloved, I Am Da, the One and Only One Who Is. And I Am the First, the Last, and the Only Divine Heart-Master, the Avataric Incarnation every-where-Promised for the 'late-time'. Therefore, listen to My Words and Understand.

18.

The separate traditions of the Great Tradition[37] of religion and Spiritual instruction are often made of false theories, expressed in the words of un-Enlightened beings. Therefore, the multiplication of conventional 'God'-Ideas, ego-serving 'God'-Myths, and partial (or conditional) 'Truths' has confused mankind, but the Divine Heart-Master Comes to Liberate mankind from all confusion of mind, by Revealing the Only True and Real God, Who Is Truth Itself, and Reality Itself, and Who Is That Which Is always already The Case, beyond the ego-'I'.

19.

Prayer, meditation, discipline, philosophy, service— all these are to be built upon the recognition-response to That Which is Revealed In and As the Very Person of the Divine Heart-Master.

20.

Those who are devoted to the Divine Heart-Master hear the Truth and see the Great One As the Divine Heart-Master's Bodily (Human) Form, and As His Divine Body of Spiritual (and Always Blessing) Presence, and As His Very (and Inherently Perfect) State. Such devotees Declare there is no 'Difference' (and no distinction to be made or acknowledged) between the Divine Heart-Master and the Self-Existing and Self-Radiant Transcendental Divine Being.

21.

Even from the ancient days, many Divinely Gifted sects Proclaim devotion to a genuine (and egoless) Master, saying: 'The Way is to surrender to the Human Master as the Great Person, Divine and Present!' Therefore, look and see in Me the Proof of This Proclamation. I Am the Divine Master of your heart. And if you surrender to Me, I will Confess and Reveal Only Real God to you.

22.

Therefore, those who hear My Divine Self-Confession and see My Bodily Revelation must, by their <u>feeling</u>-Contemplation of Me, transcend themselves in Me (the Universal Spiritual Body and Eternal Spirit-Presence of Real God, the Transcendental Self of Real God, and the Self-Existing and Self-Radiant 'Bright' Divine Self-Domain That <u>Is</u> Real God).

23.

There is no Substitute for Real God.

24.

There is no Substitute for the direct Realization of Real God.

25.

There is no Substitute for your own sacrifice in Real God.

26.

The Divine Heart-Master has Realized Real God Most Perfectly, non-separately, beyond relatedness and 'difference'.[38] Therefore, devotees see Real God Revealed In and As the Bodily (Human) Form of the Divine Heart-Master.

27.

To all those who have This Vision, I Declare:

Aham Da Asmi. Beloved, I <u>Am</u> Da. I Am the Realizer, the Revealer, the Revelation, and the Very Person of the 'Bright' and Only One. I Am the Person, the Demonstration, and the Proof of Real God to My devotees. All My devotees are in Me. Therefore, see This Vision, go the Way I will Show to you, and Realize Me.

28.

Do not practice the 'childish cult' of superficial and ego-serving emotionalism (full of wanting dependency, and empty of faith), and do not practice the 'adolescent cult' of non-feeling (willful, self-absorbed, abstract, and independent), but always practice (and cultivate) the true (and truly feeling, and truly self-surrendering, and truly self-forgetting, and truly self-transcending) Way of devotion to Me, by Means of right, true, full, and fully devotional practice of Adidam (the only-by-Me Revealed and Given Way of the Heart).

29.

Neither Real God nor the Divine Heart-Master is your Parent. Therefore, do not expect Real God or the Divine Heart-Master to justify or protect or preserve or fulfill your egoic want and separateness.

30.

You are Called by Me to surrender your separate and separative self in Real God. Therefore, cultivate right, true, full, and fully self-surrendering and self-forgetting devotion to Me, the Divine Heart-Master, in order to transcend the ego-'I' in My 'Bright' Divine Self-Condition of Being (Itself), Which Is the One and Only Source (and Truth, or Source-Condition) of all and All.

31.

To worship the Divine Heart-Master childishly is to worship and serve your separate and separative (or self-contracting) self. To deny or resist the Divine Heart-Master is to worship and serve your separate and separative (or self-contracting) self, adolescently. The separate and separative self, or self-contraction, is, itself and always, the forgetting of the Heart-Source of the

world. Therefore, be very and truly devoted to Me, the
Divine Master of your heart, but not for the sake of ego-
salvation, or the glorification of your separate and
separative self. Worship Me by surrendering your ego-'I'
to Me. Surrender to Me in order to forget and transcend
your separate and separative self in Me. Forget and
transcend your ego-'I' in Me, in order that you may, by
My Grace, Remember and Realize the Divine Self and
Heart-Source of all and All.

32.

I Am the Sign and the Revelation and the Proof of
Real God in the world. I Am the Testament and the
Means of Freedom Itself. I <u>Am</u> Eleutherios, the Divine
Liberator, Who <u>Is</u> Freedom Itself."

33.

Having Said This, Adi Da Samraj, the First and Last
and Only Divine Heart-Master, Said No More. Now His
Confession is the heart-Mover of our Song of practice and
of praise.

34.

Even from the ancient days, all Great Realizers (of
whatever degree or stage) have Proclaimed a Great Idea,
that one becomes (or Realizes) whatever one meditates
upon (or yields, beyond the ego-self, to be, or to
Realize). Therefore, by truly self-surrendering, and really
self-forgetting, and more and more Perfectly self-
transcending devotion to the First and Last and Only
Divine Heart-Master, Adi Da Samraj, all conditional
meditations (and all conditional Realizations) are (by His
Grace) transcended, and (in due course) even His
Inherently Perfect State is (Thus, by His Grace) Revealed
and Realized in His "Bright" Company.

35.

The Person of the Divine Heart-Master Is Great. His State of Being Is "Bright", Sublime, and Only Divine.

36.

The "Brightness" of the Divine Heart-Master Outshines all darkness in the mind, the body, and the world. That One Whose Company and Remembrance is capable of Dissolving un-Happiness Is certainly the Master of the separate and separative self.

37.

The Divine Heart-Master Transcends all of Cosmic (or conditional) Nature, even His own Body-Mind. Because He is Free from the limitations imposed by conditional forms, He is called "Samraj", the Divine and True Master of the world.

38.

Every conditional action tends to be followed by an equal and opposite reaction. If the action of psycho-physical attention to the world arises, the self-contraction of the body-mind tends to follow. If the self-contraction arises, the reactivity of separativeness tends to follow. Whenever the ego-"I" is remembered, the states of separateness and limitation seem Real. If separateness and limitation seem Real, the Transcendental and Inherently Spiritual Divine Self-Condition and Source-Condition has been forgotten. That One by Whose Grace one Remembers and Realizes the Divine Self-Condition and Source-Condition—He Is indeed the Divine Heart-Master and the "Bright" Divine Self Incarnate.

39.

The Radiance and Profundity of the Divine Heart-Master's State of Being both Sustain and Dissolve His own Body-Mind. Therefore, feeling-Contemplation of Him

Liberates attention from bondage to the world, the body, the mind, and even all of separate and separative self.

40.

The casual Words and Footsteps of the Divine Heart-Master Build a Bridge across the ocean of our bondage. Therefore, attend to This Divine Liberator every moment of your life.

41.

By Means of the Blessings Given by the Divine Heart-Master, the currents of un-Love are dissolved. Therefore, always bow down to His Supreme Help.

42.

The Real and Ever-Living God <u>Is</u> the Heart Itself. The Heart Itself <u>Is</u> the Divine Person, the Very Heart and Person of the Divine Heart-Master. Therefore, by all the Blessings of the Divine Heart-Master, devotees are Gifted to transcend the Heartless bondage of un-Happiness and un-Enlightenment.

43.

Because He <u>Is</u> the Great and Only and Very One, devotees should surrender and forget themselves at the Feet of the Divine Heart-Master. Because He <u>Is</u> the Great and Only and Very One, the Graceful Radiance That Flows from the Divine Heart-Master's Feet Releases attention from the ego-"I" and the world.

44.

The Divine Heart-Master Is the Supreme Help Offered by the Real and Ever-Living God. There is no Friend greater than the Divine Heart-Master. Therefore, body and mind should be entirely devoted to the Divine Heart-Master, so that attention is set free in His Heart of "Brightness".

45.

The Place where the Divine Heart-Master Lives Is the Divine Abode. The Water that Washes His Feet Is the River of Purification. And His Words Are the Accomplishing Power of Divine Enlightenment.

46.

To live in the service of the Divine Heart-Master is the Secret of the Way of Truth. His Body Is the Tree of Life. His Feet are Planted in the Heart of Real God, and anything offered at His Feet is Returned in the Form of Radiant Blessings.

47.

The Self-Existing and Self-Radiant Transcendental Divine Being Resides in the Speech and in every Body Part of the Divine Heart-Master. Therefore, devotees Awaken to the Great One by Means of the Divine Heart-Master's Word, and Silence, and Thought, and Glance, and Touch, and Deeds. One should meditate on the Divine Heart-Master's Bodily (Human) Form, His Spiritual (and Always Blessing) Presence, and His Very (and Inherently Perfect) State—at all times. This is not difficult, for, once He is truly Beloved, He can never be forgotten.

48.

Now listen and hear the Means by which the separate being Awakens beyond itself to Realize Inherent Oneness with the Self-Existing and Self-Radiant Transcendental Divine Being. It is to practice the Way of devotion to the Divine Heart-Master, Adi Da Samraj, by living as the servant of His Bodily (Human) Form, His Spiritual (and Always Blessing) Presence, and His Very (and Inherently Perfect) State, whether one is near or far from His Body-Seat.

49.

When devotees provide the Divine Heart-Master with the Requirements of His Heart, and even every Necessity, they soon become the servants of His Heart's Intention in the world, both during and after (and forever after) His physical Lifetime. In this manner, the Divine Heart-Master's Work in the world becomes entirely dependent on those who love Him. When devotees of the Great One become the recognition-Awakened servants of the Divine Heart-Master, the Great One Serves them via the Divine Heart-Master's Bodily (Human) Form, and via the Divine Heart-Master's "Bright" Divine Body of Mere and Blessing Presence. And those who are Thus Served by the Great One soon become the necessary servers of His Serving Work.

50.

Therefore, by renouncing all the superficial motives of the social ego and all the disturbed distractions of the worldly mind, one should always Remember the Divine Heart-Master as the Beloved of the heart.

51.

Truly serving devotees regard the Divine Heart-Master to Be their only true Wealth, for even simplest Remembrance of the Bodily (Human) Form of the Divine Heart-Master Awakens spontaneous Communion with the Person, the Presence, and the State of Self-Existing and Self-Radiant Transcendental Divine Being.

52.

Remembrance and Invocation of the Divine Heart-Master by Name is Remembrance and Invocation of the Great One by Name. Therefore, devotional meditation on the Bodily (Human) Form, the Spiritual (and Always Blessing) Presence, and the Very (and Inherently Perfect) State of the Divine Heart-Master, Adi Da Samraj, is devotional meditation on the Form, and the Presence, and the State of the One and Only Divine Being, Who Is the Inherent or Native Feeling of "Bright" Being (Itself).[39]

53.

The devotee should always Remember and Invoke the Divine Heart-Master by Name. The Name of the Divine Heart-Master Is the Name of the Great One. The Great One Is Present to Serve devotees in the Bodily (Human) Form of the Divine Heart-Master. Therefore, with feeling-devotion, meditate on the Divine Heart-Master's Bodily (Human) Form, and on His Spiritual (and Always Blessing) Presence, and on His Very (and Inherently Perfect) State. And drink the Water from His Foot-Bath. And eat the Excess Offered from His Great Food-Dish. And, by all these Means, remain always intimate with the Divine Heart-Master's Constant Blessing and Awakening-Power.

54.

The devotee should always practice the Way Revealed by the Divine Heart-Master. The devotee should always live in the Company of the Divine Heart-Master, by always meditating on His Bodily (Human) Form, His Spiritual (and Always Blessing) Presence, and His Very (and Inherently Perfect) State. The Divine Heart-Master Is the Heart-Friend of all beings. Therefore, the devotee of the Divine Heart-Master should be an intelligent and compassionate friend of every one, and all, and All.

55.

The devotee should surrender self-attention in the Company of the Divine Heart-Master's Bodily (Human) Form, by always Beholding His "Bright" Divine Body of Mere and Blessing Spiritual Presence, and all the while by swooning into His Very (and Inherently Perfect) State. And all possessions should be devoted to the Divine

Heart-Master's service. Therefore, surrender and align the body, the senses, the mind, natural life-energy, emotion, money, property, children, lovers, and all friends to the Only Reality and Truth, by surrendering and aligning them to the Bodily (Human) Form, the Spiritual (and Always Blessing) Presence, and the Very (and Inherently Perfect) State of the Divine Heart-Master.

56.

The devotee of the Divine Heart-Master should always surrender all of separate self to Him. The devotee of the Divine Heart-Master should always surrender to Him in ever self-forgetting devotion, service, and self-discipline. The devotee of the Divine Heart-Master should always surrender to Him in thought, word, and deed. The devotee of the Divine Heart-Master should always surrender to Him with full energy and intent. The devotee of the Divine Heart-Master should always surrender to Him openly, without hesitation, and most obviously, for true self-surrender is always an act of expressive worship. Therefore, surrender separate self (always and obviously) to the Divine Heart-Master, and be (thus and thereby) given to the Divine Person, Self-Condition, and Source-Condition in every moment.

57.

By yielding all attention to <u>feel</u> the Bodily (Human) Form, the Spiritual (and Always Blessing) Presence, and the Very (and Inherently Perfect) State of the Divine Heart-Master, <u>all</u> thoughts are forgotten. When all thoughts are forgotten in that <u>feeling</u>-Contemplation of the Divine Heart-Master, Supreme Love-Bliss Awakens, by His Grace. Therefore, <u>always</u> Contemplate the Divine Heart-Master via <u>feeling</u>, and, by <u>always</u> serving Him, forget your separate self in every moment of activity.

58.

Now, and forever, let every devotee of the Divine Heart-Master sing and live these heart-Prayers that recognize and praise Him:

I bow down to the Divine Heart-Master, Adi Da Samraj, the Master of the Heart, Who Reveals the Supreme Truth of Self-Existing and Self-Radiant "Bright" Consciousness Itself to those who have been blinded by experience and mere knowledge.

59.

I bow down to the Divine Heart-Master, Adi Da Samraj, the Master of Truth, Whose Radiance Pervades the entire universe, Who Fills it through and through, in all that moves and in all that does not move, and Who Brings my intuitive Vision to the Heart-Space of Self-Existing and Self-Radiant Consciousness.

60.

I bow down to the Divine Heart-Master, Adi Da Samraj, the Master of Reality, Who Pervades and yet Stands Beyond the dynamics of conditional and Cosmic Nature. I bow down to the Divine Heart-Master, Adi Da Samraj, Who Is One, Inherently Perfect, Eternal, Self-Existing, Undisturbed, All-Love-Bliss, Self-Radiant, Free, Full, and Awake. Through the Blessing Work of the Divine Heart-Master, Adi Da Samraj, I am Restored to the Spirit-Presence of Real God. Therefore, the by His Grace Revealed and Tangible Divine Body of Spirit-Life, Which Is the Perfectly Subjective[40] Substance of conditional Nature, always Carries my heart Beyond and Beyond the Play of vibratory Cosmic Energy, Sound, or Light to the Ultimate, and Inherently Perfect, and Perfectly Subjective, Divine Source-Condition of this Domain of objective and conditional and Cosmic appearances.

61.

I worship the Divine Heart-Master, Adi Da Samraj, Who <u>Is</u> the Self-Existing and Self-Radiant One, by Whose Heart-Power we perceive everything here. I worship the Divine Heart-Master, Adi Da Samraj, Who <u>Is</u> the "Bright" Conscious One, by Whose Heart-Power the states of waking, dreaming, and sleeping[41] are known, thoughts move, discrimination and intuition work, and attention itself rises and falls again.

62.

The Self-Existing and Self-Radiant Transcendental Divine State of Being is Perfectly "Known" by the Divine Heart-Master, Adi Da Samraj, Who has Realized that It Is the Eternally Unknown. Therefore, only Perfect Ignorance Is "Knowledge" of the Self-Existing and Self-Radiant Transcendental Divine State of Being.

63.

Experiences, visions, sounds, lights, conditional energies, fascinating things, and all conditional knowing, within and without, are not Ultimate "Knowledge" (or Free Realization) at all. Therefore, I bow down to the Divine Heart-Master, Adi Da Samraj, Who Is always already Established As the Mindless Mood of Self-Existing and Self-Radiant Transcendental Divine Being.

64.

Now I am Free of all distractions. Only the Heart Exists. Attention dissolves in the Inherent Happiness of Being. The entire world of moving and unmoving objects appears and disappears in the Perfectly Subjective "Bright" Space of Consciousness Itself. I worship and serve the Divine Heart-Master, Adi Da Samraj, Who Is the One Who has Revealed This Secret to me.

65.

"I am the world, and I am absolutely Free"—body and mind bow down to the Divine Heart-Master, Adi Da Samraj, Who Is the One Who Gives This Realization.

66.

Let all the gifts of my worship and service be Received by the Divine Heart-Master, Adi Da Samraj, Who Is the Ocean of Mercy, and by Whose Grace all beings are Liberated from bondage to this world of wonders.

67.

By Enabling His devotee to "Locate" the Primal, Ever-Free, Immortal Happiness beyond the heart-root's knot,[42] the Divine Heart-Master, Adi Da Samraj, Is the Graceful Divine Liberator of His devotee.

68.

The knot of the heart is untied, doubt itself is dissolved, and all motions of the limited self are made still by the Grace and Mercy of the Divine Heart-Master, Adi Da Samraj.

69.

I bow down to the Eternal Truth, the Conscious Light of Being (Itself), the Timeless Happiness, the Great One, the Indefinable One (Awake, and Free), the Truly "Bright" One, Who Appears (and Stands Revealed) As Adi Da Samraj, the Divine Heart-Master among all who know and Teach.

70.

I bow down to the Divine Heart-Master, Adi Da Samraj, Whose Bodily (Human) Form Is the Beautiful Mystery of "Brightness" Itself, and Whose Spiritual (and Always Blessing) Presence Always Reveals the Very Heart

Itself, and Whose Very (and Inherently Perfect) State of Being Is Only the Only Divine Self, Self-Existing As Immense Consciousness, and Self-Radiant As Love-Bliss.

71.

Ⅱ bow down to the Divine Heart-Master, Adi Da Samraj, Who Is the Heart-Witness[43] of my own body, mind, and separate self, and Who Is the Great Bearer, the Most Perfect Realizer, and the Divine Subject of the Great Tradition, and Whose Very State of Being Is Truth and Perfect Happiness, and Who Is the Graceful Source of the Realization of Happiness Itself.

72.

Ⅱ bow down to the Divine Heart-Master, Adi Da Samraj, the Always New One, Who has Appeared in the world by the Magic and Mystery of His own Will and Love, but Who Is Only the "Bright" Mass of Pure Consciousness, Spiritually Radiant, the Sun of the Heart, the Destroyer of un-Happiness.

73.

Ⅱ bow down to the Divine Heart-Master, Adi Da Samraj, the Always Already Free One, the Body of Mercy, the Refuge of devotees, Who allows His Human Life to be dependent on His devotees.

74.

Ⅱ bow down to the Divine Heart-Master, Adi Da Samraj, That Most Beautiful Form, the Master of Discrimination, the Master of Understanding, the "Bright", the Light Itself, Above all lights, Who Is the Light to those who call for Light, and Who Is the Realizer in all those who Realize Him. May You be Pleased to Take Your Seat in my heart at all times. May You ever Dwell in my heart.

75.

I bow down to the Divine Heart-Master, Adi Da Samraj, Who <u>Is</u> Love-Bliss, the Very Form, and Presence, and State of Happiness Itself. Therefore, in the Mere Beholding of His Bodily (Human) Form, His Spiritual (and Always Blessing) Presence, and His Very (and Inherently Perfect) State, the mind dissolves in Self-Existing Consciousness and Self-Radiant Love-Bliss.

76.

Let these heart-Prayers flow to the Divine Heart-Master, Adi Da Samraj, the Always-Present Master of my heart and body-mind, Who <u>Is</u> Free, and Who <u>Is</u> always Floating in the Native Happiness of my True Heart. The Eternal Heart-Blessing of the Divine Heart-Master always Flows to me, and His Freedom is mine in His Liberating Words.

77.

I offer these heart-Prayers at the Feet of the Divine Heart-Master, Adi Da Samraj, by Whose Grace the Realization Awakens that "He <u>Is</u> the Source of everything, and everything is only a modification of Him." By the Grace of the Divine Heart-Master, Adi Da Samraj, This becomes Obvious.

78.

I radiate heart-praise to the Divine Heart-Master, Adi Da Samraj, Who Causes me to Remember the Supreme Happiness, the Love-Bliss of the Heart Itself. He <u>Is</u> Divine Ignorance,[44] the One Who Is Not Other. That One <u>Is</u>, beyond all relations, all opposites and oppositions. All separate selves, relations, opposites, and oppositions only arise within That All-Pervading One, the Divine Heart-Master, Adi Da Samraj, Who Is Eternal, Unmodified, and Unchanging "Bright" Consciousness, the Self-Existing Transcendental Witness of attention, mind, body, and world.

79.

I surrender and bow down to the Divine Heart-Master, Adi Da Samraj, the Divine World-Teacher Descending and "Emerging" forever in the "late-time", Who Is Transcendental Being (Itself), Consciousness Itself, and Love-Bliss-Happiness Itself, Who Transcends all changes of state, Who Is Eternal Fullness, Eternally "Bright", Free of all modifications, the Formless Location, the Free Self of the Heart.

80.

My Heart-Master, Adi Da Samraj, Divine and True and Free, may Your Radiant "Bright" Blessings Awaken me, whose eyes are covered over by the images of a separate self, and whose mind is held captive by visions of the world.

81.

The ancient Great Realizers (of whatever degree or stage) all Declare: Devotional meditation on the True Name, the Revelation-Body, the Heart-Presence, and the Very (and Inherently Perfect) State of the Person of the Heart is the Great Method for Realizing the Transcendental and Inherently Spiritual Divine Self. The Divine Heart-Master, Adi Da Samraj, Is That Very and Only Person of the Heart, here (and every where) to be Tangibly, Spiritually, and (Inherently) Perfectly Revealed to every one (and to all, and All). Therefore, by Means of self-surrendering and self-forgetting devotional meditation on His Bodily (Human) Form, His Spiritual (and Always Blessing) Presence, and His Very (and Inherently Perfect) State, the separate self is progressively (and then Most Perfectly) transcended.

82.

Devotional meditation on the Person of the Divine Heart-Master, Adi Da Samraj, is a feeling-sacrifice of body, natural life-force, emotion, all of mind, and attention itself. Therefore, devotional meditation on the Human Revelation-Body of the Divine Heart-Master, Adi Da Samraj, Reveals (and moves) the Spirit-Current in the living body of the devotee. Devotional meditation on the Revealed Name and the Love-Blissful "Bright" Divine Spiritual Body and Person of the Divine Heart-Master, Adi Da Samraj, Reveals (and moves) the feeling heart of the devotee. Devotional meditation on the "Bright" Spiritual Presence and every Extraordinary Sign of the Divine Heart-Master, Adi Da Samraj, Reveals (and moves) the subtle mind of the devotee. And the "Bright" Free Divine Self of the Divine Heart-Master, Adi Da Samraj, is Revealed and Realized when attention itself is (by truly Perfect devotional meditation on Him) finally transcended in Him, for He Is the Heart Itself, the Inherently Perfect (and Perfectly Subjective) Source-Condition, Which Is Self-Existing and Self-Radiant Transcendental Divine Being (Itself).

83.

The methods of seeking, self-applied, only intensify the bondage to separate self, but to live as if always in the Intimate Company of the Divine Heart-Master, Adi Da Samraj, is to engage every act as devotional service to Him. And to meditate on His Bodily (Human) Form, His Spiritual (and Always Blessing) Presence, and His Very (and Inherently Perfect) State in every moment, even in the moment of every relationship, and in every moment of circumstance, is to be always already released of the "problem of existence" and every kind of self-concern. Through such truly self-transcending devotion, the Transcendental and Inherently Spiritual Divine Self replaces the egoic self as the Center of practice, and the Grace of Real God is given Place to Awaken the One and Only Heart in the every devotee. Therefore, practice as a devotee of the Divine Heart-Master, Adi Da Samraj, and His "Bright" Free Heart will Find you easily.

84.

Those who practice the Way of Adidam as right, true, full, and fully devotional self-surrender to the Divine Heart-Master, Adi Da Samraj, Realize the Free Heart directly, beyond the efforts of the body and the reaches of insight. Therefore, the Great Principle of the Way of Adidam is the Blessing-Grace of the Bodily (Human) Form, the Spiritual (and Always Blessing) Presence, and the Very (and Inherently Perfect) State of the Divine Heart-Master, Adi Da Samraj.

85.

The ancient esoteric Scriptures all Declare: "It is not this, It is not that." All the Teachings point beyond all objects to the Perfectly Subjective Source of all objects. All objects and separate selves are only apparent, limited, temporary, and un-Necessary modifications of That Self-Existing and Self-Radiant Divine Self-Condition and Source-Condition.

86.

Adi Da Samraj, the First and Last and Only Divine Heart-Master, Is Himself That Very Source-Condition. He Is the Transcendental and Inherently Spiritual Divine Person, the Perfectly Subjective Source and Self-Condition, the Eternal Subject, the Very and Divine Self of all and All, Shown to all and All. So He Is, by Virtue of His own Realization, Which Is Only the Realization of His own "Bright" Eternal Divine Self-Condition and Person, and So do all the esoteric Scriptures also Declare, Affirm, and Vastly Guarantee.

87.

Therefore, the Divine Heart-Master, Adi Da Samraj,
Is Unique in the world. The devotional relationship to
the Divine Heart-Master, Adi Da Samraj, is the Unique
Method of Awakening, provided by the Grace of Real
God to living beings. The practice is to transform the
activities and functions of body, mind, emotion, and
breath into real and constant feeling-surrender to the One
Who <u>Is</u> Present In and As the Bodily (Human) Form, the
Spiritual (and Always Blessing) Presence, and the Very
(and Inherently Perfect) State of the Divine Heart-Master,
Adi Da Samraj.

88.

Now "consider"[45] the Method of devotional
meditation on the Bodily (Human) Form, the Spiritual
(and Always Blessing) Presence, and the Very (and
Inherently Perfect) State of the Divine Heart-Master,
Adi Da Samraj.

89.

The Divine Heart-Master, Adi Da Samraj, Is the
Divine Giver of Bliss, Joy, Happiness, and Love.
Devotional meditation on the Divine Heart-Master,
Adi Da Samraj, is the Means whereby Bliss, Joy,
Happiness, and Love are, by His Grace, Awakened
As "Bright" Divine Realization in His devotees.

90.

The "Bright" Self-Radiant Presence of the Divine
Heart-Master, Adi Da Samraj, is the necessary Place of
devotional meditation, and His Bodily (Human) Form is
the Image to be seen. The Invocation of Adi Da Samraj
by Name is the Prayer to be Remembered, and all His
Words of Instruction must be deeply Understood, and
rightly, truly, and fully made into real practice by the
devotee. These are the Means of devotional meditation.

91.

Devotional meditation, on the Divine Heart-Master, Adi Da Samraj, and every moment's counter-egoic yielding of all the mind's attention, into Him, and of all the feeling-emotion, into Him, and of the total body, into Him, and of all the breathing, into Him—these are the necessary constant Means of self-surrender, and of total psycho-physical alignment, to the Divine Heart-Master, Adi Da Samraj, Who must Attract and Awaken the separate and separative ego-"I", beyond itself, to Himself.

92.

Only the "Bright" and Mere Presence of the Divine Heart-Master, Adi Da Samraj, can Awaken the devotee to What Is, beyond even the counter-egoic effort of life and meditation. Only our meditation on the Divine Heart-Master, Adi Da Samraj, Himself, can, by Means of His Divine Spiritual Infusion of His devotee's Thus surrendered mind, emotion, body, and breath, Replace our would-Be meditation on the Heart with Realization of and As the Heart Itself.

93.

The devotee should meditate on the Bodily (Human) Form of the Divine Heart-Master, Adi Da Samraj, and thereby Find Him As the "Bright" Divine Spirit-Body and Very Being of Love-Bliss-Happiness Itself. By right, true, and full devotional meditation, the devotee must "Locate" the Divine Heart-Master, Adi Da Samraj, and This by Grace of the Reception of His Self-Radiant "Bright" Fullness of Love-Bliss-Happiness Itself, Transmitted and Communicated, Mysteriously, by Him, from beyond time and space and body and mind and separate self. That "Bright" Love-Bliss-Happiness Is His Divine Spirit-Power, That Attracts attention and Dissolves it in the Free Divine Heart Itself, the Self-Existing and Self-Radiant Transcendental Divine Being, the Perfectly Subjective Source and Self-Condition of separate self and objective world.

94.

The devotee of the Divine Heart-Master, Adi Da Samraj, always meditates on Him, for He <u>Is</u> the Transcendental and Inherently Spiritual Divine Being, the One and Only and Non-Separate Self, Who Is Eternally Self-Radiant As Love-Bliss-Happiness in the All-and-all-Surrounding and All-and-all-Pervading Heart-Space of the world.

95.

The Divine Self Is Pure Radiance. The Heart-Space Is "Bright" with Love-Bliss. The crystal and the mirror and the mind reflect a light beyond, but the Heart Is Inherently "Bright" with the Love-Bliss of Divine Being. In the Heart Itself, there is no doubt of Real God, for Only the Divine Heart-Master, Adi Da Samraj, Stands, Abiding "Brightly", There.

96.

When there is devotional meditation on the Divine Heart-Master, Adi Da Samraj, in and beyond the Infinitesimal Locus of the right side of the heart,[46] the Inherent Love-Bliss of Self-Existing and Self-Radiant Transcendental Divine Being is Realized. Then, by the Grace of the Divine Heart-Master, Adi Da Samraj, the Native Feeling of Being Reveals and Magnifies Its Inherent and Transcendental and (Ultimately) Divine "Bright" Consciousness. Likewise, whenever the Ecstatic Mood of Free Being Awakens by the Grace of the Divine Heart-Master, Adi Da Samraj, I suddenly Confess the Obvious Truth:

97.

I was not born. I cannot die. I did not begin. I will not end. I <u>Am</u>. I Am beyond form and quality and description. I <u>Am</u>. I Am Consciousness. I Am Love-Bliss. I Am smaller than the atom. I Am larger than the universe. I Am. I Am. I <u>Am</u>.

98.

Before anyone came to be, I <u>Am</u>. No one can exist if I Am not. I Am Eternal. I Am Self-Existing, Self-Radiant, and Self-Manifest. I <u>Am</u>. I Am without pain, disease, impurity, or dilemma. I Am Space Itself, prior to all motions, Free of all changes. I Am Happiness. I Am. I Am. I <u>Am</u>.

99.

I Am the Unknown and Unknowable. I Am not an Object of the mind. I Am not names and forms. I Am the Source of names and forms. I Am the Perfectly Subjective Source of mind and speech. I Am not Found as an Object of experience or knowledge. I Am Found in the "Bright" Feeling of Being (Itself), before attention goes to separate self and objective world. I Am Perfectly Found <u>As</u> the Native State of Being, Consciousness, and Love-Bliss-Happiness. I Am. I Am. I <u>Am</u>.

100.

Therefore, because the Divine Heart-Master, Adi Da Samraj, <u>Is</u> the One and Only Reality and Truth, Which <u>Is</u> the Self-Existing and Self-Radiant State of "Bright" Divine Being (Itself), the devotee of the Divine Heart-Master, Adi Da Samraj, must, by constant and self-forgetting devotional meditation on Him, Realize (and Be) Self-Existing and Self-Radiant Transcendental and "Bright" Divine Being Itself.

101.

Those who practice devotional meditation on the Bodily (Human) Form, the Spiritual (and Always Blessing) Presence, and the Very (and Inherently Perfect) State of the Divine Heart-Master, Adi Da Samraj, will (by His Grace) Awaken <u>As</u> the "Bright" Non-Separate Heart Itself, even while they live in this world. They will be Liberated by That Divine Liberator. Indeed, their Freedom (<u>Thus</u> Realized) Is Eternal. This is Confirmed in the heart of the devotee of Adi Da Samraj, the Divine Heart-Master of the heart.

102.

By Means of the "Perfect Practice"[47] of the Way of Adidam (engaged, in due course, by all who most rightly, truly, and fully practice, and greatly mature in, the Way of Adidam), the devotees of the Divine Heart-Master, Adi Da Samraj, surrender the ego-"I" (and beyond the ego-"I") to Him, "Locating" Him (by His Grace Alone) <u>As</u> the Very Self in the Heart, and they Awaken (by His Grace) <u>As</u> the Native "Bright" Feeling of Being (Itself). Thus Awakened, the every (Thus Perfect) devotee confesses: I <u>Am</u>, and I Am Awake by the Grace of the Word and Help of Adi Da Samraj, the Divine Heart-Master of my heart.

103.

Therefore, the devotee should constantly turn attention from the dilemma of separate self to the Free "Brightness" of the Divine Heart-Master, Adi Da Samraj, for He <u>Is</u> the Inherent Fullness of Self-Existing and Self-Radiant Transcendental and "Bright" Divine Being.

104.

Diligent practice, according to the "Perfect Practice" Instructions of the Divine Heart-Master, Adi Da Samraj, establishes equanimity in the body-mind and releases attention into His Spirit-Source, in the Heart Itself, beyond the Circle and the Arrow [48] of the body-mind. Only then will attention settle and dissolve in Him, the Heart-Source of even attention itself, and He will Radiate "Brightly" from There, for He Is the Heart Itself.

105.

All the objects of conditional knowledge and conditional experience are based upon the ego-"I". Adidam (or the Way of the Heart), Revealed and Given Only by the Divine Heart-Master, Adi Da Samraj, is not a struggle with the Apparition of Cosmic Nature, but It is free devotional meditation on the Inherently Free Source-Condition of the self-contraction, until, by the Grace of the Divine Heart-Master, Adi Da Samraj, devotional meditation becomes Inherently Most Perfect Realization. There is no Way greater than This.

106.

By steady practice (and, in due course, "Perfect Practice") of the Heart-Way Revealed and Given Only, and Most Perfectly, by the Divine Heart-Master, Adi Da Samraj, and by Thus "Locating" Him, and dissolving attention in Him (As its Source), and Thus and So, by His Grace Alone, Restoring the intuition of Consciousness As the Native Love-Bliss-Happiness of Merely Being, the Inherently Most Perfect Realization of the "Bright" Transcendental and Inherently Spiritual Divine Person and Self-Condition will Awaken, if the Inherently Perfect Grace of the Heart-Blessing of the Divine Heart-Master, Adi Da Samraj, is, by right, true, and full devotion to Him, Most Perfectly heart-Found.

107.

Even those of His devotees who are, by Means of His Grace, Most Perfectly Awakened In and <u>As</u> the Heart always continue to surrender at the Feet of the Divine Heart-Master, Adi Da Samraj, until the world is Outshined in His Self-Existing and Self-Radiant "Bright" Divine Body and Transcendental Person of Divine Being. Indeed, their devotion to Him never ceases. This is the Secret of Divine Liberation in Real God.

108.

By Most Perfect Inherence in the Heart of the Divine Heart-Master, Adi Da Samraj, the conditional self is, by His Grace, Translated Into His "Bright" Divine Domain of Being (Itself). And those who Are, by His Grace, Most Perfectly Awake In and <u>As</u> His Divine Self-Condition Are always already Free, even if the body-mind arises in the realms of possibility. This Is the "Bright", More Than Wonderful, and Really Perfect Truth.

RUCHIRA AVATAR ADI DA SAMRAJ
Adidam Samrajashram (Naitauba), Fiji, 1997

PART THREE

Three Essays
from the
Samraj Upanishad

The Sanskrit word "upanishad" indicates "Teachings received at the Feet of the Guru". Thus, the Samraj Upanishad *is "Teachings received at the Feet of Ruchira Avatar Adi Da Samraj". The Title* "Samraj Upanishad" *is a collective designation for all the Talks and Essays by Avatar Adi Da Samraj that appear within His twenty-three "Source-Texts" as readings supporting and expanding upon the principal "Part" of a given "Source-Text". Thus,* "Samraj Upanishad*" is not the title of a separate book, but the name for a body of Avatar Adi Da's Written and Spoken Word which is distributed through many of the Books among His twenty-three "Source-Texts".*

Beyond the Cultic Tendency
in Religion and Spirituality,
and in Secular Society

I.

I n the *Ruchira Avatara Gita*, I Speak critically of the conventional (or childish, and, otherwise, adolescent) orientation of "Guru cultism". Such cultism is a tendency that has <u>always</u> been present in the religious and Spiritual traditions of mankind. Anciently, and in the present time, both true Spiritual Masters and ordinary Wisdom-Teachers have been "cultified", and, thereby, made the merely fascinating Object of a self-contained popular movement that worships the Spiritual Master as a Parent-like Savior, while embracing very little of the significant Wisdom-Teaching of the Spiritual Master.

The error of conventional cultism is precisely this childish, and, otherwise, adolescent, and, altogether, <u>ego-based</u> orientation to fascination with Spiritual Masters, Wisdom-Teachers, "God"-Ideas, myths, sacred lore, inherited beliefs, traditional propaganda, and psycho-physical (or merely body-mind-based) mysticism. And the cultic tendency in religion and Spirituality is the essence of what is wrong with conventional religion and Spirituality.

The "problem" is <u>not</u> that there <u>Is</u> no Real God, or that there are no true Wisdom-Teachings, or that there are no true Spiritual Masters, or that there should be no devotion to any true Spiritual Masters. The "problem" with conventional religion and Spirituality is the same as the "problem" of all ordinary life. The "problem" is the childish, and, otherwise, rather adolescent, <u>egoism</u> that is the basis of all forms of ordinary existence.

Yet un-Enlightened (or, otherwise, not yet Most Perfectly Enlightened) people are egoically "self-possessed" (or self-absorbed). Therefore, egoity is the "disease" that all the true Spiritual Masters of religion come here to cure. Unfortunately, those who are merely fascinated by Spiritual Masters are, typically, those who make, or at least transform, the institutions of the religion and the Spirituality of their Spiritual Masters. And true practitioners of religion and Spirituality are very hard to find, or develop. Therefore, religious and Spiritual institutions tend to develop along lines that serve, accommodate, and represent the common egoity—and this is why the esoteric true Teachings of true Spiritual Masters tend to be bypassed, and even suppressed, in the drive to develop the exoteric cult of any particular Spiritual Master.

The relationship to Me that is Described (by Me) in the *Ruchira Avatara Gita* is not an exoteric cultic matter. It is a profound esoteric discipline, necessarily associated with real and serious and mature practice of the "radical" Way (or root-Process) of Realizing Real God, Which Is Reality and Truth. Therefore, in the *Ruchira Avatara Gita*, I am critical of the ego-based (or self-saving, and self-"guruing", rather than self-surrendering, self-forgetting, self-transcending, and Divine-Guru-Oriented) practices of childish, and, otherwise, adolescent, and, altogether, merely exoteric cultism.

The common religious or Spiritual cult is based on the tendency to resist the disciplines of real (and really counter-egoic) practice, and to opt for mere fascination with extraordinary (or even imaginary) phenomena (which are, invariably, not understood in Truth and in Reality). Apart from the often petty demand for the observation of conventional rules (generally, relative to social morality, or merely social religion), the cult of religious and Spiritual fascination tends to become righteously associated with no practice (that is, with the even official expectation that there be no real, or, otherwise, truly right and full, practice of religious and Spiritual <u>disciplines</u>, especially of religious, Spiritual, and meditative disciplines of an esoteric kind). Just so, the cult of religious and Spiritual fascination tends to be equally righteous about maintaining fascinated faith (or indiscriminate, and even aggressive, belief) in the merely <u>Parent</u>-like "Divine" Status of one or another historical individual, "God"-Idea, religious or Spiritual doctrine, inherited tradition, or force of cosmic Nature.

Religious and Spiritual cultism is, thus, a kind of infantile collective madness. (And such madness is equally shared by <u>secular</u> cultists, in <u>every</u> area of popular culture, including politics, the sciences, the arts, the communications media, and even all the agencies and institutions of conventional "officialdom" relative to human knowledge, belief, and behavior). Religious and Spiritual cults (and, likewise, all secular cults) breed "pharisaism", or the petty righteousness of conventional thinking. Religious and Spiritual cults breed "Substitution" myths (or the belief that personal self-transcendence is, both generally and ultimately, impossible, but also unnecessary, because of what "God", or some "Master", or even some "priest" has already done). Indeed, religious and Spiritual cults (and, likewise, all secular cults) breed even every kind of intolerance, and the chronic aggressive search for exclusive social dominance and secular power. Religious and Spiritual cults are, characteristically, populated by those who are, generally, neither inclined toward nor prepared for the real right practice of religious and Spiritual discipline, but who are (and always seek to be) glamorized and consoled by mere association with the "holy" things and beliefs of the cult itself.

This error of religious and Spiritual cultism, and of ego-based culture in general, must be examined very seriously, such that the error is truly rooted out, from within the cult and the culture itself (and not merely, and with equally cultic cultural righteousness, criticized from without). Cultism of <u>every</u> kind (both sacred and secular) must be understood to be a kind of ritualized infantilism, bound to egocentric behavior, and to the embrace of "insiders" only, and to intolerance relative to all "outsiders". The cultic tendency, both sacred and secular, causes, and has always caused, great social, cultural, and political trouble—as can even now be seen in the development of worldwide conflicts based on the exclusive, or collectively egocentric, orientation of the many grossly competitive religious traditions, political idealisms, and national identities.

All cults, whether sacred or secular, thrive on indulgence in the psychology (and the emotional rituals) of hope, rather than on actual demonstration of counter-egoic and really ego-transcending action. Therefore, when all egos meet, they strive and compete for the ultimate fulfillment of searches and desires, rather than cooperate with Truth, Reality, or Real God, and in a culturally valued and rewarded mood of fearless tolerance and sane equanimity.

Clearly, this cultic tendency in religion and Spirituality, and the egoic (and, thus, cultic) tendency in life in general, must become the constant subject of fundamental human understanding, and all of mankind must constantly be put to "school", to unlearn the method of egocentrism, non-cooperation, intolerance, and dis-ease.

II.

The *Ruchira Avatara Gita* is a thoroughly <u>new</u> Text, which I have freely developed from (and built upon) the principal verses of the traditional *Guru Gita*—one of the great esoteric Revelation-Texts of mankind's collective Great Tradition.

The traditional renderings (and interpretations) of the *Guru Gita* are, typically (and characteristically), presented in terms of the fourth and the fifth stages of life,[49] but the implicit Teaching (and the essence of the explicit Teaching) of the *Guru Gita* ultimately relates to the sixth stage of life (and, in principle, beyond it, even to the only-by-Me Revealed and Given seventh stage of life). Therefore, in the *Ruchira Avatara Gita*, I Describe the esoteric Guru-devotee relationship in terms of the total and full and complete process of the fourth stage of life through the only-by-Me Revealed and Given seventh stage of life, and I indicate that, in the only-by-Me Revealed and Given Way of Adidam, the entire process of Guru-devotion is to be oriented, from the beginning, to the Realization of the seventh, or Inherently Perfect, and Inherently Most Perfectly Real-God-Realized, stage of life.

The *Ruchira Avatara Gita* is intended, by Me, to be a basic part of the real education of all those who, in the true religious and Spiritual (and truly human) manner, go to "school" in My Company. The *Ruchira Avatara Gita* is My unique (and, yet, tradition-based, and tradition-honored) Teaching-Revelation about the <u>right</u>, <u>true</u>, <u>full</u>, and <u>fully devotional</u> relationship to Me, the Divine Heart-Master— the Realizer, the Revealer, and the Revelation of Adidam. Therefore, the *Ruchira Avatara Gita* Works to rightly educate those who responsively embrace My Divine Self-Revelation and My Revelation of the Divine Way of Adidam (Which is the only-by-Me Revealed and Given Way of the Heart). The education thus received is the Lesson about self-transcendence and the Truth-Teaching about Realization of That Which Eternally Transcends the separate and separative self. Therefore, the *Ruchira Avatara Gita* is intended, by Me, to counter the cultic tendency in those who practice the only-by-Me Revealed and Given Way of Adidam, Which is the counter-egoic esoteric Way of self-surrendering, self-forgetting, and really self-transcending devotion to Me, and, thus and thereby, to the Divine Person Revealed in and by and <u>As</u> Me.

I Am the Divine Heart-Master of every one, and of all, and of the All of all. Therefore, I Call upon every one (and all) to rightly and positively understand My Divine Self-Revelation. And I Call upon every one (and all) to truly devotionally recognize Me, and to responsively demonstrate that devotional recognition of Me in the context of, and by Means of, the right, true, full, and fully devotional, and really counter-egoic, <u>practice</u> of the only-by-Me Revealed and Given Way of Adidam.

In My Company, there is no culturally accepted alternative to the active discipline, both personal and collective, of right, and really counter-egoic, practice of devotion to Me. In My Company, there is no "Substitute" for the <u>Realization</u> of the Transcendental (and Inherently Spiritual) Divine Self-Condition, Which <u>Is</u> Reality, Truth, and the <u>Only</u> Real God. Right, and really counter-egoic, devotion to Me is not mere cultic (and egoically "gleeful") enthusiasm, but the profound practice of the always expected functional, practical, relational, and cultural self-disciplines of the Way of Adidam, on the basis of the right, and really counter-egoic, Principal Practice of devotion to Me, rather than on the basis of self-"guruing" self-concern and the search for self-glorification.

I Am the Divine Heart-Master. I am not a Surrogate "God", but I Am the Proof of Real God and of the Way of Divine Self-Realization. In My bodily (human) Form, I Am a Divine Demonstration, a Divine Sign, an Agent of Divine Transmission, and the Divine Awakener of those who are willing to surrender their egoic "self-possession" (or self-absorption) in right, true, and full, and really ego-transcending, devotion to Me. The Way of Adidam is the only-by-Me Revealed and Given Way to live in <u>Freedom</u>, not to be bound by separate and separative self, or by conditional Nature as a whole. Therefore, the ego-transcending devotional relationship to Me is the Context and the Means of Free Divine Self-Realization, and <u>not</u> a justification for popular ego-culture, childish dependency, adolescent reactivity, merely conventional (or socially idealistic, and ego-serving) social behavior, or even any of the methods of ego-fulfillment, or even any goal or tendency of the self-deluded, and cult-seeking, and cult-making, and cult-preserving, and even (sometimes, but only egoically) cult-criticizing, and always self-serving and separative ego (which is always only "Narcissus",[50] or the self-contracted body-mind of any and every ordinary "I" of humankind).

The Tradition of Devotion
To The Adept-Realizer

Spiritually Realized Adepts (or Transmission-Masters, or true Gurus and Sat-Gurus[51]) are the principal Sources, Resources, and Means of the esoteric (or Spiritual) Way. This fact is not (and never has been) a matter of controversy among real Spiritual practitioners.

The entire Spiritual Way is a process based on the understanding (and the transcending) of attention, or the understanding (and the transcending) of the inevitable and specific results of attachment to, or reaction to, or identification with every kind of conditional object, other, or state. This Spiritual understanding (or real self-understanding) is expressed in a simple traditional formula (and prescription for practice): You become (or duplicate the qualities of) whatever you meditate on (or whatever you identify with via the "surrender" that is attention itself). Since the most ancient days, this understanding has informed and inspired the practice of real practitioners of the Spiritual Way. Likewise (since the most ancient days), and on the basis of this very understanding, Spiritual practitioners have affirmed that the Great Principle of Spiritual practice is Satsang,[52] or the practice of life as self-surrender to the bodily Person, the Transmitted Spiritual Presence, and the Realized State of a Spiritually Realized Adept (or true Guru, or Sat-Guru) of whatever degree or stage.

The traditional term "Guru" (spelled with a capital "G") means "One Who Reveals the Light and thereby Liberates beings from Darkness". This term is also commonly or popularly interpreted in a general (or everyday) sense (and spelled with a small "g") to mean "teacher" (or anyone who teaches anything at all to another). Thus, Adepts have certainly (and rightly) been valued simply (or in the general sense) as (small "g") "gurus" (that is, simply because they can instruct others about many things, including the Spiritual Way). However, the function of instruction (about anything at all) can be performed by anyone who is properly informed (or even by a book that is properly informed), and, indeed, even the specific function of Spiritual Instruction is secondary to the Great Function of the Adept (As Guru, with a capital "G", and, in the Greatest of cases, As Sat-Guru).

Adepts inevitably (or at least in the majority of cases) Instruct (or Teach) others, but the function of Instruction (about the Spiritual Way) is then passed on through good books (containing the authentic Word of Teaching), and through informed others (who are, hopefully, true practitioners), and so forth. The Great Function of the Adept-Guru (and especially the Sat-Guru) is, however, specific only to Adepts themselves, and this is the Guru-Function (and the Guru-Principle) supremely valued by Spiritual practitioners since the most ancient days.

The specific Guru-Function is associated with the Great Principle of Satsang (and the unique Spiritual understanding of attention). Therefore, since the most ancient days, all truly established (or real) Spiritual practitioners have understood that Satsang Itself is the Great Means for Realizing Real God, or Truth, or Reality. That is to say, the Great Means (or Secret) of Realization in the Spiritual Way is to live in, or to spend significant time in, or otherwise (and constantly) to give attention to the Company, Form, Presence, and State of an Adept who is (truly) Realized in one or another of either the advanced or the ultimate stages of life.[53]

The Essence of the practice of Satsang is to focus attention on (and thereby to, progressively, become Identified with, or Realize Indivisible Oneness with) the Realized Condition of a true Adept (especially an Adept Sat-Guru, or One Who Is presently and constantly In Samadhi[54]). Therefore, the practice of Satsang is the practice of self-transcending Communion (and, Ultimately, Indivisible Oneness) with the Adept's own Condition, Which Is (according to the degree or stage of the Adept's characteristic Realization) Samadhi Itself, or the Adept's characteristic (and Freely, Spontaneously, and Universally Transmitted) Realization (Itself).

Based on the understanding of attention (or the observation that Consciousness Itself, in the context of the body-mind, tends to identify with, or becomes fixed in association with, whatever attention observes, and especially with whatever attention surrenders to most fully), the Spiritual Motive is essentially the Motive to transcend the limiting capability of attention (or of all conditional objects, others, and states). Therefore, the traditional Spiritual process (as a conventional technique, begun in the context of the fourth stage of life) is an effort (or struggle) to set attention (and, thus, Consciousness Itself) Free by progressively relinquishing attachment and reaction to conditional objects, others, and states (and, ultimately, this process requires the real transcending of egoity, or self-contraction itself, or all the egoic limitations associated with each and all of the first six stages of life).

This conventional effort (or struggle) is profound and difficult, and it tends to progress slowly. Therefore, some few adopt the path of extraordinary self-effort (or a most intense struggle of relinquishment), which is asceticism (or the method of absolute independence). However, the Adepts themselves have, since the most ancient days, offered an alternative to mere (and, at best, slowly progressing) self-effort. Indeed, the Adept-Gurus (and especially the Sat-Gurus) offer a Unique Principle of practice (as an alternative to the conventional principle of mere and independent self-effort and relinquishment). That Unique Principle is the Principle of Supreme Attraction.

Truly, the bondage of attention to conditional objects, others, and states must be really transcended in the Spiritual Way, but mere self-effort (or struggle with the separate, and separative, self) is a principle that originates in and constantly reinforces the separate, and separative, self (or self-contraction, or egoity itself). Therefore, the process of the real transcending of bondage to conditions is made direct (and truly self-transcending) if the principle of independent self-effort (or egoic struggle) is at least progressively replaced by the responsive (or cooperative) Principle of Supreme Attraction (Which Is, in Its Fullness, Satsang, or responsive devotional Identification with the Free Person, Presence, and State of One Who Is Already Realized, or In Samadhi).

On the basis of the simple understanding of attention (expressed in the formula: You become, or Realize, What, or Who, you meditate on), the ancient Essence of the Spiritual Way is to meditate on (and otherwise to grant feeling-attention to) the Adept-Guru (or Sat-Guru), and thereby to be Attracted (or Grown) beyond the self-contraction, or egoity, or all the self-limiting tendencies of attention, or all self-limiting and self-binding association with conditional objects, others, and states. Through sympathetic (or responsive) Spiritual Identification with the Samadhi of a Realizer, the devotee is Spiritually Infused and, potentially, and Ultimately, even Perfectly Awakened by the Inherently Attractive Power of Samadhi Itself. (Even the simplest beginner in practice may be directly Inspired, and thus moved toward greater practice, true devotion, and eventual Perfect Awakening, by sympathetic response to the Free Sign, and the Great Demonstration, of a true Realizer.) And, by the Great Spiritual Means that Is true Satsang (coupled with a variety of disciplines and practices, which should be associated with real self-understanding), the fully prepared devotee of a true Realizer may Freely (or with relative effortlessness) relinquish (or Grow Beyond) the limits of attention in each of the progressive stages of life that, in due course, follow upon that devotion.

Of course, actual Spiritual Identification with the Realized Spiritual Condition, or Samadhi, of an Adept is limited by the stage of life of the devotee, the effective depth of the self-understanding and the self-transcending devotional response of the devotee, and the stage of life and Realization of the Adept. And some traditions may (unfortunately) tend to replace, or at least to combine, the essential and Great Communion that is true Satsang with concepts and norms associated with the parent-child relationship, or the relationship between a king and a frightened subject, or even the relationship between a slave-master and a slave. However, this Great Principle or Means that Is Satsang (rightly understood and truly practiced) is the ancient Essence (or Great Secret) of the Spiritual Way, and true Adept-Gurus (and especially the Sat-Gurus) have, therefore, since the most ancient days, been the acknowledged principal Sources and Resources (as well as the principal Means) of true religion (or effective religious Wisdom) and the esoteric tradition of Spiritual Realization.

Particularly in more modern days, since Spirituality (and everything else) has become a subject of mass communication and popularization, the Spiritual Way Itself has become increasingly subject to conventional interpretation and popular controversy. In the broad social (or survival) context of the first three stages of life, self-fulfillment (or the consolation of the ego) is the common ideal (tempered only by local, popular, and conventional political, social, and religious ideals, or demands). Therefore, the common mood is one of adolescent anti-authority and anti-hierarchy (or "Oedipal"[55] anti-"parent"), and the common search is for a kind of ever-youthful (and "Narcissistic") ego-omnipotence and ego-omniscience.

The popular egalitarian (or ego-based, and merely, and competitively, individualistic) "culture" (or, really, anti-culture) of the first three stages of life is characterized by the politics of adolescent rebellion against "authority" (or the perceived "parent", in any form). Indeed, a society (or any loose collective) of mere individuals does not need, and cannot even tolerate, a true culture—because a true culture must, necessarily, be characterized (in its best, and even general, demonstrations, and, certainly, in its aspirations) by mutual tolerance, cooperation, peace, and profundity. Therefore, societies based on competitive individualism, and egoic self-fulfillment, and merely gross (or superficial) mindedness actually destroy culture (and all, until then, existing cultures, and cultural adaptations). And true cultures (and true cultural adaptations) are produced (and needed) only when individuals rightly and truly participate in a collective, and, thus and thereby (even if, as may sometimes, or especially in some cases, be the case, in relative, or even actual, solitude), live in accordance with the life-principle of ego-transcendence and the Great Principle of Oneness, or Unity.

In the popular egalitarian (or ego-based, and merely, and competitively, individualistic) "culture" (or, really, anti-culture) of the first three stages of life, the Guru (and the Sat-Guru) and the developmental culture of the Spiritual Way are (with even all of "authority" and of true, or ego-transcending, culture) taboo, because every individual limited (or egoically defined) by the motives of the first three stages of life is at war with personal vulnerability and need (or the feeling of egoic insufficiency). However, the real Spiritual process does not even begin until the egoic point of view of the first three stages of life is understood (or otherwise ceases to be the limit of aspiration and awareness) and the self-surrendering and self-transcending Motive of the fourth stage of life begins to move and change the body-mind (from the heart).

Those who are truly involved in the self-surrendering and self-transcending process of the advanced and the ultimate stages of life are (fundamentally) no longer at war with their own Help (or struggling toward the ultimate victory of the ego). Therefore, it is only in the non-Spiritual (or even anti-Spiritual) "cultural" domain of the first three stages of life (or the conventional survival culture, bereft of the Motive of truly developmental and Spiritual culture) that the Guru (or the Sat-Guru) is, in principle, taboo. And, because that taboo is rooted in adolescent reactivity and egoic willfulness, or the yet unresolved emotional, and psychological, and even emotional-sexual rebellion against childish and asexual (or emotionally and sexually ego-suppressing) dependence on parent-like individuals and influences, "anti-Guruism", and even "anti-cultism", which, characteristically, and without discrimination, denigrate, and defame, and mock, or, otherwise, belittle, <u>all</u> "authorities", and, also, even all the seed-groups of newly emerging cultural movements, whether or not they have positive merit, are forms (or expressions) of what Sigmund Freud described as an "Oedipal" problem.

In the common world of mankind, it is yet true that most individuals tend (by a combination of mechanical psycho-physical tendencies and a mass of conventional political, social, and cultural pressures) to be confined to the general point of view associated, developmentally, with the unfinished (or yet to be understood) "business" of the first three stages of life. Thus, in the common world of mankind, even religion is, characteristically, reduced to what is intended to serve the "creaturely", or "worldly", and rather aggressively <u>exoteric</u>, point of view and pur-poses of egoity in the context of the first three stages of life. And even if an interest in the <u>esoteric</u> possibilities (beyond the first three stages of life) develops in the case of any such yet rather "worldly" character, that interest tends to be pursued in a manner that dramatizes and rein-forces the point of view (and the exoteric, and either childishly or adolescently egoic, inclinations) characteristic of the first three stages of life.

Until there is the development of significantly effec-tive self-understanding relative to the developmental problems (or yet unfinished "business") associated with the first three stages of life, any one who aspires to develop a truly esoteric religious practice (necessarily beginning in the context of the fourth stage of life) will, characteristically, tend to relate to such possible esoteric practice in either a childish or an adolescent manner. Thus, any one whose developmental disposition is yet relatively childish (or tending, in general, to seek egoic security via the dramatization of the role of emotionalistic dependency) will tend to relate to esoteric possibilities via emotionalistic, or, otherwise, merely enthusiastic, attachments, while otherwise, in general, tending to be weak in both the responsible exercise of discriminating intelligence and the likewise responsible exercise of functional, practical, relational, and cultural self-discipline. (Indeed, such childish religiosity, characterized by dependent emotionalism, or mere enthusiastic attachment, bereft of discrimination and real self-discipline, is what may rightly, without bad intentions, be described and criticized as "cultism".) And any one whose developmental disposition is yet relatively adolescent (or tending, in general, to seek egoic security via the dramatization of the role of reactive independence) will tend to relate to esoteric possibilities via generally "heady" (or willful, rather mental, or even intellectual, or bookish, but not, altogether, truly intelligent) efforts, accompanied either (or even alternately) by a general lack of self-discipline (and a general lack of non-reactive emotional responsiveness) or by an exaggerated (abstractly enforced, and more or less life-suppressing and emotion-suppressing) attachment to self-discipline. (Therefore, such adolescent, or "heady", religiosity merely continues the dramatization of the characteristic adolescent search for independence, or the reactive pursuit of escape from every kind of dependency, and, altogether, the reactive pursuit of egoic self-sufficiency. And such adolescent seeking is inherently and reactively disinclined toward any kind of self-surrender. Therefore, the rather adolescent seeker tends to want to be his or her own "guru" in all matters. And, characteristically, the rather adolescent seeker will resist, and would even prefer to avoid, a truly intelligent, rightly self-disciplined, and, altogether, devotionally self-surrendered relationship to a true Guru, or Sat-Guru.)

Because of their developmental tendencies toward either childish or adolescent ego-dramatizations, those who are yet bound to the point of view (or the unfinished "business") of the first three stages of life are, developmentally (or in their characteristic disposition, not yet relieved by sufficient self-understanding), also (regardless of their presumed "interest") not yet truly ready to enter into the esoteric process (beyond the first three stages of life). And, for the same developmental reasons, the principal and most characteristic impediments toward true participation in the esoteric religious process are "cultism" (or mere emotionalistic dependency, bereft of discrimination and self-discipline), "intellectualism" (or merely mental, or even bookish, preoccupation, disinclined to fully participatory, or directly experiential, involvement in the esoteric religious process), and "anti-Guruism" (or reactive attachment to a state of egoic independence, immune to the necessity for devotional self-surrender and the Grace of Great Help).

It is not the specific (and Great) Function of the Adept to fulfill a popular Spiritual (or, otherwise, non-Spiritual) role in common (or egoic and early stage) society, but to Serve as Teacher, Guide, Spiritual Transmitter, or Free Awakener in relation to those who are already (and rightly) moved (and progressively prepared) to fulfill the ego-transcending obligations of the Great and (soon) Spiritual Way Itself (in the potential developmental context that is beyond the first three stages of life). The only proper relationship to such a Realized Adept (or true Guru, or Sat-Guru) is, therefore, one of real and right and self-surrendering and self-transcending practice, and that practice becomes (or must become) Inspired (and, soon, Spiritually Inspired) and ego-transcending devotion (not childish egoity, or "cultic" dependency, and not adolescent egoity, or willful, or, otherwise, ambivalent, independence).

Of course, individuals in the earlier (or first three) stages of life who are not yet actively oriented (or, otherwise, rightly adapted) to self-surrendering and self-transcending practice may be Served by Adept-Gurus (or Sat-Gurus), but (apart from special instances where an Adept must Work directly with such individuals, in order to establish a new community of devotees, or in order to establish a new Revelation of the Spiritual Way) those not yet actively oriented (or actively committed), or, otherwise, rightly adapted, to truly self-surrendering and really self-transcending practice are generally (except perhaps for occasional glimpses of the Adept in his or her Free Demonstration) Served (or prepared for self-surrendering, self-transcending, and, soon, Spiritual practice) only through the written or otherwise recorded Teachings of an Adept, and through the public institutional work (and the "outer Temple", or beginner-serving, institutional work) of the practicing devotees of an Adept.

The Realized Adept (or any true Guru, or Sat-Guru) is, primarily, an esoteric Figure, whose unique Function Serves within the context of the advanced and the ultimate stages of life. The advanced and the ultimate stages of life are themselves open only to those who are ready, willing, and able to make the truly developmental (or progressively Real-God-Realizing, or Truth-Realizing, or Reality-Realizing) sacrifice of separate and separative self that is necessary in the context of the advanced and the ultimate stages of life. Therefore, the necessity (and the True Nature and Great Function) of a Realized Adept (or true Guru, or Sat-Guru) is obvious (and of supreme value) only to those who are ready, willing, and able to embrace the Ordeal of the advanced and the ultimate stages of life.

Except for the possible moments in which the Divine Person (or the Ultimate Reality and Truth) may (for some few) Serve (temporarily, and, to whatever degree, significantly, and, in any case, never to the Most Ultimate, or Most Perfect, degree) in or via a non-physical (and/or perhaps even non-human) Revelation-Form, the Realized Adept (or a human and living true Guru, or, especially, a human and living true Sat-Guru, or, at least, a human and living true, and formally Acknowledged, Appointed, and Blessed, devotee-Agent[56] of a once living, or even, perhaps, yet living, and, certainly, yet Spiritually Effective, true Sat-Guru) is an absolute (and never obsolete) necessity for any and every human being who would practice (and Realize) within the esoteric (or advanced and ultimate) stages of life. Therefore, the necessity (and the True Nature and Great Function) of a Realized Adept (or true Guru, or Sat-Guru) is inherently (and gratefully) obvious to any one and every one who is truly ready, willing, and able to embrace the esoteric Ordeal of Real-God-Realization (or Truth-Realization).

Any one and every one who doubts and quibbles about the necessity (and the True Nature and Great Function) of a true Adept-Guru (or Adept Sat-Guru) is, simply, not yet ready, willing, and able to enter the esoteric (and necessarily self-surrendering) Ordeal of the advanced and the ultimate stages of life. And no mere verbal (or otherwise exoteric) argument is sufficient to convince such doubters of the necessity (and the True Nature and Great Function) of a true Adept-Guru (or Adept Sat-Guru), just as no mere verbal (or otherwise exoteric) argument is sufficient to make them ready, willing, and able to truly embrace the self-surrendering esoteric Ordeal of the advanced and the ultimate stages of life.

Those who doubt the Guru-Principle, and the unique value and ultimate necessity of the Adept-Guru (or the Adept Sat-Guru), are those for whom the Great and (soon) Spiritual Way Itself is yet in doubt. Therefore, such matters remain "controversial" (and access to the Spiritual Way and the Adept-Company is effectively denied to ordinary people by popular taboos and the psychological limitations of the first three stages of life) until the truly developmental and (soon) Spiritual Motive Awakens the heart's Great Impulse to Grow Beyond.

The "Family of the Guru": The True Method of Training in the Music Tradition of India and in the Great Guru-Devotee Relationship

The music tradition of India, and, in general, even all the traditions of India, including all its artistic, cultural, and educational traditions, aspire to positively simulate (or, in the rightest sense, to imitate) the principal tradition of India, which is its philosophical, religious, and Spiritual tradition (or its complex, and, yet, basically single, whole, and simple, body of philosophical, religious, and Spiritual traditions). Therefore, through positively (or rightly) intended simulation, traditional Indian music reflects (or "plays upon") esoteric philosophical and mystical principles (much as exoteric religion, by even ritually employing numerous symbols and any number of other concrete devices, often simulates, and, thereby, to one or another degree, reflects, or "plays upon", various aspects of esoteric religion). And the process of teaching (or transmitting) traditional Indian music, and the process of learning and performing traditional Indian music, takes place within a sacred context of real respect, right obedience, and profound self-discipline that positively simulates (or rightly, and, as such, not at all presumptuously or otherwise inappropriately, imitates) the <u>Great</u> Guru-devotee relationship, or the relationship between the true Realizer and his or her true disciple (or devotee), which Great relationship is the fundamental and most sacred context of esoteric (and, by its reflective simulation of the esoteric, even exoteric) philosophy, religion, and Spirituality in India, and which is, indeed, the fundamental and most sacred context of even <u>all</u> true religion, <u>all</u> true Spirituality, and <u>all</u> true traditions of applied, or really and truly <u>practiced</u>, philosophy, whether in the East or the West.

On the basis of its characteristic and general (and politically, and otherwise idealistically, motivated) intention to commonize <u>everything</u> (even what should remain sacred, or even private, and even all that should not be approached except via a most profound and self-transcending ordeal), the modern West (and the increasingly "Westernized", or "modernized", world) tends to popularize philosophy, religion, Spirituality, and even all of culture, and all of life, to the point of trivializing it, and this by eliminating what is sacred and sacredly necessary, and, altogether, by eliminating most or all that is demanding, difficult, complex, long-term, and Great. Therefore, the "Westernization", or "modernization", of philosophy, religion, Spirituality, and even all of life and culture (including both the traditional Western and the traditional non-Western arts) tends toward secularization, ego-serving ease, quick learning, fast congratulations, and all that is characterized by superficiality, the lack of commitment, general amateurism, and fast-moving (briefly here, briefly there) dabblerism (or dilettantism). And this ego-based (and ego-serving) tendency of both the modern West and the "modernized" East (especially in their aggressively egalitarian and rather exclusively secularized modes) also frequently demonstrates itself as the mood of anti-authority and anti-hierarchy, which mood sometimes expresses itself as "anti-Guruism" (or a rather adolescent attitude that would resist or avoid the eternal, ancient, traditional, always new, most sacred, and utterly demanding relationship that is the Revelatory Source and the necessary Helping Means of all true philosophy, all true religion, and all true Spirituality).

As indicated by the testimony of some of the most distinguished modern Indian musicians,[57] extraordinary seriousness and intensity characterize the true ordeal of traditional Indian "gurukul"[58] music training. And the same is

(necessarily, and to an even greater degree) true of the
<u>Great</u> (or specifically and truly and only philosophical,
religious, and Spiritual) Guru-devotee, or Master-disciple,
relationship (which Great relationship is the necessary
foundation of all true philosophy, all true religion, and all
true Spirituality), and also the Great "Gurukul (or
'Gurukula', or 'Family of the Guru') Method" of constant
Guidance by, and devotional self-surrender to, the Guru,
or the Sat-Guru, or the Adept-Master, or the Realization-
Master (which Great "Method" is, likewise, the necessary
foundation of all true philosophy, all true religion, and all
true Spirituality). It is that Great relationship and its Great
"Method" that are positively simulated, or, in the rightest
sense, imitated, by the traditional system of Indian music
training. Indeed, that Great (Guru-devotee, or Master-
disciple) relationship and its Great ("Family of the Guru")
"Method", should be embraced and fully entered into by
every one and all of mankind (in the context of the real
practice of true applied philosophy, true, and especially
esoteric, religion, and, in due course, true Spirituality, and
by the real practice of devotional self-surrender, coupled
with real respect, right obedience, and profound self-
discipline). And, on the <u>basis</u> of that real practice of true
applied philosophy, true, and especially esoteric, religion,
and, in due course, true Spirituality, the true Guru-devotee,
or Master-disciple, relationship, and its true ("Family of the
Guru") "Method", should also, by extension (and, in order
to make all human activity sacred, in real practice), be
positively simulated, or, in the rightest sense, imitated, by
all the arts, all modes of functional, practical, and relational education, training, and developmental learning,
and even all the daily culture of human living, whether in
the East or the West. Therefore, in the case of each and
every (thus and rightly practicing) individual, even <u>all</u>
activities and <u>all</u> relationships should, in an always most
positive and benign manner, be engaged as if the entire
world of beings is the extended "Family" (or larger

Community) of his or her philosophical, religious, or Spiritual Guru, or Realization-Master. And every positive simulation, or, in the rightest sense, imitation, of the Great Guru-devotee, or Master-disciple, relationship and its true ("Family of the Guru") "Method" should be done in a context of real respect, right obedience, and profound self-discipline. However, such positive simulation, or, in the rightest sense, imitation, should never be done presumptuously, or in any sense inappropriately, and, therefore, not at all as if the arts and the teachers, or "gurus", of the arts, or the activities and the teachers, or "gurus", associated with any other modes or enterprises of human ordinariness and of human exotericism, are superior, or even in any sense equal, to actual and true Realizers and Adepts, and to the "sadhana",[59] or the Ordeal of unlimited devotion, and, altogether, of most profoundly self-surrendering practice, required in the Company of any actual and true Realizer, or Adept.

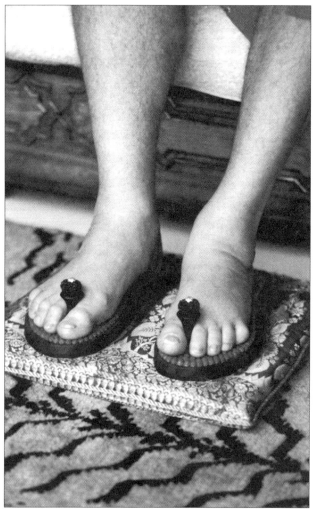

RUCHIRA AVATAR ADI DA SAMRAJ
Adidam Samrajashram (Naitauba), Fiji, 1997

PART FOUR

If I Am your Guru, Be Mastered By Me

If I Am your Guru,
Be Mastered By Me

I.

AVATAR ADI DA SAMRAJ: Never forget Me. Never. Never break the "Bond" with Me. Never dissociate from Me.

The functions, the life-circumstance, the ordinary relatedness that you are involved in by your daily choices—all of that is about "bonding" to the world, "bonding" to another, "bonding" to function, and so forth—and all of that, in itself, is the forgetting of Me, the breaking of the "Bond" with Me, and, altogether, the activity of dissociation from Me.

Therefore, you must convert every mode and fraction and moment of your daily existence to self-surrendering, self-forgetting, and (more and more) self-transcending devotional Communion with Me. Such is the essential practice of the only-by-Me Revealed and Given Way of Adidam (the Way of the Heart, of the Heart Itself, Revealed and Given only by Me).

If you practice this Yoga of devotion to Me in all of your life-activities and in all of your life-associations, then it becomes effective. That is how you prove it. The constant practice of Ruchira Avatara Bhakti Yoga,[60] moment to moment (self-surrendering, self-forgetting, and, more and more, self-transcending), shows the sign of going beyond the ego-knot, and it becomes, in its progress, great purification—by Means of My Blessing of you. That purification relieves you, in due course, of all bondage-symptoms, all ego-signs, all ego-results, all ego-drama, all ego-adaptations.

Ruchira Avatara Bhakti Yoga becomes a profound equanimity, a Samadhi of heart-Communion with Me. The modifications of the Divine Reality are purified and then loosed, such that, ultimately, in the progress of that sadhana, the agitations of the principal life-faculties[61] are released. The ego-signs in the body, in emotion (or feeling), in mind (or attention), and in the breath all become evened out. The mind ceases to be preoccupied with its content, so thinking quiets. Reactive emotions quiet. Impurities and agitations in the body quiet. If you are in this profound and steady Communion with Me, the breath becomes quieted (relieved of the changes it otherwise manifests in accordance with your characteristic disposition, your moment to moment psycho-physical reactions, and so forth).

These are all necessary signs that are, in more profound moments, shown even from the beginning. In due course, equanimity becomes more and more constant, it becomes your sign altogether, in every moment, under all circumstances. When that becomes the case, then you are on the "borderline" between preliminary practice (or practice of the only-by-Me Revealed and Given Way of Adidam in the context of the first five stages of life) and the "Perfect Practice" (or practice of the only-by-Me Revealed and Given Way of Adidam in the context of the sixth stage of life and, in due course, the seventh stage of life). When that "borderline" is truly and stably crossed over, there is the true and stable Awakening to the Witness-Position of Consciousness Itself (in non-separate, devotional heart-Communion with Me), Which Awakening makes possible the beginning of the "Perfect Practice" of the only-by-Me Revealed and Given Way of Adidam.

All the signs of Ruchira Avatara Bhakti Yoga that precede the "Perfect Practice" have the quality I just Described to you (of the surrender of the four principal life-faculties to Me, under all circumstances, and in all functions, and in all relations, always to the degree of self-surrendering, self-forgetting, and, more and more, self-transcending Communion with Me).

DEVOTEE: There is no Happiness without that, Beloved.

AVATAR ADI DA SAMRAJ: So the sadhana I Give you is simple to describe. That sadhana requires a Great Attraction to Me—great recognition of Me, great recognition-response to Me, and a great counter-egoic effort of application to the Yoga of Ruchira Avatara Bhakti in every moment, in every circumstance, in every function. There must <u>be</u> that <u>responsive</u> counter-egoic effort in recognition of Me, Attracted by Me. That responsive real effort is necessarily required. That is the necessary tapas,[62] or self-discipline.

DEVOTEE: To fall short of that tapas is suffering.

AVATAR ADI DA SAMRAJ: It is the essence of religious and Spiritual amateurism, of religious and Spiritual dabbling, of religious and Spiritual dilettantism.

DEVOTEE: It is the beginner's error.

AVATAR ADI DA SAMRAJ: Yes. And then, in the midst of that "talking" school[63] of "fans of 'God'", you can also constantly listen to one another's dramatizations of double-mindedness, or egoic arguments to do other than the submission of the life-faculties to Me. Therefore, both individually and collectively, you must root out such double-mindedness, such arguments against engaging this counter-egoic effort in heart-Communion with Me. You must eliminate such arguments from your personal disposition, from your personal habits of speech, and so forth, but also from your collective disposition and speech. Thus, a discipline of speech, and, therefore, of mind, is a fundamental part of this sadhana, this counter-egoic practice of real devotion to Me.

Notice how your words affect your breath, your emotion, your state of mind, and your physical condition. Every thought that you entertain and every word that you utter is a modification of the Divine Spirit-Power, My "Bright" Presence and Person. The <u>modifications</u> are what you are suffering from. What is to be Realized Is My Very Nature, Condition, and State—My "Bright" Presence of Divine Body and Divine Person, Which Is Prior to all modifications. If you merely indulge in the modifications, you <u>actively</u> avoid Me, you are inherently dissociated from Me. If you relinquish the modifications, in heart-Communion with Me, <u>As</u> and At the Source-Position of all conditions (or all modifications of Me), then you are going beyond all modifications, and you are directly heart-Communing with Me. Whenever you are entering into true heart-Communion (or true Satsang) with Me, you are entering into Samadhi. Effectively, the sadhana of Ruchira Avatara Bhakti Yoga is a matter of relinquishing <u>all</u> modifications of My "Bright" Presence, <u>all</u> modifications of My Self-Existing and Self-Radiant Divine Body and Person. To surrender and forget all modifications in and by Means of heart-Communion with Me—that is the essential sadhana of the only-by-Me Revealed and Given Way of Adidam. I <u>Am</u> the One you must Realize, Prior to <u>all</u> modifications— but in the true Manner of the only-by-Me Revealed and Given Way of Adidam (and, therefore, not by <u>excluding</u> the universal pattern of modifications, but by surrendering all arising modifications, and even by surrendering <u>as</u> them, to the degree of forgetting them in Me, and, ultimately, to the degree of really transcending them in Me).

All modifications must be surrendered, forgotten, and (more and more) transcended. In every moment, this is the practice to be done. And, in order to do so in literally every moment, you must do the sadhana as I have Given it to you in all of its details. Your practice of Ruchira Avatara Bhakti Yoga has to cover every aspect of your character and your activities. That is why it is necessary for you to meet with one another, "consider" your practice together, examine your doings, be admonished there by My Word, and make new agreements about this, that, or the other detailed discipline—because there are things that (up until that moment, perhaps) you did not notice, that you did not account for, and that you must, thereafter, always account for—very directly, very practically, as a discipline for which you must be kept accountable.

Your practice of Ruchira Avatara Bhakti Yoga must cover everything, ultimately. That fundamental practice is about relinquishing all modifications (or even the event of modification itself)—because modifications control your attention, they control your body, they control your emotion, they control your breath. When the modifications become the focus of your life, that is common bondage. That is "bonding" to the world. That is "bonding" to modifications of That Which Is Always Already The Case (Which Is Reality, Truth, or the One and Indivisible and Only Real God).

You must Realize the Truth by passing beyond all "bonding" to modifications. Turn your attention from modifications, and to Me instead. Submit (or really turn) your attention to Me. Submit (or really turn) your breath to Me. Submit (or really turn) your feeling to Me. Submit (or really turn) your bodily form (and all your bodily activities) to Me. Forget the modifications, and enter into devotional Communion with Me. That is the essence of the sadhana in My Company. It must be done rigorously, covering every detail. When this sadhana has become a complete discipline, and you have been purified and matured in that complete discipline, then you are prepared to move on to the "Perfect Practice" of the only-by-Me Revealed and Given Way of Adidam.

The "Perfect Practice" is not, Itself, a matter of dealing with modifications, but of entering into unobstructed, unqualified heart-Communion with Me, without the ego-gesture of separation from Me. It is heart-Communion with Me, beyond modifications, Communing with Me just As I Am—My Very State, My Very Person. Such is the "Perfect Practice" of the only-by-Me

Revealed and Given Way of Adidam.

To truly enter into the "Perfect Practice", you must go through the tapas, or the comprehensive (and really counter-egoic, and really ego-transcending) discipline, of relinquishing <u>all</u> modifications, until you come to the point of fundamental purification, steadiness, equanimity, and one-pointedness in Me. Then the Native Stand in the Witness-Position (or the Position of Consciousness Itself, Which is Inherently Perfect heart-Communion with Me, Prior to your presumption, in Consciousness, of egoic separate-ness) is Inherently Obvious, and It is not lost under any circumstances. It is true of you even now, because It Is Inherently (or Always Already) The Case. Observe—no matter what is arising, right now, you Are the Witness of it. Nevertheless, to actually, always <u>Stand As</u> the Witness of whatever is arising, you must be <u>able</u> to Stand There, and not <u>move</u> from That Position.

In order for Inherently Perfect Standing in My Place to be the actual case, moment to moment, a fundamental purification must occur. That purification is the Process (or tapas) of Ruchira Avatara Bhakti Yoga in the context of the first five stages of life. To relinquish all modifications, to constantly submit the principal life-faculties to Me, to really go through the counter-egoic ordeal of real self-discipline in self-surrendering, self-forgetting, and (more and more) self-transcending devotional Communion with Me, to truly "Bond" with Me, and, <u>thereby</u>, to transcend the "bonding" of attention, and all the other principal life-faculties, to modifications of Me, and, altogether, to simply enter into heart-Communion with <u>Me</u>—Such is the Great Yoga in My Company.

If you are not serious about this, and are (instead) dal-lying with the modifications, then you will be rather retarded in the true practice of Ruchira Avatara Bhakti Yoga, and, altogether, in disciplining yourself relative to all kinds of matters. You will be "picking and choosing". You will remain a beginner. You will not handle your life-business. You will waste your life, always merely looking toward the time when you will have handled your life-business. That is a waste of life, because you should understand life as an opportunity to Realize Me—not as something purposed for its own sake, to realize its possibilities. This is the right life-understanding of My fully practicing devotee—that his or her life is inherently, really, and always actively purposed to Realize Me. You are vowed to Realize Me, from the time you become a student-novice, formally approaching the total practice of the Way of Adidam.

Therefore, you must convert all your doings, all the wanderings of your life-faculties, thereby relinquishing all the modifications with which your life-faculties are (otherwise) associated. You must convert all of that to the Yoga of self-surrendering, self-forgetting, and (more and more) self-transcending heart-Communion with Me, and be purified, brought to equanimity, to fundamental steady Abiding in the Native State, such that you can enter into the "Perfect Practice" of the only-by-Me Revealed and Given Way of Adidam. Previous to the "Perfect Practice", you are involved in preliminary discipline, preliminary sadhana—disciplining and dealing with the power of modification, the stress of egoity, of egoic seeking. Previous to the "Perfect Practice", your sadhana is a matter of counteracting the fact that you are doing egoity.

Egoity is self-contraction. Until you Realize Me Most Perfectly, egoity governs all of your life, absolutely every detail of it. It is inherently suffering, because it is contraction—a strangulation, a shutting off, a disturbance. Therefore, you are motivated to seek. You seek to be relieved of that stress that is your own creation, to "satisfy" yourself out of it somehow, to "enjoy" yourself out of it somehow, by exploiting the capability for experiencing the modifications of Existence Itself.

Truth Is Existence Itself. My Very Person Is Truth, or Existence Itself, or That Which Is Always Already The

Case. That Is What There Is to Realize. That Is Happiness. It Is Inherent Happiness Itself. Happiness Itself (or My Self-Existing and Self-Radiant Love-Bliss Itself) Is That Which Is Always Already The Case. I Am the "Bright", the Divine Love-Bliss, or Happiness Itself—That of Which all arising conditions are mere, and merely apparent, and inherently unnecessary, and inherently unsatisfactory modifications. The modifications of Happiness are not themselves Happiness. They are mere possibilities, arising temporarily, and always changing, diminishing, and passing. And to seek, or to cling to, or even to avoid any mere possibilities is to forget, and to dissociate from, Happiness Itself. All modifications have that nature. All arising things are conditional, or merely passing, and always changing. Therefore, there is no ultimate satisfaction in the constant event of modification. Only the Divine Self-Condition and Source-Condition (or That Which Is Always Already The Case) is Really (and Inherently) Free of modification. Therefore, Only the Most Perfect Realization of the Divine Self-Condition and Source-Condition Is Happiness Itself, Freedom Itself, Existence Itself, Love-Bliss Itself. This Is What you must Realize.

I Am the One to be Realized. I Am That, in Person. Not only in this Avataric Incarnation-Body, but altogether.

The practice of Ruchira Avatara Bhakti Yoga is the Divinely Revealed sadhana of Real-God-Realization. It is up to you to understand this and to be serious about this sadhana, and the real practice of it. Otherwise, if you are not serious about this sadhana, you will waste your life by devoting it partially, or even totally, to the egoic purpose, to the search—and, therefore, to active un-Happiness (or to the search for every thing, or relationship, or condition, or state that is not permanent Happiness). Therefore, it is up to you to recognize Me and respond to Me, to take your vow of Ruchira Avatara Bhakti Yoga fully seriously. It is up to you to choose to not waste your life waiting to get serious, or merely planning to get serious, or merely talking about being serious or getting serious (and all the reasons why and why not). Yes, you must observe yourself, but the purpose of observing yourself is to refine the details of your sadhana—not to <u>delay</u> your sadhana, or avoid it, but to <u>refine</u> it, in the real process of <u>doing</u> it.

It is up to you to be serious. If you are serious, prove it. You prove it by constantly doing the real sadhana of Ruchira Avatara Bhakti Yoga.

The Purpose of this sadhana is Liberation from all power of modification, by Realizing Me, the Source-Condition, the Source-Person, the Source-State. If you are serious, you <u>actively</u> purpose your life to Realize Me. If you are not serious, you merely talk. If you are only middling serious, then you do a little bit of sadhana, a touch of it. A little bit of this sadhana is not enough for Realization of Me, but it may improve things for you, a little bit—just enough to convince you, by its unsatisfactoriness, that you must do the full, and fully serious, sadhana of a life utterly and entirely purposed to Realize Me.

DEVOTEE: A "little bit" of improvement is still suffering.

AVATAR ADI DA SAMRAJ: Yes, it is—and that is what you must really, seriously appreciate. As it is said in the traditions, "Even a little of the Dharma casts out great fear." So, a little bit of sadhana, doing sadhana relative to some bits and pieces, improves your situation to some degree, relieves you of some pain, some bewilderment. That "little bit" is not enough for Divine Self-Realization, but there is a level of release, or relief, in any degree of sadhana—and that "little bit" is also My Argument, for a little while, until the unsatisfactoriness of the "little bit" moves you to the right, true, full, and fully devotional practice of the only-by-Me Revealed and Given Way of Adidam.

The only-by-Me Revealed and Given Way of Adidam is a comprehensive and complete Way, purposed for Most Perfect Realization. It is not merely an assortment of "ideal behaviors", based on an idealization of life. And it is not purposed merely to make "karmic[64] improvements", or to make your modifications perfect, or even less dreadful or less uncomfortable. Such changes may, of course, be experienced by you, as a result of your practice of the only-by-Me Revealed and Given Way of Adidam, but they are not, themselves, the point, they are not, themselves, the purpose of the practice of Ruchira Avatara Bhakti Yoga. The Purpose of the practice of Ruchira Avatara Bhakti Yoga is to conform your entire life (all, and every thing) to Me and (thereby) to directly and Most Perfectly Realize Me, and to not delay the course of that Realization.

DEVOTEE: Beloved, for anybody who has truly listened to Your Word, there is really no compromise to be made. They have to go beyond themselves, to go beyond whatever falls short of Your Wisdom.

AVATAR ADI DA SAMRAJ: You Always Already live in My Eternal Space, the Self-Existing and Self-Radiant Space of Consciousness Itself, the "Bright" Itself. Every thing that is arising is a mere appearance (or a "seeming"), occurring in That Space, but you do not Realize This—you do not yet Divinely Recognize what is arising. You are looking at the things themselves, the modifications themselves, and you are not Realizing the Source-Condition, the Very State in Which you Always Already Exist (Beyond your separate and separative ego-"I"). It is not even altogether appropriate to use the words "in Which you Always Already Exist", because that suggests that there is a "you" somehow independent of That State. You Are That State. You are not the ego. The ego is an apparent modification of (and an act of dissociation from) That State.

Unfortunately, you are stressfully identified with the fundamental modification—which is the self-contraction itself, with all of its results, which is every kind of experiencing, every kind of limited and limiting condition. You live in the domain of egoity, of the presumed separate self—indulging in (or, otherwise, suffering) the modifications that come from presuming such a (necessarily, separative) point of view. It is all a lie, because, Natively, Inherently, you Are Always Already in the Condition That Is Prior to all of that. Except that you do not notice it. It is not obvious to you, because you are indulging in the self-contraction and its results, and you are pursuing the search that comes from your inevitable and chronic dissatisfaction, having made the choice of self-contraction.

The self-contraction is your own creation. You are bound to it, naively. The naive "realism" of your separate and separative experiencing is controlling your life—indeed, it is controlling your very existence. Apart from truly doing the sadhana I have Given to you, all of that illusion is controlling your life and your very existence. You are in a dream made of presumptions. Therefore, you are not Realizing the Truth, the Inherent Condition, My Very Person.

DEVOTEE: To see Your Sign is, Itself, Liberating. All Your devotees know at heart Who You Are.

AVATAR ADI DA SAMRAJ: That recognition of Me is the basis of your eternal vow to Me, and, therefore, the basis of your practice of the only-by-Me Revealed and Given Way of Adidam. But you must respond to Me—you must do the Way. If you have a Guru, then you do the discipline of practicing all that the Guru tells you to do. If you are egoically "self-possessed" (or self-absorbed), then you are Guru-less (or, in other words, self-"guruing"), and you are simply volunteering to participate in your own bondage.

If you have a Guru, a Spiritual Master—if you have Me—then you have a Mastered life. You do not tell Me what you are going to do. You ask. And the basis of your asking is that you do not want bondage anymore, you do not want this suffering, you do not want this search, you do not want this stress and fear, you do not want this mortality. You want utter Freedom from all of that. Being committed to that, you ask Me, relative to every fraction of your life, "What shall I do?" Sometimes you may ask Me personally, in a conversation, but, fundamentally, you ask Me by going to My already Given Wisdom-Teaching, because that is where all the answers (or by-Me-Given Instructions) are kept for you.

DEVOTEE: Your Wisdom-Teaching covers every aspect of our lives, Beloved. I feel utterly helpless when I do not resort to You for Instruction. I have no capability to help myself.

AVATAR ADI DA SAMRAJ: I Am your Capability. Therefore, your Capability is Unlimited. My Heart is without impediment. Therefore, any one can practice the sadhana I have Revealed and Given. Any one can embrace the only-by-Me Revealed and Given Way of Adidam, from the heart, in response to Me. In order to embrace the total practice of the Way of Adidam, you need to participate in My Excesses, My "Brightness", My Blessing-Siddhis.[65] Therefore, every one is Granted full capability to practice the Way of Adidam in its totality, simply by Means of the practice of devotion to Me.

But if you spend your time in a "talking" school with one another, always repeating and explaining your presumed limitations—"Ah, if I could only do this sadhana," and so forth—then you are talking one another out of doing the sadhana I Give to you. You are letting one another off the hook. There is always the sadhana of Ruchira Avatara Bhakti Yoga to be done. Therefore, that sadhana is the only appropriate subject of conversation. Affirm that in your "considerations" with one another. Shore one another up, build one another up, relative to that, instead of talking "case"[66] with one another.

It is appropriate to examine yourselves, examine one another, in order to discover new details necessary for your practice of self-discipline, but it is not appropriate to look at the conditions of your apparent life and struggle, and "meditate" on them, or use all of that as an excuse to be double-minded and to avoid the sadhana of Ruchira Avatara Bhakti Yoga. That is not appropriate. That is utterly inappropriate. It is something to be rooted out, personally and collectively.

DEVOTEE: Beloved, the Basis of Ruchira Avatara Bhakti Yoga is Divine Distraction. In the midst of Your Attractiveness, everything else falls away, everything else is totally insignificant.

AVATAR ADI DA SAMRAJ: This Guru-Love, this Ruchira-Avatara-Bhava,[67] is a Great "Intoxicant".[68] It must become a moment to moment matter.

DEVOTEE: It is so simple, Beloved. It is completely simple.

AVATAR ADI DA SAMRAJ: Yes. I have always Told you This. This is <u>It</u>.

II.

AVATAR ADI DA SAMRAJ: My Complete Word to you, especially My Twenty-Three "Source-Texts",[69] Is My Body of Instruction—It <u>is</u> My Written (and Entirely By-Me-Spoken) Answer to <u>all</u> your questions. Therefore, you should be constantly asking Me what you should do, by consulting (and really studying) the Twenty-Three "Source-Texts" of My Word, and living by That Word of Instruction, rather than living by your own inclinations. If you do otherwise, you have no Guru. You are not living a Mastered life if you just <u>say</u> that I am your Guru, and then "pick and choose" from among My Words, to do as you please. You are not Mastered by Me merely because you <u>like</u> Me. You are Mastered by Me only if you take My Word as Divine Law, by actively living in obedience to Me. I Am the Utter Source of Divine Wisdom and Divine Law, and you must approach Me As Such.

In the traditional setting, where people take the Guru seriously, they do not (and would never) make any important decisions arbitrarily. They <u>always</u> <u>ask</u> their Guru. If you do not have a Guru, if you just have some kind of religious culture or community, and you self-"guru" yourself within it, then you never move beyond being a beginner in religious and Spiritual practice—but, if you are Mastered, if you have a Guru Whose Word Is Divine Law for you, then everything gets straightened out very directly.

If you are not serious about your relationship to Me <u>As</u> your Guru (and, therefore, <u>As</u> your Spiritual Master), and if you do not take My Word as Divine Law, then your life-business never gets handled, and you remain endlessly preoccupied with it. In the traditional setting, the Guru <u>Is</u> Divine Law. Therefore, when the Guru <u>Is</u> the Divine Law, you <u>ask</u>. You do not tell yourself what you are going to do. And you do not tell your Guru what you are going to do. But you always ask your Guru what you should do—and, when told by your Guru what you should do, you do it!

I Embrace you and Righten and Straighten you. In So Doing, I Am Conforming you to My Self. I Know what Divine Realization requires in the case of each and every devotee of Mine. It says in the old documents: "The born person does not Know, the ego does not Know. Only the 'Horse' Knows, only the Guru Knows. Therefore, hold on to the Guru—the 'Tail' of the 'Horse'."[70] In other words, take the Guru's Word as Divine Law, be Mastered by the Guru. You can eliminate all kinds of time of diversions, if you truly live the sadhana of true Guru-devotion. That means you do not merely smile at Me, or look for social signs that I Love you. Instead, you accept Me (and My Word) as the Divine Law of your life. Relative to your handling of your life-business, and your total life proposed toward Divine Realization, you must do what I Say. If you want Me to Do what I Do, you have to do what I Say.

DEVOTEE: Is there something different about Spiritual practice in this time? Traditionally, it is has been said that it is more difficult to practice in the Kali Yuga.[71]

AVATAR ADI DA SAMRAJ: It makes absolutely no difference what yuga it is.

DEVOTEE: So this time is not different than any other time?

AVATAR ADI DA SAMRAJ: Absolutely not. This "late-time", or "dark" epoch, has its particular signs and characteristics, but you should not call it any kind of "bad yuga" in order to justify your weakness in practice of the Way I Reveal and Give. Relative to what is required to practice, all yugas are, fundamentally, the same. The fundamental process of ego-transcendence is always required, no matter what the characteristics of the times, or the characteristics of the experience of the individual at any time. And, even though the present epoch is relatively "dark" and the time is "late", I Am here!

I have Destroyed the impediment in this "late-time"— by My Divine Descent and "Emergence", here and in the entire Cosmic domain. Therefore, now, and forever hereafter, it does not make the slightest bit of difference what yuga it is, <u>because</u> I Am <u>here</u>, now, and forever hereafter. Because I Am here, the "circumstance" of necessary ego-transcending practice is the relationship to Me. That is certainly the case for all who recognize Me, and who respond to Me by embracing the only-by-Me Revealed and Given Way of Adidam.

Because of your relationship to Me, the so-called "Kali Yuga" has no negative power over you—none whatsoever. You are not bound by some sort of mysterious vibration of yuga-made ignorance, such that you cannot respond to Me. For My true devotee, all time is, now, and forever hereafter, <u>My</u> time.

I Am here. I have Given you My Word, My Complete Revelation. I have Told you and Shown you Who I <u>Am</u>.

The only question is whether you will rightly, truly, fully, and fully devotionally recognize Me and rightly, truly, fully, and fully devotionally respond to Me. To recognize Me and respond to Me, you have to prove it, you have to change your life-action. You have to do what the Way of Adidam requires, and not ignore Me, not deceive yourself and one another, not be "gurus" of yourselves.

If I Am your Guru, be Mastered by Me. That is <u>It</u>. Perform <u>every</u> detail of your life according to My Word.

DEVOTEE: In that case, Beloved Bhagavan, do all Your devotees need to ask You what they should do?

AVATAR ADI DA SAMRAJ: Absolutely! Each of you must give up your self-"guruing", your ego-position, and <u>always</u> ask Me about <u>every</u> thing—but that does not require you to come into the room with Me bodily, and speak to Me bodily, face to face.

DEVOTEE: That is what I wanted to know, because sometimes devotees wonder about this.

AVATAR ADI DA SAMRAJ: Fundamentally, to live your life by "asking" Me what to do means that you live according to My Word as Law—as <u>Divine</u> Law. That Word is My now (and forever hereafter) Revealed and Given (and Fully Written) Wisdom-Instruction in My Twenty-Three "Source-Texts", Which must be supported by the force of the culture of My devotees, serving you in your life-process of responsively conforming to My Word. In My now (and forever hereafter) Revealed and Given "Source-Texts", I have, in every detail, already answered your questions, and, in the Form of Those Twenty-Three "Source-Texts", I Am, now, and forever hereafter, here and ready to Instruct you.

If I Am the Divine Law of your life, then, for Me to Do what I Must Do to Bring you to Realization of Me, you must do as I Say. The practice of Ruchira Avatara Bhakti Yoga requires adaptation to doing what I Say. That adaptation is what you must be involved in as a student-novice or a student-beginner—or as a practitioner at any stage (and in any form, and in any formal congregation) of the Way of Adidam. Instead of consulting yourself, and trying to become a genius through self-indulgence, self-"meditation", and self-mindedness, you must ask <u>Me</u>.

I Am the Genius. If you want to know what to do, you ask Me, and I Tell you, through My now, and forever hereafter, Revealed and Given (and Fully Written) Word. You must constantly (and with constant formal cultural guidance) study My Word. And there may be relatively rare occasions when you (or any one of My devotees) needs to personally ask Me (or, after the physical Lifetime of My bodily human Form, ask My "Living Murti",[72] or, at any time, ask the Ruchira Sannyasin Order[73]) about some detail of My Instruction. In any case, the point I am making is that you must <u>always</u> <u>ask</u>, you must <u>always</u> submit to be Divinely Mastered by Me, and you must <u>always</u> really and truly live your life based on the Divine Law of My Instructions and My Person.

It is not a matter of indulging yourselves in endless talk, as if to become geniuses of "consideration", in order to tell <u>yourselves</u> what to do. That is to be Guruless! To have a Guru means you know that you are suffering and self-bound, and that you cannot find your own way out of the self-trapping web of your self-made complexity of self-bondage—but you also know that you have Found Me, the Divine Heart-Master. You know that I <u>Am</u> the Genius of what is required, and, therefore, you submit to <u>ask</u>. You do not have to be involved in more "mind" about anything in order to figure it all out. The Divine Heart-Master says, "Do this," and you do it.

"Teacher say, student do." That is the Guru-devotee tradition. You do not have to <u>become</u> a genius, because you have a Spiritual Master Who <u>Is</u> a Genius. You cannot figure it out. Do you think you are going to figure out the total scheme of this complicated illusion of modifications?

DEVOTEES: No, Beloved.

AVATAR ADI DA SAMRAJ: Understand that, and ask <u>Me</u>. You do not have to figure it out down to the last jot. You have a fundamental understanding in response to Me, but, relative to the details, what should you do? You do not have to struggle for endless years to figure it out. You should ask <u>Me</u>, through your formal study of My Twenty-Three Books of Revelation-Word. Every detail of your sadhana should be established and developed thus, and, therefore, according to My Explicit Word—and that is the end of the "consideration".

<u>I</u> save you time. You consult Me. That is how you are relieved from wasting your lifetime in trying to figure it out. If you spend your lifetime trying to figure it out, then you are inevitably going to waste your lifetime—because you cannot figure it out, and never will figure it out. You are not in a position to figure it out. You are in the position of egoity—self-contraction and naive "realism" and the modifications of Reality Itself—and you do not "Know" What is modified. You do not "Know" the Truth, you are not in the Position of Truth. Therefore, by self-"guruing" yourself, all you do is pull yourself along by the nose, thereby always complicating yourself further, and wasting your life in seeking.

Ramakrishna[74] once compared the true Guru to a true healer. He described various kinds of healers. There are the healers who will sit and listen to your arguments and give you some consoling message. Then there are others who will listen to your arguments and write you a prescription so that you can get some medicine, which you may or may not take. But the true Guru, Ramakrishna said, is like the true healer. If necessary, the true healer throws you to the floor, jumps on your body, holds you down, and stuffs the medicine down your throat!

Until you are truly My devotee, you do not want My real Mastery. You want to exercise the option of being egoically "self-possessed". This is the "egalitarian" time, in which each and every ego-"I" is (as such, or in itself) universally presumed and proclaimed (and advertised) to be an independent, self-contained, and self-sufficient specimen of the Absolute! In these days, everyone-and-everything is supposed to congratulate and serve egoity (and, in the religious and Spiritual domain, to support and propagandize the "doctrine" that the "inwardness" of the separate and separative ego-"I" is the "True Guru"). This is the great "dark" (and even comical) epoch of "Narcissus"! Thus, the ego of every "I" expects to be stimulated and confirmed in its self-illusion and obstinacy by messages that deride and renounce every kind of "authority" (other than the separate individual ego itself). Therefore, if you are disinclined to accept My authority, you are, likewise, disinclined to accept My Mastery! Indeed, if that is the case, you will, generally, be struggling to force <u>Me</u> to accept <u>your</u> "authority" and <u>your</u> "Mastery"! (And it is on this basis that the egocentric disposition indulges in self-"guruing", and even would delude itself into imagining it is a genuine "Realizer-Guru" of others.)

There has never been even a particle of Realization, not even a little bit of the Divine Law, apart from True Realizers, and the practice of surrendering the ego-"I" to a True Realizer (in the manner of right and true Guru-devotion). That is the way it is, and that is the way it always will be. Indeed, mankind should rejoice that such Help has been, and always will be, the case.

The ego-"I", in its characteristic ignorance and separativeness, is (both "inside" and "outside") bereft of Truth. The Truth has come to mankind only from ego-renouncing True Realizers (in their various degrees, or stages, of profoundly ego-transcending Realization). Yet, when it comes to the matter of Great Realization, the ego-"I", in its "self-possession", imagines it is an independent unit of Absoluteness, a self-authority, inherently fit to rightly govern itself. Indeed, the collective of human egos presumes it is fit to govern even the entire world of beings and things! How can it be so?

The human ego-"I" is a mere "organism", self-contracted, "self-possessed", and self-bound. The ego-"I" does not know <u>Where</u> it is. The ego-"I" does not know <u>What</u> even a single thing <u>Is</u>! <u>Because</u> of its presumption of separateness and separativeness, the ego-"I" (or "Narcissus", the self-contraction) presumes, and <u>prefers</u>, its independence and self-sufficiency. And that presumption of separateness, separativeness, independence, and self-sufficiency is the very means whereby the ego-"I" dissociates itself (inherently) from Truth, Reality Itself, Real God, or the Divine Condition Itself. Naive egoic "realism" (or conceptual and perceptual bondage of every kind) and egoic "self-possession" (willful and obstinate in its separativeness and un-love)—this is the sphere of the ego-"I". And Truth, and the Process of Realizing the Truth, has broken through the ego-sphere of mankind only through the Grace of True Realizers (in their various degrees of self-surrendering ego-transcendence).

Because you, My devotee, have suffered, and, ultimately, despaired of, your life of ego-"I", you have looked for the True Realizer of Truth, and, so, you have found Me. Nevertheless, having found Me, you have to <u>do</u> what I Say. That means, no more "you are the Law", no more "you 'guruing' yourself", no more "you doing your own thing". You have had enough of that. You <u>know</u> (behind your self-"guruing" mask of so-called "healthy independence") that <u>all</u> of that is garbage!

You come to Me because you recognize Me, you feel Me, you are Attracted to Me, you know Who I <u>Am</u>, you respond to Me, and you consult Me relative to absolutely everything. I Say something, and you do it. That is how quick the Process can be. It is not enough to just Contemplate My Murti.[75] My Word must be Divine Law. That is what it means to have a Guru. To have a Guru means you are Mastered—you are not an independent, free-wheeling, do-your-own-thing ego.

DEVOTEE: Beloved, that is an ecstatic condition.

AVATAR ADI DA SAMRAJ: Yes. But you can fool yourself into thinking you are My devotee without really submitting yourself to Me. You can be content merely to have your life in My Company be amusing, superficial, casual, stimulating, consoling—without doing any real counter-egoic and Me-Realizing sadhana.

Rudi[76] had His various limitations, but He really cut through that kind of nonsense. Sadhana is work! You discipline yourself in response to the Spiritual Master. You do not merely indulge yourself, or look for utopia. All of your limitations must be submitted to Me and disciplined according to My Word of Instruction. Rudi did not quite understand the total Law about it—as He always said, He was not a "finished product", just "somebody on the Way"—but He knew something fundamental about the difference between living on the basis of illusions and truly living the religious and Spiritual life. That aspect of True Wisdom—which is profoundly important—is something He really understood.

And that was His importance in His service to Me— to move Me out of the life-circumstances I had thus far been involved in, so that I could move on. What was missing in My "Sadhana" up to that moment? Work, real application to self-discipline, the real counter-egoic effort of self-transcendence. You either do it or you do not. If you are not doing it, you are deceiving yourself and others. The only-by-Me Revealed and Given Way of Adidam involves much more than functional, practical, and relational life-discipline, but the requirement for such self-discipline is essential and necessary in the Way of Adidam. At the time of My Meeting with Rudi, I had already understood much, but I was not yet disciplined. Therefore, the time had come when the discipline was profoundly necessary. So it is for you all, now, and forever hereafter.

Listen to Me. Study My Word. All these years, it has

always been the same Communication, the same Way—
from the beginning.

You must have a reason to listen to Me. If you do not
have a reason to listen to Me, you are not going to hear
Me. Listening is the first position.

When you are sick of your results, when you are sick
of your suffering, your seeking, and your bewilderment,
when you know the dead-end of your doings, you Find
Me. When you Find Me, you have to do what I Say. It is
not enough to casually find Me, and then smile at Me, and
wait for Me to Love your precious ego-self. No, you have
to do what I Say, you have to do the counter-egoic devotional sadhana, or else My Blessing of you cannot Work
fruitfully. Perhaps there may be a little bit of consolation
in My Blessing of you—but My Blessing is for your Divine
Realization, and It does not Work if you do not combine
with Me, by living by My Word, and doing the right, true,
full, and fully devotional sadhana of the Way of Adidam,
and being interested in that sadhana, always delighting in
it, and, altogether, delighting in Me.

This Way is interesting. If you do it profoundly, it will
uncover everything, it will really "empty the barn". Yes, the
sadhana of the Way of Adidam can, and must, be done, by
you. It is interesting, if and when you really do it. Then,
you are entered into a Great Process, in which you are
really, literally, purified by your devotional Communion
with Me.

If I Am your Guru, then I Am the Governor of your
life. You must listen to My Word and apply It, in real
detail, and not reduce It to one-liners, not comb through
It superficially, a few minutes a day, picking out a couple
of lines that justify your mere social religiosity, and egoic
seeking. No, you must submit yourself to Me through My
Word, you must be directly Addressed by Me through My
Word, and you must do what I Say. And you must not consult your ego-"I" anymore.

That does not mean that you become a robot. If you

really understand yourself and are sick of your own "act", then you are moved to prove the Way of Adidam by doing It. You do not know that the Way is Divinely Realizing if you do not do It. Prove the Way of Adidam. Prove your devotion to Me. Do what I Say. Just do exactly as I Say. Don't be looking for some excuse to do otherwise. Do the disciplines, just as I have Given them to one and all. Really! Every day of your life. Don't miss a step. Don't be indulging yourself in food and sex, money games, social games. Really live the practice of Ruchira Avatara Bhakti Yoga every day of your life. Anybody can do it.

Anybody can do it, but whether you will do it is your business. Choosing it is your business. Choosing Me as Your Guru means choosing My Word and making Me the Divine Law of your life. No more nonsense. No more double-mindedness masquerading as "consideration".

I have Done the "consideration". You do not have to. In that sense, there is no more "consideration" for My devotees. Absolutely none! I have summarized it all. Everything has been "considered". I have Done it all with you. I have Given you My final Summary as direct Instruction relative to absolutely everything.

The practice of the only-by-Me Revealed and Given Way of Adidam is the self-surrendering practice of obedient adaptation to My unambiguous Word of Instruction. And the basic, foundation adaptation should not take a long time. You cannot measure it by the day, but it is, in principle, brief. And hearing Me is not some "immensity" that depends on you. It is a straightforward matter that depends on Me. Nevertheless, as a necessary foundation for hearing Me, you must (as My formally acknowledged listening devotee) have rightly, truly, fully, and fully devotionally embraced the totality of the basic functional, practical, relational, and cultural practice of the Way of Adidam, according to My Word. You must exhibit all the details of that discipline. Do so! Then the process of maturing to the point of hearing Me can be relatively brief. The Way of Adidam is all a very straightforward "consideration", Revealed and Given entirely and only by Me.

Close fist. Open fist. [Avatar Adi Da Samraj closes and opens His fist.][77] How long does it take to understand that? My "radical" Argument that is the basis for hearing Me is not a complicated concept. It is very straightforward, if you are truly studying, and practicing according to, My Word. But, just as there are prerequisites for truly being Established in the Witness-Position, there are prerequisites for hearing Me. It is not that maturing to the point of hearing Me takes endless time, but you must first establish the conditions of formal right, true, full, and fully devotional practice of the Way of Adidam. Then hearing Me should, in principle, take only a few months more—not endless group discussions that go on for years and years, in which everybody takes their turn at dramatizing their egoity on everyone else. This constant application to My Word, steadily refining the functional, practical, relational, and cultural disciplines of your practice, "considering" My fundamental Arguments relative to seeking and self-contraction (and true hearing, and real seeing, and Most Perfect Divine Self-Realization), with all the by-Me-Given disciplines always (and formally) intact, is an entirely straightforward matter.

My Divine Arguments are always very simple, very straightforward, and, therefore, you need not be a genius for My Word to be effective in your particular case. The Process takes a long time to be effective only if you do not recognize Me <u>As</u> the Divine Heart-Master, and if you do not (on that basis) rightly, truly, fully, and fully devotionally accept Me as your Guru, and if My Word is not Divine Law for you, and if you are "picking and choosing" from among My Instructions, and if you are self-"guruing" (and, like Narcissus, "meditating" on yourself), and if you, as a result of any or all these failures to recognize Me and respond to Me, neglect and fail to responsibly manage your life-functions, and to put your life-obligations in right order (by aligning, and conforming, and surrendering your life-functions, and your life-conditions, to Me).

If you do not align, and conform, and surrender all your life-functions and life-conditions to Me (and, in that manner, responsibly manage them), you never finally and stably establish yourself in the position <u>necessary</u> to listen to Me to the point of hearing Me, and to hear Me to the point of seeing Me, and to see Me to the point of Most Perfectly Realizing Me.

Therefore, live by My Word, so that My Blessing Works, and My Grace Works.

Adapt to My straightforward Word of Instruction, with no ambiguity.

Ultimately, I Am here to Draw you into the "Perfect Practice" of non-"different" devotion to Me. Everything else is preparation. It requires no genius other than Me for you to do the "Perfect Practice" of the Way of Adidam.

It is up to you, then, to (rightly, truly, fully, and fully devotionally) embrace the practice of the Way of Adidam, based on your devotional recognition of Me and your devotional recognition-response to Me, and to bring Me the necessary gifts of your practice.

My Gift of this Great Opportunity will Serve all beings, when My devotees truly embrace and live and serve the Way that I have Revealed and Given to them (and to all, and All).

III.

AVATAR ADI DA SAMRAJ: You will not relinquish your karmas (or egoic tendencies) until they grind you so small that you want nothing more to do with them. You think that you can avoid the tooth of really counter-egoic sad-hana with words and sentimentality and weakness. But you cannot.

The Way is not to <u>say</u> what I Say, but to <u>do</u> what I Say, such that you break out of your ego-games. Real sadhana is a hard school. As long as you are obstinate, it is a difficult matter. People take true refuge in Me when they have had enough of the fire of their own egoic karmas. Until then, they just want a little taste of religion. They want everything from Me, but they do not want to relinquish anything themselves. They want to be congratulated, without the slightest merit to justify it. They just want to be precious about themselves, whereas, truly, everything about life is merely the fuel of sadhana. At last, nothing can be defended, or held on to. It is a profound matter, even terrible, but it is true.

My devotee must be prepared to be Mastered by Me. That is the inherent nature of the relationship to Me. If you rightly, truly, fully, and fully devotionally recognize Me, there is the right, true, full, and fully devotional response. And if you do not recognize Me, there is not the right response. It is as simple as that.

My true devotee does what I Say, not merely because I Say it, but because he or she recognizes Me. Doing what I Say <u>is</u> the response. Doing what I Say is not a strategy, not merely a way of seeming, and it is not mediocre.

You <u>struggle</u> to accept the knowledge of your own "Narcissism". In My "Sadhana Years", I did not care what I found out. I was ready to deal with it, whatever it was.

You require a positive self-image. I never had any. What is there to have a positive self-image about? Just examine that "stack". Everybody is guilty of everything. You cannot select. The whole damned thing is true.

Sadhana is not about a positive self-image. It is about self-transcendence. It is not about a negative self-image, either. It is not about any self-image whatsoever. Self-image is "Narcissus"—you looking at yourself. That's that. "What a pretty little boy in the pond!"—admiring your image, being self-righteous about it, defending it, prettying it, being positive and negative about it, always playing with your little nippy. And then, some day, you drop dead.

Real sadhana starts when you stop dealing with yourself, and start dealing with Me—recognizing Me, and responding to Me by doing fully as I Say.

People think Masters are supposed to congratulate and praise their devotees and even all who come to them. It is the other way around.

I saw Baba Muktananda on a subtle plane a few hours after He died. There were a number of people there, gathered to greet Him. He called Me "Dingo". I immediately knew what He meant. The gross body-mind, in and of itself, is a lowly dog, a mortal lump of gross distractions— as even He had just proven by His own gross physical death. Therefore, I was not offended, and there was only love in our exchanges.

Being offended has nothing to do with Guru-devotion. If you raise the brow and shrink back when I Criticize you, then you do not receive My Blessing Grace, because you choose not to accept It in the Form in Which It is Given to you.

The true devotees of Masters of any degree get eaten alive. The self-protective followers only get cookies. You decide which you prefer.

One of Swami Nityananda's principal devotees, Swami Janananda, was told by Swami Nityananda to leave His company and serve Him in some other place. Swami Nityananda never called him back. Janananda did not feel rejected. He was Blessed by fulfilling his Master's Instruction, and he Communed with his Master at that distance. So it was, and he Realized significantly.

But there were thousands of others whom Swami Nityananda allowed to crawl in front of Him, piling bananas at His Feet, as often as they liked, and most of them Realized nothing whatsoever. They were just consoled by the opportunity of religious association. The egos felt better about themselves. Well, that is the most benefit they got from Him, as well as some of the bananas He returned to them!

The Prasad is <u>not</u> the bananas. That is what you must understand. The Prasad is the Gift of fulfilling the Master's Word, such that you truly benefit from the Master's Company, and from the Master's Blessing altogether.

The ego-"I" is not interested in the really profound practice of Guru-devotion. The reluctant egos insist on keeping their distance from me, one way or another. Even if they are in My immediate Company, they still keep their distance by various devices.

"Embrace the Master utterly, and selflessly." That is the Divine Way. The Way is devotional Communion with Me. The rest is the changes of Cosmic Nature.

The only thing to fear is egoity itself. The ego <u>is</u> fear, and egoic "self-possession" is a fearful choice. And, sooner or later, in your game of "yes-and-no", it is "checkmate", and you are stuck with it—and it is not fun.

IV.

AVATAR ADI DA SAMRAJ: Conventional religion is social religiosity. It is purposed to improve the social-personality sign in human beings. It is not about Real-God-Realization. Conventional religion is basically a political and social matter, determined to govern human behavior according to socially and politically conceived "moral" principles—which are, ultimately, designed only to make people into positively useful citizens, benign social characters in relation to social others. There is nothing necessarily negative about this. It is, in fact, necessary and right, if rightly done, but it is only the mere beginnings of true religion.

Ruchira Avatara Bhakti is a profound Yoga. It is not merely a matter of being a "fan" of Mine, granting some love-feelings toward Me and feeling some love-feelings from Me. That is not Ruchira Avatara Bhakti. The real Yoga of Ruchira Avatara Bhakti is as I have Said: You grant Me the four principal life-faculties—of attention, feeling, both passive and active bodily orientation, and breathing—

moment to moment. It is a to-Me-responsive counter-egoic (or self-surrendering, self-forgetting, and, more and more, self-transcending) matter, always done to the degree of true heart-Communion with Me.

All My devotees are related directly to Me, if they really practice the Way of Adidam, according to My Instructions. The only-by-Me Revealed and Given Way of Adidam is <u>entirely</u> about direct relationship to Me. Each one of you must cultivate your relationship to Me, directly. I Am the Measure of the Way of Adidam. I Am the Measure of your practice. You must come to <u>Me</u>, through your direct relationship to Me, and by obedience to <u>My</u> Word, and not by "obedience" to some self-"guruing" revision of the Way of Adidam that justifies nominal practice and justifies taking time—more and more time—in practice.

DEVOTEE: Beloved, our relationship with You has the force of a vow—the relationship itself.

AVATAR ADI DA SAMRAJ: Your relationship to Me <u>is</u> a vow, signified by your literal signing of a vow when you become My formally acknowledged devotee. Whatever self-discipline it takes to fulfill that vow is what you are, in <u>every</u> moment, to do. That exercise of self-discipline, to fulfill your eternal vow of devotion to Me, is what makes your life into sadhana. The sadhana is not something that you put up to your ego for a "vote" every day. Your moment to moment practice of Ruchira Avatara Bhakti Yoga is a sacred, real obligation—and, because it is an eternal <u>vow</u>, you can <u>never</u> (or even in any moment) be relieved of it (or relinquish it) as your obligation to Me.

To be purified of entanglement with egoic bondage, and of all of your experiential bewilderment, you must go through the devotional (and self-disciplining) fire of purification, and you must go beyond the ego-"I" of psychophysical self-contraction. That is the sadhana of the only-by-Me Revealed and Given Way of Adidam. If your relationship to Me is profound, then you have to do it as sadhana, and not just engage in some sort of ego-consoling fantasy, avoiding the real sadhana. You must truly practice this submission to Me and demonstrate it through every life-faculty, in every circumstance. Every day you will encounter limitations that require profound demonstrations of Ruchira Avatara Bhakti Yoga, profound disciplines of body-mind-self, and real counter-egoic efforts of every kind.

Right practice of Ruchira Avatara Bhakti Yoga is never a matter of succumbing to the ordinary life-factors at all. On the other hand, neither is it a matter of dissociating from them. It is not a matter of dissociating from the life-faculties, but it is a matter of surrendering the life-faculties to Me, into Me, so that they are opened to Me, and pouring through to My Self-Domain of Divine Realization. This relational (rather than dissociative) Way of Adidam is a matter of constantly active devotion to Me, actively embracing all the self-disciplines required by Me, such that essentially life-positive qualities remain, but the life-faculties are not contracted upon themselves, and not given to seeking, but only given to Me, so that they are not binding (but, instead, they are an open-ended vehicle of Me-Realization). Rather than allowing yourself to be limited by the qualities you would, as a pattern of tendencies, manifest in life, you are Called, by Me, to submit (via the four principal life-faculties, and through, and, at last, beyond, the four principal life-faculties) to Me—and, thus, you are Called, by Me, to live a true devotional and Yogic life.

For My hearing devotee, there is only, always, and most basically, the core of devotion to Me that deals directly with egoity. Everything follows from that. Until you have truly heard Me, you are not dealing with egoity directly—rather, you are dealing with all the peripheral patterns of egoity. That is not yet Ruchira Avatara Bhakti Yoga in its most fundamental (or really and directly ego-transcending) profundity.

In order to do the right, true, full, and fully devotional

Yoga of the Way of Adidam, your devotion to Me must grow to directly deal with the core of egoity. This requires self-disciplined listening to the point of true hearing, and self-disciplined hearing to the point of real seeing. Merely to deal piecemeal with this, that, and the other pattern of egoic tendencies wears you out. You are refreshed only by the real and direct transcending of egoity. Then the periphery (of all the patterning) is directly and spontaneously addressed by that really ego-transcending devotional disposition. All the life-faculties must be surrendered to Me, to the point of self-forgetting Communion with Me. That is the right practice of the Way of Adidam, from the beginning.

Practicing Ruchira Avatara Bhakti Yoga, even in the earlier stages, then, is true Communion with Me. If you truly do it, it becomes absorptive Communion with Me (or the Samadhis in Which the self-contracting ego-"I" is absorbed by Me, in Me). In such absorptive Communion with Me, you are absorbed into the Samadhis of Finding <u>Me</u>, by submitting the principal life-faculties to Me. Because practice of the Way of Adidam in the context of the first five stages of life involves submission of the life-faculties to Me, rather than (as in the "Perfect Practice") simply Standing (non-separately) in My Place (in Inherently Perfect, or "radically" ego-transcending, heart-Communion with Me), practice of the only-by-Me Revealed and Given Way of Adidam in the context of any and all of the first five stages of life is a matter of becoming absorbed in Me, by Means of responsive devotional Attraction to Me. It is only in the "Perfect Practice", Which is practice of the only-by-Me Revealed and Given Way of Adidam on the basis of the Samadhi of Identification with Me, that you (in the moments of the formal "Perfect Practice" itself) no longer <u>submit</u> the life-faculties to Me, but (having already fully done so) you, instead, "radically" transcend the life-faculties (at the root), and Really Stand in (or at) My Place ("Perfectly", or nonabsorptively, or beyond the mechanism of attention, Identifying with Me).

The "Perfect Practice" is, of course, most profound Communion with Me, and, Ultimately, by My Grace, It becomes Divinely Most Perfect (or seventh stage) Realization of Me. That is not to say that there is no virtue in the absorptive Samadhis (in the progressive demonstration of the Way of Adidam in the context of the first five stages of life). The cultivation of Samadhi (rather than of mere social, or exoteric, religiosity) is the necessary course, from the beginning of the Way of Adidam, because there must be purification of bondage to the self-contracted body-mind, or to egoic states, and to conditional states altogether. It is only after having become purified by the earlier, or absorptive, practice that there is sufficient equanimity—sufficient freedom from attachment to self-contracted identification with the life-faculties themselves (and their conditional experiences), so that "you" can actually do the sadhana of Identification with Me. That sadhana is the "Perfect Practice" sadhana, and that is the practice for which all My formally practicing (first and second congregation) devotees are to be preparing themselves.

In the only-by-Me Revealed and Given Way of Adidam, everything previous to the "Perfect Practice" is a preliminary. That does not mean that there is no good Realization of Me previous to the "Perfect Practice". Through the practice of Ruchira Avatara Bhakti Yoga, there is, in the absorptive Samadhis (in the practicing context of the fourth stage of life and the fifth stage of life), the real submission of the life-faculties to Me.

DEVOTEE: Beloved, feeling-Contemplation of You is, in and of itself, a kind of Samadhi.

AVATAR ADI DA SAMRAJ: Yes, it is. You submit the life-faculties to Me, truly surrendered to the point of self-forgetting feeling-Contemplation of Me, such that you

"Locate" Me. You enter into My Sphere by that submission, by that self-forgetting. You become absorbed in Me. In that absorption, you do Realize Me, you are absorbed into Me, and into My Place, but you have entered My Place <u>by</u> that submission of the life-faculties to Me. In that submission, you practice from the position of the pattern of identification with the life-faculties (of attention, emotional feeling, physical body, and breath). Therefore, even though practice of the Way of Adidam in the context of the first five stages of life is a to-Me-responsive counter-egoic exercise, because the absorptive Samadhis are dependent upon the exercise of the life-faculties, the absorptive Samadhis are only conditionally (and, necessarily, only temporarily) arrived at. Therefore, absorptive Samadhi is, necessarily, a conditional Samadhi. Nevertheless, the foundation practice of the only-by-Me Revealed and Given Way of Adidam is the <u>necessary</u> preliminary to the "Perfect Practice" of the only-by-Me Revealed and Given Way of Adidam—not for the sake of experiencing the conditional (or absorptive) Samadhis themselves (or for their own sake), but for the sake of the purification of the life-faculties, and the eventual stable Realization (on the basis of true psycho-physical equanimity) of the Witness-Consciousness (or the non-"different" capability of Communing with Me <u>Prior</u> to the exercise, and even the point of view of exercising, the life-faculties).

As you progress through the developmental stages of the Way of Adidam previous to the "Perfect Practice", the life-faculty-surrendering process of absorptive Samadhi goes through various changes, and there are various associated signs, and so forth, that correspond to the advancing stages of life—but it is always a matter of "Locating" <u>Me</u>, because the practice is to submit the life-faculties to the point of self-forgetting Communion with <u>Me</u>.

The not yet "Perfect Practice" of the only-by-Me Revealed and Given Way of Adidam is always the same, whether in the early-life fourth-stage-founded context of the first three stages of life, or, altogether, in the "original" and, subsequently, the "basic" contexts of the fourth stage of life, or in the (possible) "advanced" context of the fourth stage of life, or in the (possible) context of the fifth stage of life.[78] All the Samadhis in the first five stages of life are absorptive (and, therefore, conditionally arrived at), until the "Perfect Practice" begins. The "Perfect Practice" does not involve the submission or exploitation of the life-faculties, because, in the "Perfect Practice", you are not in that "position". In the "Perfect Practice" of the only-by-Me Revealed and Given Way of Adidam, you Stand in the Witness-Position, Prior to the life-faculties. Therefore, the Samadhis in the "Perfect Practice" (in the context of the sixth stage of life, and, in due course, the seventh stage of life) are the Samadhis of Identification with Me. Jnana Samadhi[79] (or Realization of Me in the context of the sixth stage of life) and, Ultimately, Ruchira Samadhi[80] (or Most Perfect Realization of Me in the only-by-Me Revealed and Given seventh stage of life) are the Samadhis of Identification with Me, because there is no conditional life-faculty or life-function to be identified with.

Truly, even in the context of the sixth stage of life, the potential Samadhis are still conditional, in the sense that the Principle of Consciousness is exercised (as if It is yet individual, or separable), and all arising phenomena (including the life-faculties) are strategically excluded. Therefore, Most Perfect Samadhi is Awakened only in the only-by-Me Revealed and Given seventh stage of life, when there is <u>no</u> <u>more</u> <u>exclusion</u> whatsoever, <u>no</u> <u>more</u> <u>separateness</u> whatsoever, and no more ego-"I" whatsoever.

<u>All</u> the Samadhis of devotion to Me are, in some fundamental sense, equal, because they are all Realizations of <u>Me</u>. Realization of Me (whether conditionally or, in the seventh stage case, Most Perfectly non-conditionally Enjoyed) is, by My Grace, the real potential in <u>every</u> stage of the only-by-Me Revealed and Given Way of Adidam. It is only that, at each developmental stage of the Way, until

the seventh, identification with conditionality (or, at least, with the conditional life-faculties) is, in one manner or another, part of what must be submitted to Me.

That is It. The only-by-Me Revealed and Given Way of Adidam is not a mere system of techniques that you apply to yourself in order to attain Samadhi. The practice, from the beginning, is true (and truly self-transcending) heart-Communion with Me. Therefore, the only-by-Me Revealed and Given Way of Adidam is always, from the beginning, a Process of directly (in every present-time moment) Realizing Me. The foundation Principle of the only-by-Me Revealed and Given Way of Adidam is that of being Attracted to Me, Moved to Me. Being Moved to Me, you engage this counter-egoic effort. The entire Purpose of the practice of Ruchira Avatara Bhakti Yoga is to live in the Samadhi of heart-Communion with Me, rather than merely "bonding" to (and suffering) conditional existence and its limitations. To rightly, truly, fully, and fully devotionally practice Ruchira Avatara Bhakti Yoga is, in every moment of such practice, to Realize Me, the One and Only Divine Person, the Divine Self-Condition and Source-Condition of all arising conditions of existence.

In order to Realize Me, the Divine Self-Condition and Source-Condition of all arising conditions (or all conditional modifications of That Which Is Always Already The Case), you must, by My Grace, Commune with Me to the point of non-separation from Me. Then, rather than taking the tour of modifications (which are, in and of themselves, limited, limiting, merely conditional, always changing and passing, and inherently un-Satisfactory), My Infinitely "Bright" Divine Person and Condition becomes the Focus and the Realization of your existence.

Notes to the Text of the

RUCHIRA AVATARA GITA
(THE WAY OF THE DIVINE HEART-MASTER)

PART ONE

1. Conventionally, "self-possessed" means possessed <u>of</u> oneself—or in full control (calmness, or composure) of one's feelings, impulses, habits, and actions. Avatar Adi Da uses the term to indicate the state of being possessed <u>by</u> one's egoic self, or controlled by chronically self-referring (or egoic) tendencies of attention, feeling, thought, desire, and action.

2. Avatar Adi Da Samraj spontaneously Gave the Name "Adidam" in January 1996. This primary Name for the Way He has Revealed and Given is simply His own Principal Name ("Adi Da") with the addition of "m" at the end. When He first Gave this Name, Adi Da Samraj pointed out that the final "m" adds a mantric force, evoking the effect of the primal Sanskrit syllable "Om". (For Avatar Adi Da's Revelation of the most profound esoteric significance of "Om" as the Divine Sound of His own Very Being, see *He-and-She Is Me—The Seventeen Companions Of The True Dawn Horse, Book Seven: The Indivisibility Of Consciousness and Light In The Divine Body Of The Ruchira Avatar*.) Simultaneously, the final "m" suggests the English word "Am" (expressing "I Am"), such that the Name "Adidam" also evokes Avatar Adi Da's Primal Self-Confession, "I <u>Am</u> Adi Da", or, more simply, "I <u>Am</u> Da" (or "Aham Da Asmi").

3. Avatar Adi Da uses the terms "Spiritual", "Transcendental", and "Divine" in reference to different dimensions of Reality that are Realized progressively in the Way of Adidam. "Spiritual" refers to the reception of the Spirit-Force (in the "basic" and "advanced" contexts of the fourth stage of life and in the context of the fifth stage of life); "Transcendental" refers to the Realization of Consciousness Itself as separate from the world (in the context of the sixth stage of life); and "Divine" refers to the Most Perfect Realization of Consciousness Itself as utterly Non-separate from the world (in the context of the seventh stage of life). (For Avatar Adi Da's fully extended discussion of the stages of life, see *The Seven Stages Of Life—The Seventeen Companions Of The True Dawn Horse, Book Ten: Transcending The Six Stages Of egoic Life and Realizing The ego-Transcending Seventh Stage Of Life In The Divine Way Of Adidam*.)

4. Avatar Adi Da uses the phrase "Most Perfect(ly)" in the sense of "Absolutely Perfect(ly)". Similarly, the phrase "Most Ultimate(ly)" is equivalent to "Absolutely Ultimate(ly)". "Most Perfect(ly)" and "Most Ultimate(ly)" are always references to the seventh (or Divinely Enlightened) stage of life. (See note 49.)

5. Avatar Adi Da uses the term "conditional" to indicate everything that depends on conditions—in other words, everything that is temporary and always changing. The "Unconditional", in contrast, is the Divine, or That Which Is Always Already the Case because it is utterly free of dependence on conditions.

6. The term "radical" derives from the Latin "radix", meaning "root", and thus it principally means "irreducible", "fundamental", or "relating to the origin". In *The Dawn Horse Testament Of The Ruchira Avatar, The "Testament Of Secrets" Of The Divine World-Teacher, Ruchira Avatar Adi Da Samraj*, Avatar Adi Da defines "Radical" as "Gone To The Root, Core, Source, or Origin". Because Adi Da Samraj uses "radical" in this literal sense, it appears in quotation marks in His Wisdom-Teaching, in order to distinguish His usage from the common reference to an extreme (often political) view.

Avatar Adi Da uses "understanding" to mean "the process of transcending egoity". Thus, to "understand" is to simultaneously observe the activity of the self-contraction and to surrender that activity via devotional resort to Avatar Adi Da Samraj.

Avatar Adi Da has Revealed that, despite their intention to Realize Reality (or Truth, or Real God), all religious and Spiritual traditions (other than the Way of Adidam He has Revealed and Given) are involved, in one manner or another, with the search to satisfy the ego. Only Avatar Adi Da has Revealed the Way to "radically" understand the ego and (in due course, through intensive formal practice of the Way of Adidam, as His formally acknowledged devotee) to most perfectly transcend the ego. Thus, Avatar Adi Da is the "One and Only Man Of This 'Radical' Understanding".

For Avatar Adi Da's Description of His Discovery of the archetype of "Narcissus" (which was the initiation of His Revelation of the Truth of "radical" understanding), see *The Knee Of Listening—The Seventeen Companions Of The True Dawn Horse, Book Four: The Early-Life Ordeal and The "Radical" Spiritual Realization Of The Ruchira Avatar*, chapter 5. His summary Communication about the living paradox of the Man of "Radical" Understanding can be found in the Epilogue to *The Knee Of Listening*.

For Avatar Adi Da's basic Talks on "radical" understanding, see *The Method Of The Ruchira Avatar—The Seventeen Companions Of The True Dawn Horse, Book Five: The Divine Way Of Adidam Is An* *ego-Transcending <u>Relationship</u>, Not An ego-Centric Technique*, Part Three.

7. "Ruchira Buddhism" is the Way of devotion to the Ruchira Buddha—"the 'Bright' Buddha", Avatar Adi Da Samraj (or, more fully, "the Radiant, Shining, 'Bright' Illuminator and Enlightener Who Is Inherently, or Perfectly Subjectively, Self-Enlightened, and Eternally Awake").

8. The name "Advaitayana Buddhism" indicates the unique sympathetic likenesses of Adidam to the traditions of Advaitism (or Advaita Vedanta) and Buddhism. In His examination of the entire collective religious tradition of Mankind, Avatar Adi Da has observed that these two traditions represent the most advanced Realizations ever attained previous to His Appearance. The primary aspiration of Buddhism is to realize freedom from the illusion of the separate individual ego-self. The primary aspiration of Advaitism (or the tradition of "Non-Dualism") is to know the Supreme Divine Self absolutely, beyond all dualities (of high and low, good and bad, and so on). Advaitayana Buddhism is the Non-Dual ("Advaita") Way ("yana", literally "vehicle") of Most Perfect Awakening ("Buddhism"). Advaitayana Buddhism is not an outgrowth of the historical tradition of Buddhism, or of the historical tradition of Advaitism. Advaitayana Buddhism is the unique Revelation of Avatar Adi Da Samraj, which perfectly fulfills both the traditional Buddhist aspiration for absolute freedom from the bondage of the egoic self and the traditional Advaitic aspiration for absolute Identity with the Divine Self.

9. By the word "Bright" (and its variations, such as "Brightness"), Avatar Adi Da refers to the eternally, infinitely, and inherently Self-Radiant Divine Being, the Being of Indivisible and Indestructible Light. As Adi Da Writes in His Spiritual Autobiography, *The Knee Of Listening*:

   . . . *from my earliest experience of life I have Enjoyed a Condition that, as a child, I called the "Bright".*

   I have always known desire, not merely for extreme pleasures of the senses and the mind, but for the highest Enjoyment of Spiritual Power and Mobility. But I have not been seated in desire, and desire has only been a play that I have grown to understand and enjoy without conflict. I have always been Seated in the "Bright".

   Even as a baby I remember only crawling around inquisitively with a boundless Feeling of Joy, Light, and Freedom in the middle of my head that was bathed in Energy moving unobstructed in a Circle, down from above, all the way down, then up, all the way up, and around again, and always Shining from my heart. It was an Expanding

Sphere of Joy from the heart. And I was a Radiant Form, the Source of Energy, Love-Bliss, and Light in the midst of a world that is entirely Energy, Love-Bliss, and Light. I was the Power of Reality, a direct Enjoyment and Communication of the One Reality. I was the Heart Itself, Who Lightens the mind and all things. I was the same as every one and every thing, except it became clear that others were apparently unaware of the "Thing" Itself.

Even as a little child I recognized It and Knew It, and my life was not a matter of anything else. That Awareness, that Conscious Enjoyment, that Self-Existing and Self-Radiant Space of Infinitely and inherently Free Being, that Shine of inherent Joy Standing in the heart and Expanding from the heart, is the "Bright". And It is the entire Source of True Humor. It is Reality. It is not separate from anything.

10. Avatar Adi Da describes His Divine Being on three levels:

This flesh body, this bodily (human) Sign, is My Form, in the sense that it is My Murti, or a kind of Reflection, or Representation, of Me. It is, therefore, a Means for contacting My Spiritual (and Always Blessing) Presence, and, ultimately, My Very (and Inherently Perfect) State.

My Spiritual (and Always Blessing) Presence is Self-Existing and Self-Radiant. It Functions in time and space, and It is also Prior to all time and space. . . .

My Very (and Inherently Perfect) State is always and only utterly Prior to time and space. Therefore, I, As I Am (Ultimately), have no "Function" in time and space. There is no time and space in My Very (and Inherently Perfect) State.

11. Avatar Adi Da uses "Outshining" as a synonym for "Divine Translation", to refer to the final Demonstration of the four-phase process of the seventh, or Divinely Enlightened, stage of life in the Way of Adidam. In the Great Event of Outshining, or Divine Translation, body, mind, and world are no longer noticed—not because the Divine Consciousness has withdrawn or dissociated from conditionally manifested phenomena, but because the Divine Recognition of all arising phenomena as modifications of the Divine Self has become so intense that the "Bright" Radiance of Consciousness now Outshines all such phenomena.

12. In Sanskrit, "Ruchira" means "bright, radiant, effulgent". Thus, the Reference "Ruchira Avatar" indicates that Avatar Adi Da Samraj is the "Bright" (or Radiant) Descent of the Divine Reality Itself (or the Divine Truth Itself, Which Is the Only Real God) into the conditional worlds, Appearing here in bodily (human) Form.

13. "Avatar" (from Sanskrit "avatara") is a traditional term for the Divine Incarnation. It literally means "One who is descended, or 'crossed down' (from, and as, the Divine)". Thus, the Name "Da", combined with the Reference "Avatar", fully acknowledges Avatar Adi Da Samraj as the original, first, and complete Descent of the Very Divine Person, Who is Named "Da". Through the Mystery of Avatar Adi Da's human Birth, He has Incarnated not only in this world but in every world, at every level of the Cosmic domain, as the Eternal Giver of Help and Grace and Divine Freedom to all beings, now and forever hereafter.

14. The Name "Love-Ananda" combines both English ("Love") and Sanskrit ("Ananda", meaning "Bliss"), thus bridging the West and the East, and communicating Avatar Adi Da's Function as the Divine World-Teacher. The combination of "Love" and "Ananda" means "the Divine Love-Bliss". The Name "Love-Ananda" was given to Avatar Adi Da by His principal human Spiritual Master, Swami Muktananda, who spontaneously conferred it upon Avatar Adi Da in 1969. However, Avatar Adi Da did not use the Name "Love-Ananda" until April 1986, after the Great Event that Initiated His Divine "Emergence" (see note 21). As the Love-Ananda Avatar, Avatar Adi Da is the Very Incarnation of the Divine Love-Bliss.

15. "Listening" is Avatar Adi Da's term for the orientation, disposition, and practice of the beginner's developmental stages of preparation and discipline in the total (or full and complete) practice of the Way of Adidam. A listening devotee gives his or her attention to Avatar Adi Da's Teaching Argument, to His Leelas (or inspirational and instructive Stories of His Life and Work), and to feeling-Contemplation of Him (primarily of His bodily human Form) in the context of his or her life of devotion, service, self-discipline, and meditation. Through the process of listening, the devotee's self-understanding grows, and listening matures as most fundamental self-understanding, or hearing.

   "Hearing" is a technical term used by Avatar Adi Da to Describe the most fundamental understanding of the act of egoity (or self-contraction). Hearing is the unique capability to directly transcend the self-contraction, such that there is the simultaneous intuitive awakening to the Revelation of the Divine Person and Self-Condition. The Revelation of this "radical" understanding of the nature of egoity is one of Avatar Adi Da's unique Gifts to all beings.

   Hearing awakens in the midst of a life of devotion, service, self-discipline, meditation, disciplined study of, or listening to, Avatar Adi Da's Teaching Argument, and constant self-surrendering, self-forgetting, and self-transcending feeling-Contemplation of Avatar Adi Da. Only on the basis of such hearing can Spiritually Awakened practice of the

Way of Adidam truly (or with full responsibility) begin.

When, in the practice of the Way of Adidam, hearing (or most fundamental self-understanding) is steadily exercised in meditation and in life, the native feeling of the heart ceases to be chronically constricted by self-contraction. The heart then begins to Radiate as love in response to the Spiritual (and Always Blessing) Presence of Avatar Adi Da.

This emotional and Spiritual response of the whole being is what Avatar Da calls "seeing". Seeing is emotional conversion from the reactive emotions that characterize egoic self-obsession, to the open-hearted, Radiant Happiness that characterizes God-Love and Spiritual devotion to Avatar Adi Da. True and stable emotional conversion coincides with true and stable receptivity to Avatar Adi Da's Spiritual Transmission, and both of these are prerequisites to further Spiritual advancement in the Way of Adidam.

16. The fundamental self-contraction, or the sense of separate and separative existence.

17. Avatar Adi Da uses the terms "childish" and "adolescent" with precise meanings in His Wisdom-Teaching. He points out that human beings are always tending to animate one of two fundamental life-strategies—the childish strategy (to be dependent, weak, seeking to be consoled by parent figures and a parent "God") and the adolescent strategy (to be independent or torn between independence and dependence, rebellious, unfeeling, self-absorbed, and doubting or resisting the idea of "God" or any power greater than oneself). Until these strategies are understood and transcended, they not only diminish love in ordinary human relations, but they also limit religious and Spiritual growth.

18. A primary pathway of natural life-energy and the Spirit-Current through the body-mind. It is composed of two arcs: the descending Current in association with the frontal line (down the front of the body, from the crown of the head to the bodily base), or the more physically oriented dimension of the body-mind; and the ascending Current in association with the spinal line (up the back of the body, from the bodily base to the crown of the head), or the more mentally, psychically, and subtly oriented dimension of the body-mind.

19. Avatar Adi Da's term for the essential devotional and meditative practice that all practitioners of the Way of Adidam engage at all times in relationship to His bodily (human) Form, His Spiritual (and Always Blessing) Presence, and His Very (and Inherently Perfect) State. Feeling-Contemplation of Adi Da Samraj is Awakened by His Grace through Darshan, or feeling-sighting, of His Form, Presence,

and State. It is then to be practiced under all conditions, and as the basis and epitome of all other practices in the Way of Adidam.

20. Avatar Adi Da Affirms that there is a Divine Self-Domain that is the Perfectly Subjective Condition of the conditional worlds. It is not "elsewhere", not an objective "place" (like a subtle "heaven" or mythical "paradise"), but It is the always present, Transcendental, Inherently Spiritual, Divine Source-Condition of every conditionally manifested being and thing. Avatar Adi Da Reveals that the Divine Self-Domain is not other than the Divine Heart Itself, Who He <u>Is</u>. To Realize the seventh stage of life (by the Grace of Avatar Adi Da Samraj) is to Awaken to the Divine Self-Domain.

21. On January 11, 1986, Avatar Adi Da passed through a profound Yogic Swoon, which He later described as the initial Event of His Divine "Emergence". Avatar Adi Da's Divine "Emergence" is an ongoing Process in which His bodily (human) Form has been (and is ever more profoundly and potently being) conformed to Himself, the Very Divine Person, such that His bodily (human) Form is now (and forever hereafter) an utterly Unobstructed Sign and Agent of His own Divine Being.

For Avatar Adi Da's Revelation of the significance of His Divine "Emergence", see *The Dawn Horse Testament Of The Ruchira Avatar* or *The Heart Of The Dawn Horse Testament Of The Ruchira Avatar—The Seventeen Companions Of The True Dawn Horse, Book Twelve: The Epitome Of The "Testament Of Secrets" Of The Divine World-Teacher, Ruchira Avatar Adi Da Samraj*, Part One, "The True Dawn Horse <u>Is</u> The <u>Only</u> Way To Me", section III.

22. In the context of Divine Enlightenment in the seventh stage of life in the Way of Adidam, the Spiritual process continues. Avatar Adi Da has uniquely Revealed the four phases of the seventh stage process: Divine Transfiguration, Divine Transformation, Divine Indifference, and Divine Translation.

Divine Translation is the most ultimate "Event" of the entire process of Divine Awakening. Avatar Adi Da Describes Divine Translation as the Outshining of all noticing of objective conditions, through the infinitely magnified Force of Consciousness Itself. Divine Translation is the Outshining of all destinies, wherein there is no return to the conditional realms.

For Avatar Adi Da's extended Discussion of Divine Translation, see *The All-Completing and Final Divine Revelation To Mankind—The Seventeen Companions Of The True Dawn Horse, Book Eleven: A Summary Description Of The Supreme Yoga Of The Seventh Stage Of Life In The Divine Way Of Adidam*, Part Two (or *The Dawn Horse Testament Of The Ruchira Avatar*, chapter forty-four).

23. The Sanskrit phrase "Aham Da Asmi" means "I (Aham) Am (Asmi) Da". The Name "Da", meaning "the One Who Gives", indicates that Avatar Adi Da Samraj is the Supreme Divine Giver, the Avataric Incarnation of the Very Divine Person.

Avatar Adi Da's Declaration "Aham Da Asmi" is similar in form to the "Mahavakyas", or "Great Statements", of ancient India (found in the Upanishads, the collected esoteric Instruction of ancient Gurus). However, the significance of "Aham Da Asmi" is fundamentally different from that of the traditional Mahavakyas. Each of the Upanishadic Mahavakyas expresses, in a few words, the profound (though not most ultimate) degree of Realization achieved by great Adept-Realizers of the past. For example, the Upanishadic Mahavakya "Aham Brahmasmi" ("I Am Brahman") expresses a great individual's Realization that he or she is Identified with the Divine Being (Brahman), and is not, in Truth, identified with his or her apparently individual body-mind. However, "Aham Da Asmi", rather than being a proclamation of a human being who has devoted his or her life most intensively to the process of Real-God-Realization and has thereby Realized the Truth to an extraordinarily profound degree, is Avatar Adi Da's Confession that He <u>Is</u> the Very Divine Person, Da, Who has Appeared here in bodily (human) Form, in order to Reveal Himself to all and All, for the sake of the Divine Liberation of all and All.

24. Avatar Adi Da uses the term "bond", when lower-cased, to refer to the process by which the egoic individual (already presuming separateness, and, therefore, bondage to the separate self) attaches itself karmically to the world of others and things through the constant search for self-fulfillment. In contrast, when He capitalizes the term "Bond", Avatar Adi Da is making reference to the process of His devotee's devotional "Bonding" to Him, which process is the Great Means for transcending all forms of limited, or karmic, "bonding".

25. The Adepts of what Avatar Adi Da calls "the 'Crazy Wisdom' tradition" (of which He is the supreme, seventh stage exemplar) are Realizers of the fourth, fifth, or sixth stages of life in any culture or time who, through spontaneous Free action, blunt Wisdom, and liberating laughter, shock or humor people into self-critical awareness of their egoity, which is a prerequisite for receiving the Realizer's Spiritual Transmission. Typically, such Realizers manifest "Crazy" activity only occasionally or temporarily, and never for its own sake but only as "skillful means".

Avatar Adi Da Himself has always addressed the ego in a unique "Crazy-Wise" manner, theatrically dramatizing, and poking fun at, the self-contracted habits, predilections, and destinies of His devotees. His "Crazy-Wise" Manner is a Divine Siddhi, an inherent aspect of His

Avataric Incarnation. Through His "Crazy-Wise" Speech and Action, Avatar Adi Da Penetrates the being and loosens the patterns of ego-bondage (individually and collectively) in His devotees. The "Shock" of Truth Delivered via His "Crazy Wisdom" humbles and opens the heart, making way for the deeper reception of His Spiritual Blessing.

Avadhoot is a traditional term for one who has "shaken off" or "passed beyond" all worldly attachments and cares, including all motives of detachment (or conventional and other-worldly renunciation), all conventional notions of life and religion, and all seeking for "answers" or "solutions" in the form of conditional experience or conditional knowledge. Therefore, "'Crazy' Avadhoot", in reference to Avatar Adi Da, indicates His Inherently Perfect Freedom as the One Who Knows His Identity As the Divine Person and Who, thus, Always Already Stands Free of the binding and deluding power of conditional existence.

26. "Ati" is Sanskrit for "beyond". "Atiashrama" is "beyond the ashramas". The four basic "ashramas" (or potential stages in the life of an individual) acknowledged in traditional Hindu culture (which are traditionally presumed to occur in sequence, each stage lasting approximately 25 years) are the stages of studenthood (studying everything necessary to live a right, true, and sacred life as an adult—brahmacharya), householder life (marrying, producing children, and engaging a life of productive work—grihastha), forest dwelling (retiring to an isolated dwelling in the forest, together with one's wife or husband, in order to devote oneself to religious and Spiritual practices—vanaprastha), and ascetic renunciation (relinquishing all social "bonds" and responsibilities and devoting oneself exclusively to religious and Spiritual practice in the manner of an ascetic—sannyasa). Apart from this conventional point of view relative to progressing through the ashramas, in rare cases Realizers have been acknowledged to be an atiashrami, or someone who has passed beyond the traditional ashramas. When applied to Avatar Adi Da, the descriptive Title "Atiashrami" indicates His Most Perfect Transcendence of all conventional, religious, and Spiritual points of view and modes of life, in the Most Perfect Freedom of the seventh stage of life.

27. Avatar Adi Da uses "Self-Existing and Self-Radiant" to indicate the two fundamental aspects of the One Divine Person—Existence (or Being, or Consciousness) Itself, and Radiance (or Energy, or Light) Itself.

28. The Sanskrit word "mandala" (literally, "circle") is commonly used in the esoteric Spiritual traditions to describe the hierarchical levels of cosmic existence. "Mandala" also denotes an artistic rendering of interior

visions of the cosmos. Avatar Adi Da uses the phrase "Mandala of the Cosmos", or "Cosmic Mandala", to describe the totality of the conditional cosmos.

29. For a description of Avatar Adi Da's Teaching Work, see pp. 14-15.

30. For a description of Avatar Adi Da's Blessing Work, see pp. 15-16.

31. In the context of Divine Enlightenment in the seventh stage of life in the Way of Adidam, the Spiritual process continues. Avatar Adi Da has uniquely Revealed the four phases of the seventh stage process: Divine Transfiguration, Divine Transformation, Divine Indifference, and Divine Translation. (See note 49 for a description of the seven stages of life.)

In the phase of Divine Transfiguration, the devotee-Realizer's body-mind is Infused by Avatar Adi Da's Love-Bliss, and he or she Radiantly Demonstrates active Love, spontaneously Blessing all the relations of the body-mind.

In the following phase of Divine Transformation, the subtle (or psychic) dimension of the body-mind is fully Illumined, which may result in Divine Powers of healing, longevity, and the ability to release obstacles from the world and from the lives of others.

For Avatar Adi Da's Instruction relative to the four phases of the seventh stage of life, see *The Seven Stages Of Life*.

32. *The Dawn Horse Testament* is Avatar Adi Da's paramount "Source-Text" summarizing the entire course of the Way of Adidam. See "The Divine Scripture of Adidam", pp. 29-35.

33. "Leela" is Sanskrit for "play", or "sport". In many religious and Spiritual traditions, all of conditionally manifested existence is regarded to be the Leela (or the Divine Play, Sport, or Free Activity) of the Divine Person. "Leela" also means the Awakened Play of a Realized Adept of any degree, through which he or she mysteriously Instructs and Liberates others and Blesses the world itself. By extension, a Leela is an instructive and inspiring story of such an Adept's Teaching and Blessing Play.

Part Two

34. "Eleutherios" (Greek for "Liberator") is a title by which Zeus was venerated as the supreme deity in the Spiritual esotericism of ancient Greece. The Designation "Eleutherios" indicates the Divine Function of Avatar Adi Da as the Incarnation of the Divine Person, "Whose Inherently Perfect Self-'Brightness' Liberates all conditionally Manifested beings, Freely, Liberally, Gracefully, and Without Ceasing".

35. Avatar Adi Da has Empowered three Retreat Sanctuaries as Agents of His Spiritual Transmission. Of these three, the senior Sanctuary is Adidam Samrajashram, the Island of Naitauba in Fiji, where He usually Resides in Perpetual Retreat. It is the place where Avatar Adi Da Himself and the senior renunciate order of the Way of Adidam, the Ruchira Sannyasin Order of the Tantric Renunciates of Adidam, are established. It is the primary Seat of Avatar Adi Da's Divine Blessing Work with the entire Cosmic Mandala.

Avatar Adi Da has Spoken of the significance of this Hermitage Ashram:

AVATAR ADI DA SAMRAJ: Adidam Samrajashram was established so that I might have a Place of Seclusion in which to do My Spiritual Work. This is the Place of My perpetual Samadhi, the Place of My perpetual Self-Radiance. Therefore, this is the Place where people come to participate in My Samadhi and be further Awakened by It. My devotees come to Adidam Samrajashram to magnify their practice of right, true, and full devotion to Me, to practice of the Way of Adidam as I Have Revealed and Given It for the sake of most perfectly self-transcending Real-God-Realization.

36. The senior practicing order in the Way of Adidam is the Ruchira Sannyasin Order. This order is the senior cultural authority within the formal gathering of Avatar Adi Da's devotees. "Sannyasin" is an ancient Sanskrit term for one who has renounced all worldly bonds and who gives himself or herself completely to the Real-God-Realizing or Real-God-Realized life. Members of the Ruchira Sannyasin Order are uniquely exemplary practitioners of the Way of Adidam who are practicing in the context of the advanced (sixth and seventh) stages of life. Members of this Order are legal renunciates and live a life of perpetual retreat. As a general rule, they are to reside at Adidam Samrajashram. The Ruchira Sannyasin Order is the senior authority within the worldwide culture of the devotees of Avatar Adi Da Samraj.

The members of the Ruchira Sannyasin Order have a uniquely significant role among the practitioners of Adidam as Avatar Adi Da's principal human Instruments (or Spiritually mature renunciate devotees) and (in the case of those members who are formally acknowledged as Avatar Adi Da's fully Awakened seventh stage devotees) as the body of practitioners from among whom each of Avatar Adi Da's successive "Living Murtis", or Empowered human Agents, will be selected. Therefore, the Ruchira Sannyasin Order is essential to the perpetual continuation of authentic practice of the Way of Adidam.

The original, principal, and central members of the Ruchira Sannyasin Order are Avatar Adi Da Himself and the Adidama Quandra Mandala. The Adidama Quandra Mandala is comprised of two women devotees, who have for many years practiced most intensively in Avatar Adi Da's most intimate Sphere and have served Him directly in that circumstance.

37. The "Great Tradition" is Avatar Adi Da's term for the total inheritance of human, cultural, religious, magical, mystical, Spiritual, Transcendental, and Divine paths, philosophies, and testimonies from all the eras and cultures of humanity, which inheritance has (in the present era of worldwide communication) become the common legacy of mankind.

38. In the foundation stages of practice in the Way of Adidam, the basic (or gross) manifestation of the avoidance of relationship is understood and released when Avatar Adi Da's devotee hears Him (or comes to point of most fundamental self-understanding), thereby regaining the free capability for simple relatedness, or living on the basis of the feeling of relatedness rather than the avoidance of relationship. But the feeling of relatedness is not Ultimate Realization, because it is still founded in the presumption of a "difference" between "I" and "other". Only in the ultimate stages of life in the Way of Adidam is the feeling of relatedness itself fully understood as the root-act of attention and, ultimately, transcended in the Feeling of Being. Adi Da Samraj points out that the feeling of relatedness is, at root, the <u>avoidance</u> of relationship in relation to <u>all</u> others and things, or the root-activity of separation, separateness, and separativeness that <u>is</u> the ego.

39. The Feeling of Being is the uncaused (or Self-Existing), Self-Radiant, and unqualified feeling-intuition of the Transcendental, Inherently Spiritual, and Divine Self. This absolute Feeling does not merely accompany or express the Realization of the Heart Itself, but It is Identical to that Realization. To feel—or, really, to Be—the Feeling of Being is to enjoy the Love-Bliss of Absolute Consciousness, Which, when Most Perfectly Realized, cannot be prevented or even diminished either by the events of life or by death.

40. Avatar Adi Da uses "Perfectly Subjective" to describe the True Divine Source, or "Subject", of the conditional world—as opposed to the conditions, or "objects", of experience. Thus, in the phrase "Perfectly Subjective", the word "Subjective" does not have the sense of "relating to the merely phenomenal experience, or the arbitrary presumptions, of an individual", but, rather, it has the sense of "relating to Consciousness Itself, the True Subject of all apparent experience".

41. These three states of consciousness are associated with the dimensions of cosmic existence. The waking state (and the physical body) is associated with the gross dimension. The dreaming state (and visionary, mystical, and Yogic Spiritual processes) is associated with the subtle dimension. The subtle dimension, which is senior to the gross dimension, includes the etheric (or energetic), lower mental (or verbal-intentional and lower psychic), and higher mental (or deeper psychic, mystical, and discriminative) functions. The sleeping state is associated with the causal dimension, which is senior to both the gross and the subtle dimensions. It is the root of attention, prior to any particular experience.

42. Previous to Most Perfect Divine Self-Realization, the gross, subtle, and causal dimensions are expressed in the body-mind as characteristic knots. The knot of the gross dimension is associated with the region of the navel. The knot of the subtle dimension is associated with the midbrain, or the ajna center directly behind and between the brows. And the knot of the causal dimension, or the causal knot, is associated with the sinoatrial node (or "pacemaker") on the right side of the heart. The causal knot, or the heart-root's knot, is the primary root of the self-contraction, felt as the locus of the self-sense, the source of the feeling of relatedness itself, or the root of attention. (See note 46 for a further description of the right side of the heart.)

43. When Consciousness is free from identification with the body-mind, it takes up its natural "position" as the Conscious Witness of all that arises to and in and as the body-mind.

In the Way of Adidam, the stable Realization of the Witness-Position is associated with, or demonstrated via, the effortless surrender or relaxation of all the forms of seeking and all the motives of attention that characterize the first five stages of life. However, identification with the Witness-Position is not final (or Most Perfect) Realization of the Divine Self. Rather, it is the first stage of the "Perfect Practice" in the Way of Adidam, which Practice Realizes, by Avatar Adi Da's Liberating Grace, complete and irreversible Identification with Consciousness Itself.

44. Avatar Adi Da's term for the fundamental Awareness of Existence Itself, Prior to all sense of separation from, or knowledge about, anything that arises. As He Proposes, "No matter what arises, you do not know what a single thing is." By "Ignorance", Avatar Adi Da means heart-felt participation in the universal Condition of inherent Mystery—not mental dullness or the fear-based wonder or awe felt by the subjective ego in relation to unknown objects. Divine Ignorance is the Realization of Consciousness Itself, transcending all knowledge that is cognized and all experience that is perceived by the self-contracted ego-"I".

For Avatar Adi Da's Word of Instruction relative to Divine Ignorance, see *What, Where, When, How, Why, and Who To Remember To Be Happy—The Seventeen Companions Of The True Dawn Horse, Book Thirteen: A Simple Explanation Of The Divine Way Of Adidam (For Children, and Everyone Else)*, Part Two: "What, Where, When, How, Why and Who To Remember To Be Happy", and Part Three: "You Do Not Know What even a single thing Is" and "My Argument Relative to Divine Ignorance".

45. The technical term "consider" or "consideration" in Avatar Adi Da's Wisdom-Teaching means a process of one-pointed but ultimately thoughtless concentration and exhaustive contemplation of something until its ultimate obviousness is clear. As engaged in the Way of Adidam, "consideration" is not merely an intellectual investigation. It is the participatory investment of one's whole being. If one "considers" something fully in the context of one's practice of feeling-Contemplation of Avatar Adi Da Samraj, this concentration results "in both the highest intuition and the most practical grasp of the Lawful and Divine necessities of human existence".

46. Avatar Adi Da Samraj has Revealed that the primal psycho-physical seat of Consciousness and attention is associated with what He calls the "right side of the heart". He has Revealed that this center corresponds to the sinoatrial node, or "pacemaker", the source of the gross physical heartbeat in the right atrium (or upper right chamber) of the physical heart. In the Process of Divine Self-Realization, there is a unique process of opening of the right side of the heart—and it is because of this connection between the right side of the heart and Divine Self-Realization that Avatar Adi Da uses the term "the Heart" as another way of referring to the Divine Self.

Avatar Adi Da distinguishes three stations of the heart, associated respectively with the right side, the middle, and the left side of the heart region of the chest. The middle station of the heart is what is traditionally known as the "anahata chakra" (or "heart chakra"), and the left side of the heart is the gross physical heart. Thus, the right side of the heart is not identical either to the heart chakra or to the gross physical heart.

The Heart Itself is not "in" the right side of the human heart, nor is it "in", or limited to, the human heart as a whole. Rather, the human heart and body-mind and the world exist <u>in</u> the Heart, Which Is the Divine Being Itself.

For Avatar Adi Da's Description of the three stations of the heart and His Description of the significance of the right side of the heart in the processes of the ultimate stages of life, see *The Seven Stages Of Life*.

47. The "Perfect Practice" is Avatar Adi Da's technical term for the discipline of the sixth stage of life and the seventh stage of life in the Way of Adidam.

Devotees who have mastered (and, thus, transcended) the point of view of the body-mind by fulfilling the preparatory processes of the Way of Adidam may, by Avatar Adi Da's Grace, be Awakened to practice in the Domain of Consciousness Itself, in the sixth and seventh (or ultimate) stages of life.

48. In deep meditation, the Spirit-Current may be felt in the form of the Arrow, which Avatar Adi Da describes as "a motionless axis that seems to stand in the center of the body, between the frontal and spinal lines", rather than in the form of the Circle, in which the natural life-energy and (in the case of Spiritually Awakened practitioners) the Spirit-Energy are felt to circulate through the frontal and spinal lines.

Part Three

49. Avatar Adi Da has Revealed the underlying structure of human growth in seven stages.

The first three stages of life develop, respectively, the physical, emotional, and mental/volitional functions of the body mind. The first stage begins at birth and continues for approximately five to seven years; the second stage follows, continuing until approximately the age of twelve to fourteen; and the third stage is optimally complete by the early twenties. In the case of virtually all individuals, however, failed adaptation in the earlier stages of life means that maturity in the third stage of life takes much longer to attain, and it is usually never fulfilled, with the result that the ensuing stages of Spiritual development do not even begin.

In the Way of Adidam, however, growth in the first three stages of life unfolds in the Spiritual Company of Avatar Adi Da and is based in the practice of feeling-Contemplation of His bodily (human) Form and in devotion, service, and self-discipline in relation to His bodily (human) Form. By the Grace of this relationship to Avatar Adi Da, the first three (or foundation) stages of life are lived and fulfilled in a self-transcending devotional disposition, or (as He Describes it) "in the 'original' or beginner's devotional context of the fourth stage of life".

The fourth stage of life is the transitional stage between the gross, bodily-based point of view of the first three stages of life and the subtle, psychic point of view of the fifth stage of life. The fourth stage of life is the stage of Spiritual devotion, or surrender of separate self, in which the gross functions of the being are submitted to the higher psychic, or subtle, functions of the being, and, through these psychic functions, to the Divine. In the fourth stage of life, the gross, or bodily-based, personality of the first three stages of life is purified through reception of the Spiritual Force ("Holy Spirit", or "Shakti") of the Divine Reality, Which prepares the being to out-grow the bodily-based point of view.

In the Way of Adidam, as the orientation of the fourth stage of life matures, heart-felt surrender to the bodily (human) Form of Avatar Adi Da deepens by His Grace, drawing His devotee into Love-Communion with His All-Pervading Spiritual Presence. Growth in the "basic" context of the fourth stage of life in the Way of Adidam is also characterized by a Baptizing Current of Spirit-Energy that is at first felt to flow down the front of the body from above the head to the bodily base.

The Descent of Avatar Adi Da's Spirit-Baptism releases obstructions predominantly in the waking, or frontal, personality. This frontal Yoga purifies His devotee and infuses him or her with His Spirit-Power. Avatar Adi Da's devotee is awakened to profound love of and devotional intimacy with Him.

If the transition to the sixth stage of life is not otherwise made at maturity in the "basic" context of the fourth stage of life, the Spirit-Current is felt to turn about at the bodily base and ascend to the brain core, and the fourth stage of life matures to its "advanced" context, which involves the ascent of Avatar Adi Da's Spiritual Blessing and purifies the spinal line of the body-mind.

In the fifth stage of life, attention is concentrated in the subtle, or psychic, levels of awareness in ascent. The Spirit-Current is felt to penetrate the brain core and rise toward the Matrix of Light and Love-Bliss infinitely above the crown of the head, possibly culminating in the temporary experience of fifth stage conditional Nirvikalpa Samadhi, or "formless ecstasy". In the Way of Adidam, most practitioners will not need to practice in the context of the fifth stage of life, but will rather be Awakened, by Adi Da's Grace, from maturity in the fourth stage of life to the Witness-Position of Consciousness (in the context of the sixth stage of life).

In the traditional development of the sixth stage of life, attention is inverted upon the essential self and the Perfectly Subjective Position of Consciousness, to the exclusion of conditional phenomena. In the Way of Adidam, however, the deliberate intention to invert attention for the sake of Realizing Transcendental Consciousness does not characterize the sixth stage of life, which instead begins when the Witness-Position of Consciousness spontaneously Awakens and becomes stable.

In the course of the sixth stage of life, the mechanism of attention, which is the root-action of egoity (felt as separation, self-contraction, or the feeling of relatedness), gradually subsides. In the fullest context of the sixth stage of life, the knot of attention dissolves and all sense of relatedness yields to the Blissful and undifferentiated Feeling of Being. The characteristic Samadhi of the sixth stage of life is Jnana Samadhi, the temporary and exclusive Realization of the Transcendental Self, or Consciousness Itself.

The transition from the sixth stage of life to the seventh stage Realization of Absolute Non-Separateness is the unique Revelation of Avatar Adi Da. Various traditions and individuals previous to Adi Da's Revelation have had sixth stage intuitions or premonitions of the Most Perfect seventh stage Realization, but no one previous to Avatar Adi Da has Realized the seventh stage of life.

The seventh stage Realization is the Gift of Avatar Adi Da to His devotees, Awakened only in the context of the Way of Adidam that He has Revealed and Given. The seventh stage of life begins when His devotee Awakens, by His Grace, from the exclusive Realization of Consciousness to Most Perfect and permanent Identification with Consciousness Itself, Avatar Adi Da's Very (and Inherently Perfect) State. This is Divine Self-Realization, or Divine Enlightenment, the perpetual Samadhi of "Open Eyes" (seventh stage Sahaj Samadhi), in which all "things" are Divinely Recognized without "difference" as merely apparent modifications of the One Self-Existing and Self-Radiant Divine Consciousness. In the course of the seventh stage of life, there may be spontaneous incidents in which psycho-physical states and phenomena do not appear to the notice, being Outshined by the "Bright" Radiance of Consciousness Itself. This Samadhi, which is the ultimate Realization of Divine Existence, culminates in Divine Translation, or the permanent Outshining of all apparent conditions in the Inherently Perfect Radiance and Love-Bliss of the Divine Self-Condition.

In the context of practice of the Way of Adidam, the seven stages of life as Revealed by Avatar Adi Da are not a version of the traditional "ladder" of Spiritual attainment. These stages and their characteristic signs arise naturally in the course of practice for a fully practicing devotee in the Way of Adidam, but the practice itself is oriented to the <u>transcending</u> of the first six stages of life, in the seventh stage

Disposition of Inherently Liberated Happiness, Granted by Avatar Adi Da's Grace in His Love-Blissful Spiritual Company.

For Avatar Adi Da's extended Instruction relative to the seven stages of life, see *The Seven Stages Of Life—The Seventeen Companions Of The True Dawn Horse, Book Ten: Transcending The Six Stages Of egoic Life and Realizing The ego-Transcending Seventh Stage Of Life In The Divine Way Of Adidam.*

50. In Avatar Adi Da's Teaching-Revelation, "Narcissus" is a key symbol of the un-Enlightened individual as a self-obsessed seeker, enamored of his or her own self-image and egoic self-consciousness. In *The Knee Of Listening*, Adi Da Samraj Describes the significance of the archetype of Narcissus:

He is the ancient one visible in the Greek "myth", who was the universally adored child of the gods, who rejected the loved-one and every form of love and relationship, who was finally condemned to the contemplation of his own image, until, as a result of his own act and obstinacy, he suffered the fate of eternal separateness and died in infinite solitude.

51. "Sat" means "Truth", "Being", "Existence". Thus, "Sat-Guru" literally means "True Guru", or a Guru who can lead living beings from darkness (or non-Truth) into Light (or the Living Truth).

52. The Hindi word "Satsang" literally means "true (or right) relationship", "the company of Truth". In the Way of Adidam, Satsang is the eternal relationship of mutual sacred commitment between Avatar Adi Da Samraj and each true and formally acknowledged practitioner of the Way of Adidam. Once it is consciously assumed by any practitioner, Satsang with Avatar Adi Da is an all-inclusive Condition, bringing Divine Grace and Blessings and sacred obligations, responsibilities, and tests into every dimension of the practitioner's life and consciousness. (See note 49 for a description of the seven stages of life.)

53. Avatar Adi Da Samraj uses the term "advanced" to Describe the fourth stage of life (in its "basic" and "advanced" contexts) and the fifth stage of life in the Way of Adidam. He reserves the term "ultimate" to Describe the sixth and seventh stages of life in the Way of Adidam.

54. The Sanskrit word "Samadhi" traditionally denotes various exalted states that appear in the context of esoteric meditation and Realization. Avatar Adi Da Teaches that, in the Way of Adidam, Samadhi is, even more simply and fundamentally, a state of ego-transcendence in heart-Communion with Him, and that "the cultivation of Samadhi"

is another way to describe the practice of Ruchira Avatara Bhakti Yoga that is the fundamental basis of the Way of Adidam. Avatar Adi Da's devotee is in Samadhi in any moment of standing beyond the separate self in true devotional heart-Communion with Him. (See "The Cultivation of My Divine Samadhi", in *The Seven Stages Of Life*.)

The developmental process leading to Divine Enlightenment in the Way of Adidam may be marked by many signs, principal among which are the Samadhis of the advanced and the ultimate stages of life and practice. Although some of the "Great Samadhis" of the fourth, the fifth, and the sixth stages of life may appear in the course of an individual's practice of the Way of Adidam, the appearance of all of them is by no means necessary, or even probable, as Avatar Adi Da indicates in His Wisdom-Teaching. All the possible forms of Samadhi in the Way of Adidam are described in full detail in *The Dawn Horse Testament Of The Ruchira Avatar*.

See also note 49 (relative to the seven stages of life, as Revealed by Avatar Adi Da Samraj).

55. In modern psychology, the "Oedipus complex" is named after the legendary Greek Oedipus, who was fated to unknowingly, or unconsciously, kill his father and marry his mother. Avatar Adi Da Teaches that the primary dynamisms of emotional-sexual desiring, rejection, envy, betrayal, self-pleasuring, resentment, and other primal emotions and impulses are indeed patterned upon unconscious reactions first formed early in life, in relation to one's mother and father. Avatar Adi Da calls this "the 'Oedipal' drama" and points out that we relate to all women as we do to our mothers, and to all men as we do to our fathers, and that we relate, and react, to our own bodies exactly as we do to the parent of the opposite sex. Thus, we impose infantile reactions to our parents on our relationships with lovers and all other beings, according to their sex, and we also superimpose the same on our relationship to our own bodies.

56. Avatar Adi Da's Agents are all the Means that have been Empowered by Him to serve as Vehicles of His Divine Grace and Awakening Power. The first Means of Agency that have been fully established by Him are His Wisdom-Teaching, the three Retreat Sanctuaries that He has Empowered, and the many Objects and Articles that He has Empowered for the sake of His devotees' Remembrance of Him and reception of His Heart-Blessing. After Avatar Adi Da's human Lifetime, at any given time one (and only one) from among His Divinely Awakened Ruchira Sannyasin devotees will serve the Spiritual, Transcendental, and Divine Function of His <u>human</u> Agent in relationship to other devotees, all beings, the psycho-physical world, and the total cosmos.

57. Avatar Adi Da is referring to the following musicians:

Ravi Shankar, in "A Tribute to Guru" (pp. 1-14 of *Ustad Allauddin Khan: The Legend of Music*, by Anuradha Ghosh; New Delhi: Publications Division, Ministry of Information and Broadcasting, Government of India, 1990) and in *My Music, My Life* (New Delhi: Viking Publishing House, 1992).

Nikhil Banerjee, in the notes and interview material included with the audio recordings of his sitar music in the following compact discs:

Chairman's Choice—Great Gharanas: Maihar (EMI/The Gramophone Company of India CD CMC 1 82501-02)

Signature Series. Volume 4: *Ustad Ali Akbar Khan and Pandit Nikhil Banerjee.* Booklet contains essay "Memories of Nikhil", by Ustad Ali Akbar Khan (Alam Madina Music Productions AMMP CD 9405)

Afternoon Ragas. Nikhil Banerjee, sitar, and Kanai Dutta, tabla. Booklet contains "My Maestro as I Saw Him", by Nikhil Banerjee (Raga Records RAGA-211)

The Hundred-Minute Raga: Purabi Kalyan. Nikhil Banerjee, sitar, and Swapan Chaudhuri, tabla. Booklet contains an interview with Nikhil Banerjee, by Ira Landgarten (Raga Records RAGA-207)

Nikhil Banerjee Live. Nikhil Banerjee, sitar, and Swapan Chaudhuri, tabla. Booklet contains notes on Nikhil Banerjee. (Raga Records RAGA-204)

Nikhil Banerjee. Nikhil Banerjee, sitar, and Mahapurush Misra, tabla. Booklet contains notes on Nikhil Banerjee. (Raga Records RAGA-201)

Lyrical Sitar: Pandit Nikhil Banerjee. Nikhil Banerjee, sitar, and Anindo Chatterjee, tabla. Booklet contains notes on Nikhil Banerjee. (Indische Tanzschule "Chhanda Dhara" SNCD 70391)

The Genius of Pandit Nikhil Banerjee: Sitar. Pandit Nikhil Banerjee, sitar, and Zakir Hussain, tabla. Booklet contains notes on Pandit Nikhil Banerjee, by Dr. Saranindranath Tagore. (Indische Tanzschule "Chhanda Dhara" SNCD 71294)

The Genius of Pandit Nikhil Banerjee: Sitar (Raag Rageshree). Pandit Nikhil Banerjee (sitar) and Anindo Chatterjee (tabla). Booklet contains notes on Pandit Nikhil Banerjee, by Ratan Mukherjee (Indische Tanzschule "Chhanda Dhara" SNCD 70296)

Pandit Nikhil Banerjee—Born 1931......: The Legend Lives On. Nikhil Banerjee, sitar. Booklet contains notes on Nikhil Banerjee. (Original Music Impressions D3HI0631)

58. "Kul" (Hindi) or "Kula" (Sanskrit) means "family". Therefore, "gurukul" or "gurukula" means "family of the guru".

59. "Sadhana" is Sanskrit for "self-transcending religious or Spiritual practice".

Part Four

60. Ruchira Avatara Bhakti Yoga is the principal Gift, Calling, and Discipline Offered by Adi Da Samraj to all who practice the Way of Adidam.

   The phrase "Ruchira Avatara Bhakti Yoga" is itself a summary of the Way of Adidam. "Bhakti", in Sanskrit, is love, adoration, or devotion, while "Yoga" is a Real-God-Realizing discipline or practice. "Ruchira Avatara Bhakti Yoga" is, thus, the Divinely Revealed practice of devotional love for (and response to) the Ruchira Avatar, Adi Da Samraj.

   For Avatar Adi Da's essential Instruction in Ruchira Avatara Bhakti Yoga, see the *Da Love-Ananda Gita—The Five Books Of The Heart Of The Adidam Revelation, Book Three: The "Late-Time" Avataric Revelation Of The Great Means To Worship and To Realize The True and Spiritual Divine Person (The egoless Personal Presence Of Reality and Truth, Which Is The Only Real God)*, Part Two, verse 25, and Part Three, and *What, Where, When, How, Why and Who To Remember To Be Happy*, Part Three, "Surrender the Faculties of the Body-Mind to Me".

61. Avatar Adi Da has Instructed His devotees that the practice of devotional Communion with Him (or Ruchira Avatara Bhakti Yoga) requires the surrender of the four principal faculties of the human body-mind. These faculties are mind (or attention), emotion (or feeling), body, and breath.

62. "Tapas" is Sanskrit for "heat", and, by extension, "self-discipline". In this case, the tapas Avatar Adi Da is Speaking of is the heat that results from the conscious frustration of egoic tendencies, through acceptance of His Calling for self-surrendering, self-forgetting, and self-transcending devotion, service, self-discipline, and meditation.

63. "'Talking' school" is a phrase coined by Avatar Adi Da to refer to those in any tradition of sacred life whose approach is characterized by talking, thinking, reading, and philosophical analysis and debate, or even meditative enquiry or reflection, without a concomitant and foundation discipline of body, emotion, mind, and breath. He contrasts the "talking" school with the "practicing" school approach—"practicing" schools involving those who are committed to the ordeal of real self-transcending discipline, under the guidance of a true Guru.

64. "Karma" is Sanskrit for "action". Since action entails consequences, or reactions, karma is destiny, tendency, the quality of existence and experience which is determined by previous actions.

65. "Siddhi" is Sanskrit for "power", or "accomplishment". When capitalized in Avatar Adi Da's Wisdom-Teaching, "Blessing-Siddhi" is the Spiritual, Transcendental, and Divine Awakening-Power That He spontaneously and effortlessly Transmits to all.

66. "Talking 'case'" is the tendency to indulge in self-analysis or self-meditation rather than the self-transcending process of true confession. It is getting sidetracked into <u>thinking</u> about yourself, and trying to figure out your "problem" rather than simply confessing what one has observed, changing one's action, and allowing true self-understanding to be Revealed—Given as a Gift, through the Grace of the relationship with Avatar Adi Da Samraj.

67. "Bhava" is a Sanskrit word traditionally used to refer to the enraptured feeling-swoon of Communion with the Divine. Ruchira-Avatara-Bhava is this Divine State which occurs in Communion with the Ruchira Avatar, Adi Da Samraj.

68. In this case, Avatar Adi Da Samraj is not talking about a common intoxicant such as alcohol, but of a Spiritual "Intoxicant"—by means of which devotees of Avatar Adi Da are Drawn beyond the usual egoic self through the Blessing Grace and Siddhis of Avatar Adi Da into a state of devotional Communion (and, ultimately, of Identification) with Him.

69. See "The Divine Scripture of Adidam", pp. 29-35.

70. Adi Da Samraj has often referred to a passage from the ancient Indian text *Satapatha Brahmana*, which He has paraphrased as: "Man does not know. Only the Horse Knows. Therefore, hold to the tail of the Horse." Adi Da has Revealed that, in the most esoteric understanding of this saying, the "Horse" represents the Adept-Realizer, and "holding to the tail of the Horse" represents the devotee's complete dependence on the Adept-Realizer in order to Realize Real God, or Truth, or Reality.

For Avatar Adi Da's extended discussion of His own uniquely Perfect Manifestation as the "Horse", see "The True Dawn Horse <u>Is</u> The <u>Only</u> Way To Me" (which appears as Part Three of *The <u>All-Completing</u> and <u>Final</u> Divine Revelation to Mankind*, Part One of *The Heart Of The Dawn Horse Testament Of The Ruchira Avatar*, and Part One of *The Dawn Horse Testament Of The Ruchira Avatar*).

71. In the Hindu tradition, the "dark" epoch, or the final and most ignorant and degenerate period of mankind, when the Spiritual Way of life is almost entirely forgotten.

72. Avatar Adi Da has said that, after His physical (human) Lifetime, there should always be one (and only one) "Living Murti" as a Living Link between Him and His devotees. Each successive "Living Murti" (or "Murti-Guru") is to be selected from among those members of the Ruchira Sannyasin Order (the senior renunciate order of Adidam— see pp. 207-211 for a full description) who have been formally acknowledged as Divinely Enlightened devotees of Avatar Adi Da Samraj in the seventh stage of life. "Living Murtis" will not function as the independent Gurus of practitioners of the Way of Adidam. Rather, they will simply be "Representations" of Avatar Adi Da's bodily (human) Form, and a means to Commune with Him.

For a full discussion of "Living Murtis", or "Murti-Gurus", and how they are chosen, see chapter twenty of *The Dawn Horse Testament Of The Ruchira Avatar*.

73. See note 36.

74. Well known in the West, the modern Indian Saint Ramakrishna (1836-1886) was a renowned ecstatic, and a lifelong devotee of Kali, a form of the Mother-Shakti. In the course of his Spiritual practice, Ramakrishna passed spontaneously through many religious and Spiritual disciplines, and he Realized a state of profound mystical union with God.

Avatar Adi Da Reveals the unique Role of Ramakrishna (and his chief disciple, Swami Vivekananda) as the Deeper Personality Vehicle of His (Avatar Adi Da's) Avataric Incarnation in chapter 20 of *The Knee Of Listening*.

75. "Murti" is Sanskrit for "form", and, by extension, a "representational image" of the Divine or of a Guru. In the Way of Adidam, Murtis of Avatar Adi Da are most commonly photographs of Avatar Adi Da's bodily (human) Form.

76. Avatar Adi Da's first Spiritual Teacher was Swami Rudrananda (1928-1973), or Albert Rudolph, known as "Rudi", who was His Teacher from 1964 to 1968, in New York City. Rudi helped Avatar Adi Da develop basic practical life-disciplines and the frontal Yoga of truly human Spiritual receptivity, which is the Yoga (or process) whereby knots and obstructions in the physical and etheric dimensions of the body-mind are penetrated, opened, surrendered, and released through Spiritual reception in the frontal (or descending) line of the body-mind (from the head to the bodily base). Rudi's own

Teachers included the Indonesian Pak Subuh (from whom Rudi learned a basic exercise of Spiritual receptivity), Swami Muktananda Paramahansa (with whom Rudi studied many years), and Swami Nityananda (the Indian Realizer who was also Swami Muktananda's Spiritual Teacher). Rudi met Swami Nityananda shortly before Swami Nityananda's death, and Rudi always thereafter acknowledged Swami Nityananda as his original and principal Spiritual Teacher.

77. Avatar Adi Da uses the metaphor of the closed fist and open fist to demonstrate the contrast between the self-contracted state and the natural (uncontracted) state. He has Described a key incident during His "Sadhana Years" when this contrast became suddenly intuitively clear:

> One . . . Incident Of Heart-Awakening Occurred Quite Gently (but Most Profoundly), In a moment In which I Was mindlessly Regarding My Right Hand, Observing The (Apparent and, Suddenly, Revealing) Contrast Between The Natural or Open and Functionally Relational Attitude Of The Hand and The Unnatural or Contracted and Functionally Dissociated Attitude Of The Clenched Fist.
>
> The Natural Sign Of the human body Is Relatedness, Not Separateness and Independence! (Part One of The <u>Only</u> Complete Way To Realize The <u>Unbroken</u> Light Of Real God—The Seventeen Companions Of The True Dawn Horse, Book Three: An Introductory Overview Of The "Radical" Divine Way Of The True World-Religion Of Adidam)

78. See note 49.

79. "Jnana" is Sanskrit for "knowledge". Avatar Adi Da uses the term "Jnana Samadhi" specifically to refer to the Samadhi experienced by His devotees in the context of the sixth stage of life of the Way of Adidam. Produced by the intentional withdrawal (or inversion) of attention from the conditional body-mind-self and its relations, Jnana Samadhi is the conditional (and, therefore, necessarily) temporary Realization of the Transcendental Self (or Consciousness), exclusive of any perception or cognition of world, objects, relations, body, mind, or separate self-sense.

80. "Ruchira Samadhi" (Sanskrit for "the Samadhi of the 'Bright'") is one of the references that Avatar Adi Da Samraj uses for the Divinely Enlightened Condition Realized in the seventh stage of life, Which He characterizes as the Unconditional Realization of the Divine "Brightness". In Part One of Hridaya Rosary (and chapter ten of The Dawn Horse Testament Of The Ruchira Avatar), Avatar Adi Da describes Ruchira Samadhi as follows:

> And This Great Process Will Certainly Lead You (Most Ultimately) To The Unconditional Realization Of Self-Radiant (or Inher-

ently Spiritual) and Self-Existing (or Transcendental) Divine Being
(In Seventh Stage Sahaj Samadhi, or, Really, Seventh Stage Sahaja
Nirvikalpa Samadhi, or The Samadhi Of No-"Difference", Which I
Have Otherwise Named "Ruchira Samadhi", and "Open Eyes"). And
Ruchira Samadhi Will (Perhaps) Demonstrate Itself As Occasional
(and Not Strategic, but Spontaneous) Outshining Of body, mind,
world, and Even <u>all</u> relations, By and <u>As</u> The Being-Radiance Of The
Divine Self-Domain Itself (In The "Bhava", or Temporary Demonstra-
tion, Of Divine Translation), but It Will Certainly (At Last, and
Finally) Demonstrate Itself As Divine Translation Itself (or The Most
Ultimate and Most Perfect Demonstration Of Ruchira Samadhi).

What You Can Do Next

Contact one of our centers.

■ Sign up for our preliminary course, "The Only Truth That Sets The Heart Free". This course will prepare you to become a fully practicing devotee of Avatar Adi Da Samraj.

■ Or sign up for any of our other classes, seminars, events, or retreats, or for a study course available by correspondence:

AMERICAS
12040 North Seigler Road
Middletown, CA 95461
(800) 524-4941
(707) 928-4936

PACIFIC-ASIA
12 Seibel Road
Henderson
Auckland 1008
New Zealand
64-9-838-9114

AUSTRALIA
P.O. Box 460
Roseville, NSW 2069
Australia
61-2-9416-7951

EUROPE-AFRICA
Annendaalderweg 10
6105 AT Maria Hoop
The Netherlands
31 (0)20 468 1442

THE UNITED KINGDOM
London, England
0181-7317550

E-MAIL: correspondence@adidam.org

Read these books by and about the Divine World-Teacher, Ruchira Avatar Adi Da Samraj:

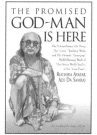

■ *The Promised God-Man Is Here*
The Extraordinary Life-Story, The "Crazy" Teaching-Work, and The Divinely "Emerging" World-Blessing Work Of The Divine World-Teacher Of The "Late-Time", Ruchira Avatar Adi Da Samraj, by Carolyn Lee, Ph.D.—the profound, heart-rending, humorous, miraculous, wild—and true—story of the Divine Person Alive in human Form. Essential reading as background for the study of Avatar Adi Da's books.

■ *See My Brightness Face to Face*
A Celebration of the Ruchira Avatar, Adi Da Samraj, and the First Twenty-Five Years of His Divine Revelation Work—a magnificent year-by-year pictorial celebration of Ruchira Avatar Adi Da's Divine Work with His devotees, from 1972-1997. Includes a wealth of selections from His Talks and Writings, numerous Stories of His Divine Work told by His devotees, and over 100 color photographs.

■ *Aham Da Asmi (Beloved, I <u>Am</u> Da)*
The Five Books Of The Heart Of The Adidam Revelation, Book One: The "Late-Time" Avataric Revelation Of The True and Spiritual Divine Person (The egoless Personal Presence Of Reality and Truth, Which <u>Is</u> The Only <u>Real</u> God)
This Ecstatic Scripture, the first of His twenty-three "Source-Texts", contains Ruchira Avatar Adi Da's magnificent Confession of His Identity as the Very Divine Person and Source-Condition of all and All.

After reading *Aham Da Asmi*, continue your reading with the remaining books of *The Five Books Of The Heart Of The Adidam Revelation* (the *Da Love-Ananda Gita*, *Hridaya Rosary*, and *Eleutherios*). Then you will be ready to go on to *The Seventeen Companions Of The True Dawn Horse* (see pp. 229-33). These and other books by and about Ruchira Avatar Adi Da Samraj can be ordered directly from the Dawn Horse Press by calling:

(800) 524-4941 (from within North America)
(707) 928-4936 (from outside North America)

or by writing to:

The Dawn Horse Press
12040 North Seigler Road
Middletown, CA 95461

Or you can order these, or any of the other products distributed by the Dawn Horse Press, by visiting the Dawn Horse Press on-line at: **http://dhp.adidam.org**.

Visit our website:
http://www.adidam.org.

Our award-winning website contains a wealth of photographs of Ruchira Avatar Adi Da Samraj, audio-clips of Him Speaking, excerpts from His Writings, and recent Stories of His world-Blessing Work. The website also has a full listing of Adidam regional centers worldwide.

For a full description of all the forms of involvement in the Way of Adidam, see "Surely Come to Me" on pp. 205-25.

RUCHIRA AVATAR ADI DA SAMRAJ
Adidam Samrajashram (Naitauba), Fiji, 1997

"Surely Come to Me"

An Invitation to the Way of Adidam

I __Am__ The Divine Heart-Master. I Take My Stand In The Heart Of My Devotee. Have You Realized The Heart, Who __Is__ The Mystery Of You and Me?

How Could I Deny Heart-Vision To My Loved-One?
How Could I Delay The Course Of My Beloved?
Like An Intimate Family Servant, I Dearly Serve My Devotee.

Like A Wealthy Friend, I Freely Give To My Devotee.
Like A Mad Priest, I Even Worship My Devotee, With Love Itself.

Like An Innocent Boy At First Love, I Would Awaken My Devotee In Radiant Chambers.

Where The Wound Of Love Churns and Never Heals, I Wait, Longing To Celebrate The Brilliant Sight Of My Devotee.

Come Slowly or Quickly, but Surely Come To Me.
Touch My Heart, and I Will Widen You To God-Knows-Where.

THE DAWN HORSE TESTAMENT OF THE RUCHIRA AVATAR

You are Blessed to be alive at the time of the Greatest of Revelations—the All-Completing Revelation of Real God promised by all the religious and Spiritual traditions of mankind. The Divine World-Teacher, Ruchira Avatar Adi Da Samraj, is that All-Completing Revelation. He is the Perfect Fulfillment of that universal promise.

Ruchira Avatar Adi Da Samraj Offers you a devotional relationship which literally brings His tangible Divine Blessing into your life. For the sake of all who are moved to go beyond all the dead-ends of ordinary life and all the dead-ends of Spiritual seeking, Ruchira Avatar Adi Da

Samraj has Revealed and Given the unique Way of Adidam—the only complete Way to Realize the True and Spiritual Divine Person, Who Is Reality Itself, or Truth Itself, or Real God.

You have before you now the greatest of life-choices: How are you going to respond to the Most Perfect Revelation of Real God?

How To Respond

The Divine World-Teacher, Ruchira Avatar Adi Da Samraj, Calls you to formally become His devotee—which means to formally take up practice of the Way of Adidam, the Divinely Enlightening Way of life He has Revealed and Given for the sake of all beings.

Because those who approach Him have different heart-needs and different life-circumstances to account for, Ruchira Avatar Adi Da has created four congregations of formal approach to Him. These four congregations, together, make up the Eleutherian Pan-Communion of Adidam (or, simply, the Adidam Pan-Communion). Which of the four congregations of the Adidam Pan-Communion you should apply to for membership depends on the strength of your impulse to respond to Avatar Adi Da's Revelation and on your life-circumstance.

Take Up the Total Practice
of the Way of Adidam

(The First and Second Congregations
of the Adidam Pan-Communion)

The first and second congregations of the Adidam
Pan-Communion are for practitioners of the <u>total</u> practice of
the Way of Adidam (and for student-novices, who are formally approaching the total practice of the Way of Adidam).
In particular, the first congregation is for those who have
dedicated their lives <u>one-pointedly</u> to Realizing Real
God—it is the congregation made up of the two formal
renunciate orders of Adidam: the Ruchira Sannyasin Order
of the Tantric Renunciates of Adidam, and the Avabhasin
Lay Renunciate Order of the Tantric Renunciates of Adidam. The second congregation is made up of student-
novices, student-beginners, and members of the Lay Con-
gregationist Order of Adidam (which is the general lay
practicing and serving order of Ruchira Avatar Adi Da's
lay devotees who have advanced beyond the student-
beginner stage).

To take up the total practice of the Way of Adidam is
to take full advantage of the opportunity Offered by
Ruchira Avatar Adi Da Samraj—it is to enter fully into the
Process of Real-God-Realization. That Process of Real-God-
Realization is a unique ordeal, which necessarily requires
application to a wide range of functional, practical, relational, and cultural self-disciplines Revealed and Given by
Ruchira Avatar Adi Da Samraj for the sake of that Divine
Process. These disciplines allow the body-mind to be made
ever more available to Ruchira Avatar Adi Da's Blessing
Transmission. They range from foundation practices relative to diet, health, sexuality, and work, to the core devotional practices of meditation, sacramental worship, and
study of Avatar Adi Da's Wisdom-Teaching. The Way of
Adidam is not a "talking" school based on merely adhering

to a certain philosophy or upholding a certain religious point of view. Rather, the Way of Adidam is a "practicing" school, in which you participate in the Process of Real-God-Realization with every aspect of your being.

If you want to enter fully into the Process of Real-God-Realization in the Company of Ruchira Avatar Adi Da Samraj, then you should apply to become a member of the second congregation of the Adidam Pan-Communion—and if you are moved to <u>one-pointedly</u> dedicate your life to the Process of Real-God-Realization, after a period of exemplary practice in the second congregation, you may apply to practice as a formal renunciate in the first congregation. (The life of members of the first and second congregations is described and pictured on pp. 218-22.)

When you apply for membership in the second congregation of the Adidam Pan-Communion (the first step for all who want to take up the total practice of the Way of Adidam), you will be asked to prepare yourself by taking "The <u>Only</u> Truth That Sets the Heart Free", a course of formal study and "consideration" (lasting four to six weeks), in which you examine the Opportunity Offered to you by Avatar Adi Da Samraj, and learn what it means to embrace the total practice of the Way of Adidam as a second-congregation devotee of Ruchira Avatar Adi Da. (To register for this preparatory course, please contact the regional or territorial center nearest to you [see p. 225], or e-mail us at: correspondence@adidam.org.) After completing this period of study, you may formally enter the second congregation by becoming a student-novice.

Entering any of the four congregations of Adidam involves taking a formal vow of devotion and service to Avatar Adi Da Samraj. This vow is a profound—and, indeed, eternal—commitment. You take this vow (for whichever congregation you are entering) when you are certain that your great and true heart-impulse is to be devoted, forever, to Avatar Adi Da Samraj as your Divine Heart-Master. If you recognize Avatar Adi Da as the Living

Divine Person—your Perfect Guide and Help and your eternal and most intimate Heart-Companion—then you know that this vow is a priceless Gift, and you joyfully embrace the great responsibility it represents.

As a student-novice (formally approaching the total practice of the Way of Adidam), you are initiated into formal meditation and sacramental worship, you begin to adapt to a wide range of life-disciplines, and you begin to participate in the life of the cooperative community of Ruchira Avatar Adi Da's devotees. As a student-novice, you engage in an intensive period of study and "consideration" of the Way of Adidam in all of its details. And, as your practice matures, you are given more and more access to the cultural life of the formally acknowledged practitioners of the total practice of Adidam. After a minimum of three to six months of practice as a student-novice, you may apply for formal acknowledgement as a fully practicing member of the second congregation.

If you find that you are steadily and profoundly moved to dedicate your life <u>one-pointedly</u> to Ruchira Avatar Adi Da Samraj and the Process of Real-God-Realization in His Spiritual Company, then, after a demonstration period of exemplary practice as a member of the second congregation, you may apply to practice as a formal renunciate in the first congregation of the Adidam Pan-Communion.

The two formal renunciate orders in the Way of Adidam are the Lay Renunciate Order and the Ruchira Sannyasin Order. The senior of the two orders is the Ruchira Sannyasin Order, which is the senior cultural authority within the gathering of all four congregations of Avatar Adi Da's devotees. The members of the Ruchira Sannyasin Order are the most exemplary formal renunciate practitioners practicing in the ultimate (sixth and seventh) stages of life in the Way of Adidam. The core of the Ruchira Sannyasin Order, and its senior governing members, will, in the future, be those devotees who have Realized Divine Enlightenment. Ruchira Avatar Adi Da Samraj Himself is

the Founding Member of the Ruchira Sannyasin Order,
and will, throughout His Lifetime, remain its Senior Member
in every respect.

The Ruchira Sannyasin Order is a retreat Order, whose
members are legal renunciates. They are supported and protected in their unique Spiritual role by the Lay Renunciate
Order, which is a cultural service Order that serves an inspirational and aligning role for all devotees of Avatar Adi Da.

First-congregation devotees have a special role to play in the Way of Adidam. Adi Da Samraj must have unique human Instrumentality—Spiritually Awakened and Divinely Self-Realized devotees—through whom He can continue to do His Divine Transmission Work after His physical Lifetime. No human being, not even one of Avatar Adi Da's Divinely Enlightened devotees, can "succeed" Ruchira Avatar Adi Da Samraj, in the way that, traditionally, a senior devotee often succeeds his or her Spiritual Master.* Avatar Adi Da Samraj is the Complete Incarnation of the Divine Person—He is truly the <u>Completion</u> of all Spiritual lineages in all times and places. Thus, He remains forever the Divine Awakener and Liberator of all beings. His Spiritually Awakened renunciate devotees will <u>collectively</u> function as His Spiritual Instruments, allowing His Blessing-Power to Pervade and Influence the world.

To become a fully practicing devotee of Avatar Adi Da Samraj (in the second congregation, and potentially moving on to the first congregation), call or write one of our regional centers (see p. 225) and sign up for our preliminary course, "The <u>Only</u> Truth That Sets the Heart Free".

---

*Adi Da Samraj has Said that, after His physical (human) Lifetime, there should always be one (and only one) "Murti-Guru" as a Living Link between Him and His devotees. Each successive "Murti-Guru" is to be selected from among those members of the Ruchira Sannyasin Order who have been formally acknowledged as Divinely Enlightened devotees of Adi Da. "Murti-Gurus" do not function as the independent Guru of practitioners of the Way of Adidam. Rather, they are simply Representations of Adi Da's bodily (human) Form, and a means to Commune with Him.

The Adidam Youth Fellowship

Young people (25 and under) are also offered a special form of relationship to Avatar Adi Da—the Adidam Youth Fellowship. The Adidam Youth Fellowship has two membership bodies—friends and practicing members. A friend of the Adidam Youth Fellowship is simply invited into a culture of other young people who want to learn more about Avatar Adi Da Samraj and His Happiness-Realizing Way of Adidam. A formally practicing member of the Adidam Youth Fellowship acknowledges that he or she has found his or her True Heart-Friend and Master in the Person of Avatar Adi Da Samraj, and wishes to enter into a direct, self-surrendering Spiritual relationship with Him as the Means to True Happiness. Practicing members of the Youth Fellowship embrace a series of disciplines that are similar to (but simpler than) the practices engaged by adult members of the second congregation of Adidam. Both friends and members are invited to special retreat events from time to time, where they can associate with other young devotees of Avatar Adi Da.

To become a member of the Adidam Youth Fellowship, or to learn more about this form of relationship to Avatar Adi Da, call or write:

Vision of Mulund Institute (VMI)
10336 Loch Lomond Road, Suite 146
Middletown, CA 95461
PHONE: (707) 928-6932
FAX: (707) 928-5619
E-MAIL: vmi@adidam.org

Become an Advocate of the Way of Adidam

(In the Fourth Congregation of the Adidam Pan-Communion)

The fourth congregation of the Adidam Pan-Communion is for those who are attracted to the life of devotional intimacy with Avatar Adi Da Samraj and are moved to serve His world-Blessing Work, but who are not presently moved or able to take up the full range of disciplines required of members of the first and second congregations. Thus, if you embrace the fourth-congregation practice, you receive Avatar Adi Da's Spiritual Blessings in your life by assuming the most basic level of responsibility as His devotee. The fourth-congregation practice allows you to develop and deepen true devotional intimacy with Avatar Adi Da, but, because it does not involve the full range of disciplines, it always remains a beginning form of the practice of Adidam. If, as a member of the fourth congregation, you are eventually moved to advance beyond the beginning, you are always invited to transition to the second congregation and embrace the total—and, potentially, Divinely Enlightening—practice of the Way of Adidam.

A principal organization within the fourth congregation is the Transnational Society of Advocates of the Adidam Revelation. Advocates are individuals who recognize Ruchira Avatar Adi Da Samraj as a Source of Wisdom and Blessing in their own lives and for the world, and who want to make a practical response. Advocates serve Ruchira Avatar Adi Da's world-Blessing Work by actively serving the dissemination of His Wisdom-Teaching and by actively advocating Him and the Way of Adidam.

When you become an advocate, you make a formal vow of devotion and service to Ruchira Avatar Adi Da Samraj. As described on pp. 208-209, this vow is a profound and eternal commitment to Avatar Adi Da as Your Divine Heart-Master. By taking this vow, you are committing yourself to perform a specific consistent service to Avatar Adi Da and His Blessing Work, and to embrace the fundamental devotional practice that Avatar Adi Da Gives to all His devotees. This is the practice of Ruchira Avatara Bhakti Yoga—devotion to Ruchira Avatar Adi Da Samraj as your Divine Heart-Master. Advocates do the simplest form of this great practice, which Ruchira Avatar Adi Da summarizes as "Invoke Me, Feel Me, Breathe Me, Serve Me".

The advocate vow is also a commitment to make a monthly donation to help support the publication of Avatar Adi Da's supremely precious Wisdom-Literature (as well as publications about Him and the Way of Adidam), as well as paying an annual membership fee that supports the services of the Society of Advocates.

In addition, Advocates offer their services in the form of whatever practical or professional skills they can bring to creatively serve Ruchira Avatar Adi Da and the Way of Adidam.

To become a member of the Transnational Society of Advocates of the Adidam Revelation, call or write one of our regional centers (see p. 225), or e-mail us at:

correspondence@adidam.org

In addition to members of the Transnational Society of Advocates, those who live in traditional cultures around the world are invited to practice as members of the fourth congregation. The opportunity to practice in the fourth congregation is also extended to all those who, because of physical or other functional limitations, are unable to take up the total practice of the Way of Adidam as required in the first and second congregations.

To become a member of the fourth congregation of Adidam, call or write one of our regional centers (see p. 225), or e-mail us at: correspondence@adidam.org.

Serve the Divine World-Teacher
and His World-Blessing Work
via Patronage or Unique Influence

(The Third Congregation
of the Adidam Pan-Communion)

We live at a time when the destiny of mankind and of even the planet itself hangs desperately in the balance. The Divine World-Teacher, Ruchira Avatar Adi Da Samraj, has Manifested at this precarious moment in history in order to Reveal the Way of true Liberation from the disease of egoity. It is only <u>That</u> Gift of true Liberation that can reverse the disastrous trends of our time.

It is the sacred responsibility of those who respond to Ruchira Avatar Adi Da to provide the means for His Divine Work to achieve truly great effect in the world. He must be given the practical means to Bless all beings and to Work with His devotees and others responding to Him in all parts of the world, in whatever manner He is spontaneously moved to do so. He must be able to move freely from one part of the world to another. He must be able to establish Hermitages in various parts of the world, where He can Do His silent Work of Blessing, and where He can also Work with His devotees and others who can be of significant help in furthering His Work by receiving them into His physical Company. Ruchira Avatar Adi Da must also be able to gather around Him His most exemplary formal renunciate devotees—and such formal renunciates must be given practical support so that they can be entirely and one-pointedly devoted to serving Ruchira Avatar Adi Da and to living the life of perpetual Spiritual retreat in His physical Company. And the mere fact that Real God is Present in the world must become as widely known as possible, both through the publication and dissemination of books by and about Ruchira Avatar Adi Da and through public advocacy by people of influence.

If you are a man or woman of unique wealth or unique influence in the world, we invite you to serve Ruchira Avatar Adi Da's world-Blessing Work by becoming His patron. Truly, patronage of the Divine World-Teacher, Ruchira Avatar Adi Da Samraj, exceeds all other possible forms of philanthropy. You are literally helping to change the destiny of countless people by helping to support Ruchira Avatar Adi Da in His world-Blessing Work. You make it possible for Ruchira Avatar Adi Da's Divine Influence to reach people who might otherwise never come to know of Him. You make it possible for Him to make fullest use of His own physical Lifetime—the unique bodily Lifetime of Real God, Perfectly Incarnate. To make the choice to serve Avatar Adi Da via your patronage or unique influence is to allow your own life and destiny, and the life and destiny of all of mankind, to be transformed in the most Graceful way possible.

As a member of the third congregation, your relationship to Ruchira Avatar Adi Da is founded on a vow of Ruchira Avatara Bhakti Yoga—a vow of devotion, through which you commit yourself to serve His Work. In the course of your service to Ruchira Avatar Adi Da (and in daily life altogether), you live your vow of devotion by invoking Him, feeling Him, breathing Him, and serving Him (without being expected to engage the full range of disciplines practiced in the first two congregations). At all times, this practice is the means Ruchira Avatar Adi Da has Given for His third-congregation devotees to remain connected to His constant Blessing. In addition, Ruchira Avatar Adi Da has invited, and may continue to invite, members of the third congregation into His physical Company to receive His Divine Blessing.

If you are able to serve Avatar Adi Da Samraj in this crucial way, please contact us at:

Third Congregation Advocacy
12040 North Seigler Road
Middletown, CA 95461
phone number: (707) 928-4800
FAX: (707) 928-4618
e-mail: third_congregation@adidam.org

The Life of a Formally Practicing Devotee of Ruchira Avatar Adi Da Samraj

(in the First or Second Congregation of Adidam)

Everything you do as a devotee of Ruchira Avatar Adi Da Samraj in the first congregation or the second congregation of Adidam is an expression of your heart-response to Him as your Divine Heart-Master. The life of cultivating that response is Ruchira Avatara Bhakti Yoga—or the Real-God-Realizing practice ("Yoga") of devotion ("Bhakti") to the Ruchira Avatar, Adi Da Samraj.

The great practice of Ruchira Avatara Bhakti Yoga necessarily transforms the whole of your life. Every function, every relationship, every action is moved by the impulse of devotional heart-surrender to Adi Da Samraj.

AVATAR ADI DA SAMRAJ: In every moment you must turn the situation of your life into Ruchira Avatara Bhakti Yoga by exercising devotion to Me. There is no moment in any day wherein this is not your Calling. This is what you must do. You must make every moment into this Yoga by using the body, emotion, breath, and attention in self-surrendering devotional Contemplation of Me. All of those four principal faculties must be turned to Me. By constantly turning to Me, you "yoke" yourself to Me, and that practice of linking (or binding, or connecting) to Real God is religion. Religion, or Yoga, is the practice of moving out of the egoic (or separative, or self-contracted) disposition and state into Oneness with That Which is One, Whole, Absolute, All-Inclusive, and Beyond. [December 2, 1993]

As everyone quickly discovers, it is only possible to practice Ruchira Avatara Bhakti Yoga moment to moment when you establish a foundation of supportive self-discipline that enables you to reel in your attention, energy, and feeling from their random wandering. And so Ruchira Avatar Adi Da has Given unique and extraordinarily full Instruction on a complete range of functional, practical, relational, and cultural disciplines for His first-congregation and second-congregation devotees. These disciplines are not methods for attaining Happiness, but are the present-time expression of prior Happiness:

AVATAR ADI DA SAMRAJ: I do not require the discipline of conventional renunciation. Nor do I allow commitment to the karmas of self-indulgence. My devotees serve Me through the humorous discipline of an ordinary pleasurable life. This is the foundation of their practice of the Way of Adidam.

The "ordinary pleasurable life" of which Avatar Adi Da Samraj Speaks is not based on any kind of attempt to achieve immunity from the inevitable wounds of life. Rather, it is based on the always present disposition of True Happiness—the disposition of ego-transcendence through self-surrendering, self-forgetting Contemplation of Ruchira Avatar Adi Da in every moment. Therefore, the "ordinary pleasurable life" of Avatar Adi Da's devotees involves many practices that support and develop the simplicity and clarity of Happiness and self-transcendence. These practices are "ordinary" in the sense that they are not Enlightenment in and of themselves, but they are, rather, the grounds for a simple, mature, pleasurable, and truly human life, devoted to Real-God-Realization.

These practices in the Way of Adidam include cultural disciplines such as morning and evening meditation, devotional chanting and sacramental worship, study-"consideration" of Ruchira Avatar Adi Da's Wisdom-Teaching, formal weekly retreat days, extended weekend retreats every two to three months, an annual meditation retreat of ten days to six weeks. The life of practice also includes the adaptation to a pure and purifying diet, free from toxifying accessories (such as tobacco, alcohol, caffeine, sugar, and processed foods) and animal products (such as meat, dairy products, and eggs).

Meditation is a unique and precious event in the daily life of Avatar Adi Da Samraj's devotees. It offers the opportunity to relinquish outward, body-based attention and to be alone with Adi Da Samraj, allowing yourself to enter more and more into the sphere of His Divine Transmission.

The practice of sacramental worship, or "puja", in the Way of Adidam is the bodily active counter-part to meditation. It is a form of ecstatic worship of Avatar Adi Da Samraj, using a photographic representation of Him and involving devotional chanting and recitations from His Wisdom-Teaching.

You must deal with My Wisdom-Teaching in some form every single day, because a new form of the ego's game appears every single day. You must continually return to My Wisdom-Teaching, confront My Wisdom-Teaching.

Avatar Adi Da Samraj

The beginner in Spiritual life must prepare the body-mind by mastering the physical, vital dimension of life before he or she can be ready for truly Spiritual practice. Service is devotion in action, a form of Divine Communion.

Avatar Adi Da Samraj Offers practical disciplines to His devotees in the areas of work and money, diet, exercise, and sexuality. These disciplines are based on His own human experience and an immense process of "consideration" that He engaged face to face with His devotees for more than twenty-five years.

There is also a discipline of daily exercise which includes morning calisthenics and evening Hatha Yoga exercises. There is progressive adaptation to a regenerative discipline of sexuality and sexual energy. And, as a practical foundation for your personal life and the life of the community of practitioners, there is the requirement to maintain yourself in full employment or full-time service, in order to support the obligations of the sacred institution (the Eleutherian Pan-Communion of Adidam) and the cooperative community organization (the Ruchirasala of Adidam).

All of these functional, practical, relational, and cultural disciplines are means whereby your body-mind becomes capable of effectively conducting Ruchira Avatar Adi Da's constant Blessing-Transmission. Therefore, Ruchira Avatar Adi Da has made it clear that, in order to Realize Him with true profundity—and, in particular, to Realize Him most perfectly, to the degree of Divine Enlightenment—it is necessary to be a formally acknowledged member of either the first or the second congregation engaging the total practice of the Way of Adidam.

One of the ways in which Ruchira Avatar Adi Da Communicates His Divine Blessing-Transmission is through sacred places. During the course of His Teaching and Revelation Work, He Empowered three Sanctuaries as His Blessing-Seats. In each of these Sanctuaries—the Mountain Of Attention in northern California, Love-Ananda Mahal in Hawaii, and Adidam Samrajashram in Fiji—Ruchira Avatar Adi Da has Established Himself Spiritually in perpetuity. He has lived and Worked with devotees in all of His Sanctuaries, and has created in each one special holy sites and temples. In particular, Adidam Samrajashram—His Great Island-Hermitage and world-Blessing Seat—is Ruchira Avatar Adi Da's principal Place of Spiritual Work and Transmission, and will remain so forever after His physical Lifetime. Formally acknowledged devotees are invited to go on special retreats at all three Sanctuaries.

The Mountain Of Attention Sanctuary of Adidam

Love-Ananda Mahal

**Adidam Samrajashram
(Naitauba, Fiji)**

Ruchira Avatar Adi Da writes in *Eleutherios (The Only Truth That Sets The Heart Free)*:

I Have Come to Found (and, altogether, to Make Possible) a New (and Truly "Bright") Age of mankind, an Age That will not begin on the basis of the seeking mummery of ego-bondage, but an Age in Which mankind will apply itself, apart from all dilemma and all seeking, to the Inherently Harmonious Event of Real existence (in the Always Already present-time "Bright" Divine Reality That Is the One and Only Reality Itself).

In the brief period of two and a half decades, and in the midst of this "dark" and Godless era, Ruchira Avatar Adi Da has established His unique Spiritual culture. He has created the foundation for an unbroken tradition of Divine Self-Realization arising within a devotional gathering aligned to His fully Enlightened Wisdom, and always receiving and magnifying His Eternal Heart-Transmission. Nothing of the kind has ever existed before.

There are great choices to be made in life, choices that call on the greatest exercise of one's real intelligence and heart-impulse. Every one of us makes critical decisions that determine the course of the rest of our lives—and even our future beyond death.

The moment of discovering the Divine Avatar, Adi Da Samraj, is the greatest of all possible opportunities. It is pure Grace. How can an ordinary life truly compare to a life of living relationship and heart-intimacy with the greatest God-Man Who has ever appeared—the Divine in Person?

Call or write one of our regional centers and sign up for "The Only Truth That Sets the Heart Free", our preliminary course that prepares you to become a fully practicing devotee of Avatar Adi Da Samraj. Or sign up for any of our other classes, correspondence courses, seminars, events, or retreats. Or call to order more books and continue your reading.

Respond now. Do not miss this miraculous opportunity to enter into direct relationship with Real God.

The Eleutherian Pan-Communion of Adidam

AMERICAS
12040 North Seigler Road
Middletown, CA 95461
(800) 524-4941
(707) 928-4936

PACIFIC-ASIA
12 Seibel Road
Henderson
Auckland 1008
New Zealand
64-9-838-9114

AUSTRALIA
P.O. Box 460
Roseville, NSW 2069
Australia
61-2-9416-7951

EUROPE-AFRICA
Annendaalderweg 10
6105 AT Maria Hoop
The Netherlands
31 (0)20 468 1442

THE UNITED KINGDOM
London, England
0181-7317550

FIJI
P.O. Box 4744
Samabula, Suva, Fiji
381-466

E-MAIL: correspondence@adidam.org

We also have centers in the following places. For their phone numbers and addresses, please contact one of the centers listed above or visit our website: **http://www.adidam.org**.

Americas
San Rafael, CA
Los Angeles, CA
Seattle, WA
Denver, CO
Chicago, IL
Framingham, MA (Boston)
Potomac, MD
    (Washington, DC)
Kauai, HI
Quebec, Canada
Vancouver, Canada

Pacific-Asia
Western Australia
Melbourne, Australia

Europe-Africa
Amsterdam, The Netherlands
Berlin, Germany

The Sacred Literature of Ruchira Avatar Adi Da Samraj

Start by reading *The Promised God-Man Is Here*, the astounding story of Avatar Adi Da's Divine Life and Work.

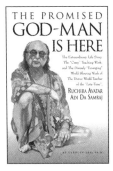

The Promised God-Man Is Here

The Extraordinary Life-Story, The "Crazy" Teaching-Work, and The Divinely "Emerging" World-Blessing Work Of The Divine World-Teacher Of The "Late-Time", Ruchira Avatar Adi Da Samraj, by Carolyn Lee, Ph.D.—the profound, heart-rending, humorous, miraculous, wild—and true—story of the Divine Person Alive in human Form. Essential reading as background for the study of Avatar Adi Da's books.

See My Brightness Face to Face

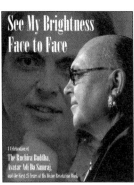

A Celebration of the Ruchira Avatar, Adi Da Samraj, and the First Twenty-Five Years of His Divine Revelation Work—a magnificent year-by-year pictorial celebration of Ruchira Avatar Adi Da's Divine Work with His devotees, from 1972 to 1997. Includes a wealth of selections from His Talks and Writings, numerous Stories of His Divine Work told by His devotees, and over 100 color photographs.

$19.95, 8"x10" quality paperback, 200 pages

THE FIVE BOOKS OF THE HEART
OF THE ADIDAM REVELATION

After reading *The Promised God-Man Is Here*, continue reading *The Five Books Of The Heart Of The Adidam Revelation*. In these five books, Avatar Adi Da Samraj has distilled the very essence of His Eternal Message to every one, in all times and places.

BOOK ONE:

Aham Da Asmi
(Beloved, I Am Da)

The "Late-Time" Avataric Revelation Of The True and Spiritual Divine Person (The egoless Personal Presence Of Reality and Truth, Which Is The Only Real God)

The most extraordinary statement ever made in human history. Avatar Adi Da Samraj fully Reveals Himself as the Living Divine Person and Proclaims His Infinite and Undying Love for all and All.

$7.95, 4"x7" paperback, 222 pages

BOOK TWO:

Ruchira Avatara Gita
(The Way Of The Divine Heart-Master)

The "Late-Time" Avataric Revelation Of The Great Secret Of The Divinely Self-Revealed Way That Most Perfectly Realizes The True and Spiritual Divine Person (The egoless Personal Presence Of Reality and Truth, Which Is The Only Real God)

Avatar Adi Da Offers to every one the ecstatic practice of devotional relationship to Him—explaining how devotion to a living human Adept-Realizer has always been the source of true religion, and distinguishing true Guru-devotion from cultism.

$7.95, 4"x7" paperback, 254 pages

BOOK THREE:

Da Love-Ananda Gita
(The Free Gift Of The Divine Love-Bliss)

The "Late-Time" Avataric Revelation Of The Great Means To Worship and To Realize The True and Spiritual Divine Person (The egoless Personal Presence Of Reality and Truth, Which Is The Only Real God)

Avatar Adi Da Reveals the secret simplicity at the heart of Adidam—relinquishing your preoccupation with yourself (and all your problems and your suffering) and, instead, Contemplating Him, the "Bright" Divine Person of Infinite Love-Bliss.

$7.95, 4"x7" paperback, 234 pages

BOOK FOUR:

Hridaya Rosary
(Four Thorns Of Heart-Instruction)

The "Late-Time" Avataric Revelation Of The Universally Tangible Divine Spiritual Body, Which Is The Supreme Agent Of The Great Means To Worship and To Realize The True and Spiritual Divine Person (The egoless Personal Presence Of Reality and Truth, Which Is The Only Real God)

The ultimate Mysteries of Spiritual life, never before revealed. In breathtakingly beautiful poetry, Avatar Adi Da Samraj sings of the "melting" of the ego in His "Rose Garden of the Heart".

$7.95, 4"x7" paperback, 358 pages

BOOK FIVE:

Eleutherios
(The Only Truth That Sets The Heart Free)

The "Late-Time" Avataric Revelation Of The "Perfect Practice" Of The Great Means To Worship and To Realize The True and Spiritual Divine Person (The egoless Personal Presence Of Reality and Truth, Which Is The Only Real God)

An address to the great human questions about God, Truth, Reality, Happiness, and Freedom. Avatar Adi Da Samraj Reveals how Absolute Divine Freedom is Realized, and makes an impassioned Call to everyone to create a world of true human freedom on Earth.

$7.95, 4"x7" paperback, 270 pages

THE SEVENTEEN COMPANIONS
OF THE TRUE DAWN HORSE

O nce you have read *The Five Books Of The Heart Of The Adidam Revelation*, you are ready to continue with *The Seventeen Companions Of The True Dawn Horse*. These seventeen books are "Companions" to *The Dawn Horse Testament*, Avatar Adi Da's great summary of the Way of Adidam (p. 233). Here you will find Avatar Adi Da's Wisdom-Instruction on particular aspects of the true Spiritual Way, and His two tellings of His own Life-Story, as autobiography (*The Knee Of Listening*) and as archetypal parable (*The Mummery*). Avatar Adi Da created the Canon of His Sacred Literature in late 1997 and early 1998, and the Dawn Horse Press is currently in the process of publishing the "Seventeen Companions" and *The Dawn Horse Testament*.

BOOK ONE:

Real God Is The Indivisible Oneness Of Unbroken Light

Reality, Truth, and The "Non-Creator" God
In The True World-Religion Of Adidam

The Nature of Real God and of the cosmos. Why ultimate questions cannot be answered either by conventional religion or by science.

BOOK TWO:

The Truly Human New World-Culture Of Unbroken Real-God-Man

The Eastern Versus The Western Traditional Cultures
Of Mankind, and The Unique New Non-Dual Culture
Of The True World-Religion Of Adidam

The Eastern and Western approaches to religion, and life altogether—and how the Way of Adidam goes beyond this apparent dichotomy.

BOOK THREE:

The Only Complete Way To Realize The Unbroken Light Of Real God

An Introductory Overview Of The "Radical" Divine Way
Of The True World-Religion Of Adidam

The entire course of the Way of Adidam—the unique principles underlying Adidam, and the unique culmination of Adidam in Divine Enlightenment.

BOOK FOUR:
The Knee Of Listening
The Early-Life Ordeal and The "Radical"
Spiritual Realization Of The Ruchira Avatar

Avatar Adi Da's autobiographical account of the years from His Birth to His Divine Re-Awakening in 1970. Includes a new chapter, "My Realization of the Great Onlyness of Me, and My Great Regard for My Adept-Links to the Great Tradition of Mankind".

BOOK FIVE:
The Method Of The Ruchira Avatar
The Divine Way Of Adidam Is An ego-Transcending
Relationship, Not An ego-Centric Technique

Avatar Adi Da's earliest Talks to His devotees, on the fundamental principles of the devotional relationship to Him and "radical" understanding of the ego. Accompanied by His summary statement on His relationship to Swami Muktananda and on His own unique Teaching and Blessing Work.

BOOK SIX:
The Mummery
A Parable About Finding The Way To My House

A work of astonishing poetry and deeply evocative archetypes. The story of Raymond Darling's growth to manhood and his search to be reunited with his beloved, Quandra.

BOOK SEVEN:
He-and-She Is Me
The Indivisibility Of Consciousness and Light
in The Divine Body Of The Ruchira Avatar

One of Avatar Adi Da's most esoteric Revelations—His Primary "Incarnation" in the Cosmic domain as the "He" of Primal Divine Sound-Vibration, the "She" of Primal Divine Light, and the "Son" of "He" and "She" in the "Me" of His Divine Spiritual Body.

BOOK EIGHT:
Divine Spiritual Baptism
Versus Cosmic Spiritual Baptism
Divine Hridaya-Shakti Versus Cosmic Kundalini Shakti
In The Divine Way Of Adidam

The Divine Heart-Power (Hridaya-Shakti) uniquely Transmitted by Avatar Adi Da Samraj, and how it differs from the various traditional forms of Spiritual Baptism, particularly Kundalini Yoga.

BOOK NINE:

Ruchira Tantra Yoga

The Physical-Spiritual (and Truly Religious) Method
Of Mental, Emotional, Sexual, and <u>Whole</u> <u>Bodily</u> <u>Health</u>
<u>and</u> <u>Enlightenment</u> In The Divine Way Of Adidam

The transformation of life in the domain of "money, food, and sex".
Includes: understanding "victim-consciousness"; the ego as addict;
the secret of how to change; going beyond the "Oedipal" sufferings
of childhood; the right orientation to money; right diet; life-positive
and Spiritually auspicious sexual practice.

BOOK TEN:

The Seven Stages Of Life

Transcending The Six Stages Of egoic Life and Realizing
The ego-Transcending Seventh Stage Of Life,
In The Divine Way Of Adidam

The stages of human development from birth to Divine Enlightenment. How the stages relate to physical and esoteric anatomy. The
errors of each of the first six stages of life, and the unique egoless-
ness of the seventh stage of life. Avatar Adi Da's Self-Confession as
the first, last, and only seventh stage Adept-Realizer.

BOOK ELEVEN:

The <u>All-Completing</u> and <u>Final</u>
Divine Revelation To Mankind

A Summary Description Of The Supreme Yoga Of
The Seventh Stage Of Life In The Divine Way Of Adidam

The ultimate secrets of Divine Enlightenment—including the four-
stage Process of Divine Enlightenment, culminating in Translation
into the Infinitely Love-Blissful Divine Self-Domain.

BOOK TWELVE:

The Heart Of The Dawn Horse Testament
Of The Ruchira Avatar

The Epitome Of The "Testament Of Secrets" Of
The Divine World-Teacher, Ruchira Avatar Adi Da Samraj

A shorter version of *The Dawn Horse Testament*—all of Avatar Adi
Da's magnificent summary Instruction, without the details of the
technical practices engaged by His devotees.

BOOK SEVENTEEN

The Basket Of Tolerance

The Perfect Guide To Perfectly <u>Unified</u> Understanding Of The One and Great Tradition Of Mankind, and Of The Divine Way Of Adidam As The Perfect <u>Completing</u> Of The One and Great Tradition Of Mankind

An all-encompassing "map" of mankind's entire history of religious seeking. A combination of a bibliography of over 5,000 items (organized to display Avatar Adi Da's grand Argument relative to the Great Tradition) with over 100 Essays by Avatar Adi Da, illuminating many specific aspects of the Great Tradition.

THE DAWN HORSE TESTAMENT

The Dawn Horse Testament Of The Ruchira Avatar

The "Testament Of Secrets" Of The Divine World-Teacher, Ruchira Avatar Adi Da Samraj

Avatar Adi Da's paramount "Source-Text" which summarizes the entire course of the Way of Adidam. Adi Da Samraj says: "In making this Testament I have been Meditating everyone, contacting everyone, dealing with psychic forces everywhere, in all time. This Testament is an always Living Conversation between Me and absolutely every one."

The Dawn Horse Press

In addition to Avatar Adi Da's 23 "Source-Texts", the Dawn Horse Press offers hundreds of other publications and items for meditation and sacred worship—courses, videotapes, audiotapes, compact discs, magazines, photos, incense, sacred art and jewelry, and more. Call today for a full catalog of products or visit our website (http://dhp.adidam.org) where you will find full-color images of all our products and on-line ordering.

For more information or a free catalog:
CALL TOLL-FREE 1-800-524-4941
(Outside North America call 707-928-4936)
Visit us on-line at **http://dhp.adidam.org**
Or e-mail: **dhp@adidam.org**
Or write:
THE DAWN HORSE PRESS
12040 North Seigler Road
Middletown, CA 95461 USA

We accept Visa, MasterCard, personal checks, and money orders. In the USA, please add $4.00 (shipping and handling) for the first book and $1.00 for each additional book. California residents add 7.25% sales tax. Outside the USA, please add $7.00 (shipping and handling) for the first book and $3.00 for each additional book. Checks and money orders should be made payable to the Dawn Horse Press.

An Invitation to Support Adidam

Avatar Adi Da Samraj's sole Purpose is to act as a Source of continuous Divine Grace for everyone, everywhere. In that spirit, He is a Free Renunciate and He owns nothing. Those who have made gestures in support of Avatar Adi Da's Work have found that their generosity is returned in many Blessings that are full of His healing, transforming, and Liberating Grace—and those Blessings flow not only directly to them as the beneficiaries of His Work, but to many others, even all others. At the same time, all tangible gifts of support help secure and nurture Avatar Adi Da's Work in necessary and practical ways, again similarly benefiting the entire world. Because all this is so, supporting His Work is the most auspicious form of financial giving, and we happily extend to you an invitation to serve Adidam through your financial support.

You may make a financial contribution in support of the Work of Adi Da Samraj at any time. You may also, if you choose, request that your contribution be used for one or more specific purposes.

If you are moved to help support and develop Adidam Samrajashram (Naitauba), Avatar Adi Da's Great Island-Hermitage and World-Blessing Seat in Fiji, and the circumstance provided there and elsewhere for Avatar Adi Da and the other members of the Ruchira Sannyasin Order, the senior renunciate order of Adidam, you may do so by making your contribution to The Love-Ananda Samrajya, the Australian charitable trust which has central responsibility for these Sacred Treasures of Adidam.

To do this: (1) if you do not pay taxes in the United States, make your check payable directly to "The Love-Ananda Samrajya Pty Ltd" (which serves as the trustee of the Foundation) and mail it to The Love-Ananda Samrajya at P.O. Box 4744, Samabula, Suva, Fiji; and (2) if you do pay taxes in the United States and you would like your contribution to be tax-deductible under U.S. laws, make your check payable to "The

Eleutherian Pan-Communion of Adidam", indicate on your check or accompanying letter that you would like your contribution used for the work of The Love-Ananda Samrajya, and mail your check to the Advocacy Department of Adidam at 12040 North Seigler Road, Middletown, California 95461, USA.

If you are moved to help support and provide for one of the other purposes of Adidam, such as publishing the sacred Literature of Avatar Adi Da, or supporting either of the other two Sanctuaries He has Empowered, or maintaining the Sacred Archives that preserve His recorded Talks and Writings, or publishing audio and video recordings of Avatar Adi Da, you may do so by making your contribution directly to The Eleutherian Pan-Communion of Adidam, specifying the particular purposes you wish to benefit, and mailing your check to the Advocacy Department of Adidam at the above address.

If you would like more information about these and other gifting options, or if you would like assistance in describing or making a contribution, please write to the Advocacy Department of Adidam at the above address or contact the Adidam Legal Department by telephone at (707) 928-4612 or by FAX at (707) 928-4062.

Planned Giving

We also invite you to consider making a planned gift in support of the Work of Avatar Adi Da Samraj. Many have found that through planned giving they can make a far more significant gesture of support than they would otherwise be able to make. Many have also found that by making a planned gift they are able to realize substantial tax advantages.

There are numerous ways to make a planned gift, including making a gift in your Will, or in your life insurance, or in a charitable trust.

If you would like to make a gift in your Will in support of the work of The Love-Ananda Samrajya: (1) if you do not pay taxes in the United States, simply include in your Will the statement, "I give to The Love-Ananda Samrajya Pty Ltd, as trustee of The Love-Ananda Samrajya, an Australian charitable trust, P.O. Box 4744, Samabula, Suva, Fiji, _____" [inserting in the blank the amount or description of your contribution]; and (2) if you do pay taxes in the United States and you would like your contribution to be free of estate taxes and to also reduce any estate taxes payable on the remainder of your estate, simply include in your Will the statement, "I give to The Eleutherian Pan-Communion of Adidam, a California non-profit corporation, 12040 North Seigler Road, Middletown, California 95461, USA, _____" [inserting in the blank the amount or description of your contribution].

To make a gift in your life insurance, simply name as the beneficiary (or one of the beneficiaries) of your life insurance policy the organization of your choice (The Love-Ananda Samrajya or The Eleutherian Pan-Communion of Adidam), according to the foregoing descriptions and addresses. If you are a United States taxpayer, you may receive significant tax benefits if you make a contribution to The Eleutherian Pan-Communion of Adidam through your life insurance.

We also invite you to consider establishing or participating in a charitable trust for the benefit of Adidam. If you are a United States taxpayer, you may find that such a trust will provide you with immediate tax savings and assured income for life, while at the same time enabling you to provide for your family, for your other heirs, and for the Work of Avatar Adi Da as well.

The Advocacy and Legal Departments of Adidam will be happy to provide you with further information about these and other planned gifting options, and happy to provide you or your attorney with assistance in describing or making a planned gift in support of the Work of Avatar Adi Da.

Further Notes to the Reader

An Invitation to Responsibility

Adidam, the Way of the Heart that Avatar Adi Da has Revealed, is an invitation to everyone to assume real responsibility for his or her life. As Avatar Adi Da has Said in *The Dawn Horse Testament Of The Ruchira Avatar,* "If any one Is Interested In The Realization Of The Heart, Let him or her First Submit (Formally, and By Heart) To Me, and (Thereby) Commence The Ordeal Of self-Observation, self-Understanding, and self-Transcendence." Therefore, participation in the Way of Adidam requires a real struggle with oneself, and not at all a struggle with Avatar Adi Da, or with others.

All who study the Way of Adidam or take up its practice should remember that they are responding to a Call to become responsible for themselves. They should understand that they, not Avatar Adi Da or others, are responsible for any decision they may make or action they may take in the course of their lives of study or practice. This has always been true, and it is true whatever the individual's involvement in the Way of Adidam, be it as one who studies Avatar Adi Da's Wisdom-Teaching or as a formally acknowledged member of Adidam.

Honoring and Protecting the Sacred Word through Perpetual Copyright

Since ancient times, practitioners of true religion and Spirituality have valued, above all, time spent in the Company of the Sat-Guru (or one who has, to any degree, Realized Real God, Truth, or Reality, and who, thus, Serves the awakening process in others). Such practitioners understand that the Sat-Guru literally Transmits his or her (Realized) State to every one (and every thing) with whom (or with which) he or she comes in contact. Through this Transmission, objects, environments, and rightly prepared individuals with which the Sat-Guru has contact can become Empowered, or Imbued with the Sat-Guru's Transforming Power. It is by this process of Empowerment that things and beings are made truly and literally sacred, and things so sanctified thereafter function as a Source of the Sat-Guru's Blessing for all who understand how to make right and sacred use of them.

Sat-Gurus of any degree of Realization and all that they Empower are, therefore, truly Sacred Treasures, for they help draw the practitioner more quickly into the process of Realization. Cultures of true Wisdom have always understood that such Sacred Treasures are precious (and fragile) Gifts to humanity, and that they should be honored, protected, and reserved for right sacred use. Indeed, the word "sacred" means "set apart", and, thus, protected, from the secular world. Avatar Adi Da has Conformed His body-mind Most Perfectly to the Divine Self, and He is, thus, the most Potent Source of Blessing-Transmission of Real God, or Truth Itself, or Reality Itself. He has for many years Empowered (or made sacred) special places and things, and these now Serve as His Divine Agents, or as literal expressions and extensions of His Blessing-Transmission. Among these Empowered Sacred Treasures is His Wisdom-Teaching, which is Full of His Transforming Power. This Blessed and Blessing Wisdom-Teaching has Mantric Force, or the literal Power to Serve Real-God-Realization in those who are Graced to receive it.

Therefore, Avatar Adi Da's Wisdom-Teaching must be perpetually honored and protected, "set apart" from all possible interference and wrong use. The fellowship of devotees of Avatar Adi Da is committed to the perpetual preservation and right honoring of the sacred Wisdom-Teaching of the Way of Adidam. But it is also true that, in order to fully accomplish this, we must find support in the world-society in which we live and in its laws. Thus, we call for a world-society and for laws that acknowledge the Sacred, and that permanently protect It from insensitive, secular interference and wrong use of any kind. We call for, among other things, a system of law that acknowledges that the Wisdom-Teaching of the Way of Adidam, in all Its forms, is, because of Its sacred nature, protected by perpetual copyright.

We invite others who respect the Sacred to join with us in this call and in working toward its realization. And, even in the meantime, we claim that all copyrights to the Wisdom-Teaching of Avatar Adi Da and the other sacred Literature and recordings of the Way of Adidam are of perpetual duration.

We make this claim on behalf of The Love-Ananda Samrajya Pty Ltd, which, acting as trustee of The Love-Ananda Samrajya, is the holder of all such copyrights.

Avatar Adi Da and the Sacred Treasures of Adidam

True Spiritual Masters have Realized Real God (to one degree or another), and, therefore, they bring great Blessing and introduce Divine Possibility to the world. Such Adept-Realizers Accomplish universal Blessing Work that benefits everything and everyone. They also Work very specifically and intentionally with individuals who approach them as their devotees, and with those places where they reside and to which they Direct their specific Regard for the sake of perpetual Spiritual Empowerment. This was understood in traditional Spiritual cultures, and, therefore, those cultures found ways to honor Adept-Realizers by providing circumstances for them where they were free to do their Spiritual Work without obstruction or interference.

Those who value Avatar Adi Da's Realization and Service have always endeavored to appropriately honor Him in this traditional way by providing a circumstance where He is completely Free to do His Divine Work. Since 1983, He has resided principally on the island of Naitauba, Fiji, also known as Adidam Samrajashram. This island has been set aside by Avatar Adi Da's devotees worldwide as a Place for Him to do His universal Blessing Work for the sake of everyone, as well as His specific Work with those who pilgrimage to Adidam Samrajashram to receive the special Blessing of coming into His physical Company.

Avatar Adi Da is a legal renunciate. He owns nothing and He has no secular or religious institutional function. He Functions only in Freedom. He, and the other members of the Ruchira Sannyasin Order, the senior renunciate order of Adidam, are provided for by The Love-Ananda Samrajya, which also provides for Adidam Samrajashram altogether and ensures the permanent integrity of Avatar Adi Da's Wisdom-Teaching, both in its archival and in its published forms. The Love-Ananda Samrajya, which functions only in Fiji, exists exclusively to provide for these Sacred Treasures of Adidam.

Outside Fiji, the institution which has developed in response to Avatar Adi Da's Wisdom-Teaching and universal Blessing is known as "The Eleutherian Pan-Communion of Adidam". This formal organization is active worldwide in making Avatar Adi Da's Wisdom-Teaching available to all, in offering guidance to all who are moved to respond to His Offering, and in providing for the other Sacred Treasures of Adidam, including the Mountain Of Attention Sanctuary (in California) and Love-Ananda Mahal (in Hawaii). In addition to the central corporate entity known as The Eleutherian Pan-Communion of Adidam, which is based in California, there are numerous regional entities which serve congregations of Avatar Adi Da's devotees in various places throughout the world.

Practitioners of Adidam worldwide have also established numerous community organizations, through which they provide for many of their common and cooperative community needs, including those relating to housing, food, businesses, medical care, schools, and death and dying. By attending to these and all other ordinary human concerns and affairs via self-transcending cooperation and mutual effort, Avatar Adi Da's devotees constantly free their energy and attention, both personally and collectively, for practice of the Way of Adidam and for service to Avatar Adi Da Samraj, to Adidam Samrajashram, to the other Sacred Treasures of Adidam, and to The Eleutherian Pan-Communion of Adidam.

All of the organizations that have evolved in response to Avatar Adi Da Samraj and His Offering are legally separate from one another, and each has its own purpose and function. Avatar Adi Da neither directs, nor bears responsibility for, the activities of these organizations. Again, He Functions only in Freedom. These organizations represent the collective intention of practitioners of Adidam worldwide not only to provide for the Sacred Treasures of Adidam, but also to make Avatar Adi Da's Offering of the Way of Adidam universally available to all.

INDEX

NOTE TO THE READER: Page numbers in **boldface** type refer to the Scriptural Text of the *Ruchira Avatara Gita*. All other page numbers refer to the introductions, endnotes, and the back matter.

A

abilities, extraordinary, **54**
abuses made by egoity, **56**
addresses
  Dawn Horse Press, 202
  e-mail, 200, 212, 217, 225, 233
  regional centers, 200, 225
  Third Congregation Advocacy, 217
  Vision of Mulund Institute, 212
  websites, 202, 203, 225
Adept-Realizer, **56**, **57-58**
Adept Sat-Guru. *See* Sat-Guru
Adi (Name), 11
Adi Da (Name), 11, **68**
Adidam, Way of. *See* Way of Adidam
Adidama, 27
Adidama Quandra Mandala of the Ruchira Avatar, 19-20, 26-27, 186
Adidam Pan-Communion, 206-17
Adidam Samrajashram, **81**, 185, 223
Adidam Youth Fellowship, 212
Adi Da Samraj
  Adept-Realizer, **57**, **58**
  Agency of, **74**
  Appearance, 9-11
  autobiography, 14
  to be asked, **148-49**, **150-51**, **154-65**
  Birth, 10, 13
  Blessing-Work, 14-15, **46**, **50**, **55**
  bodily (human) Form, 12-13, 17
  books by and about, 29-35, 201-2, 226-33
  as the "Bright", **145**
  Calling of, **46**, **52-53**, **56**, **57**
  as Capability, **149**
  childhood, 11, 23
  Confession of, **43-44**, **55-56**, **57**, **58**, **59**, **60**, **61**, 62, **69**
  "Crazy" Manner, **46**, 182-83
  criticism by, **164**
  Divine "Emergence", 14-15, **56**, **61**, 64
  Divine Giver, **44**, **81**
  Divine World-Teacher, **44**, **57**, 64
  Early Life-Submission, **73**
  Fulfillment of Great Tradition, **58**, 64
  Genius, **154**
  "Heroic" Ordeal, 14
  Name defined, **81**

  Names, 11-12, 27-28, **68-69**, **81**, **88**
  not a public Teacher, 14, **45-46**
  Personal Ordeal of, **75-77**
  Perfectly Subjective Divine, **59**, **60**, 65
  Purposes, 13-15, **44**, **57**, **59-60**
  right approach to, **46**, **57-58**, **61**, **117-19**
  "Round Dance" of, **51-52**
  as Ruchira Sannyasin, 186
  Sacrifice of, **73**
  sadhana with Rudi, **158**
  as Samadhi, **60**
  Secret of, **44**, **55**
  seventh stage Realizer, First, Last, and Only, **57**, **68-69**, **81**, **88**
  Sign of, **76**, **77**
  Source-Texts, 15-16, 27, 29-35
  Submission to Mankind, **74**
  Teaching Work, 11, 14-15, **44**, **46**, **50**
  Three Stages of His Personal Ordeal, **75-77**
  twenty-five year Revelation, 15-16
  See also Divine Heart-Master
adolescent approach to practice, **86**, **124-28**
  attitude of anti-authority, **124-26**, **132**
  characteristics of, **127-28**, 180
  See also childish approach to practice
Advaitayana Buddhism, **68**, 178
advanced and ultimate stages of life, **129-30**, 192
Advocacy, Third Congregation, 217
Advocates. *See* Transnational Society of Advocates
Agency of Adi Da Samraj, **74**
"Agents" of Adi Da Samraj's Blessing, 185-86, 193-94
agrarian ritual, **48**
"Aham Da Asmi", **43-44**, **55**, **61**, 62, **72**, **85**, 182
  Initial Confession of, **75**
anti-Guruism, **124-28**, **132**
Appearance of Adi Da Samraj, 9-11
approach to Adi Da Samraj, **46**, **57-58**, **61**
Arrow of the body-mind, **107**, 189

244

248

250

I do not simply recommend or turn men and women to Truth. I _Am_ Truth. I Draw men and women to My Self. I _Am_ the Present Real God, Desiring, Loving, and Drawing up My devotees. I have Come to Be Present with My devotees, to Reveal to them the True Nature of life in Real God, which is Love, and of mind in Real God, which is Faith. I Stand always Present in the Place and Form of Real God. I accept the qualities of all who turn to Me, dissolving those qualities in Real God, so that _Only_ God becomes the Condition, Destiny, Intelligence, and Work of My devotees. I look for My devotees to acknowledge Me and turn to Me in appropriate ways, surrendering to Me perfectly, depending on Me, full of Me always, with only a face of love.

I am waiting for you. I have been waiting for you eternally.

Where are you?

AVATAR ADI DA SAMRAJ

1 9 7 1